KAFKA AT THE BEACH

a layman's handbook for those falsely accused of felonies

by

Steve Bevilacqua

Published by Arden Venice Press, Venice, CA

For Blodg

fuck, there's no coffee...

As the tires screech and the car runs me down, a hundred scenes flash through my brain. Surf bands, bikini girls, drug addicts in love...These scenes aren't from my life. They're from the unfinished movie sitting in a mountain of machinery in what used to be my living room.

I stumble back and land on my ass, and the bag of coffee hits the asphalt. I yell "Yo!" at the murderous Toyota and the driver sticks her fist out the window, thrusting an angry middle finger at me while speeding toward the gaggle of little girls in frilly Communion dresses leaving St. Clement's Church.

*The Layman's Handbook for Those Falsely Accused of Felonies, page 4...Pay close attention during your **incident** as it will be the subject of tediously obsessive scrutiny for months to come...*

It's a bright Sunday morning in Venice Beach, California, and the summer crowds are filling the streets, even though it's only May 7th. I've been working all night at a jerry-rigged editing system in the tiny apartment I share with my girlfriend Tamara. With our low-budget movie long out of money, and my credit cards all dead and buried, three days ago I was thrown out of our editing space and forced to cram everything into the living room. The furniture's piled high against the walls to make room for the editing system. The place now looks like the lair of some cable-obsessed monster.

The movie seemed like a good idea at the time but now I'm hopelessly in debt and nowhere near finished. And we're out of coffee, so I walk down to the Rose Café to get some, completely unaware that this errand is about to devour the next year of my life.

The bag of coffee is purchased without incident and I head home to get back to work. I reach the corner of 3rd and Rose Avenue and begin crossing the street. I'm almost safely at the curb when the shriek of rubber makes me jump and I see the crusted black Corolla about to kill me. I jump back but the car swipes my thigh and knocks me down.

As Ms. Finger's car races away, I pick up the coffee and get back on my feet. My knees suddenly buckle and my heart starts pounding. That was close. I wipe some crud from her fender off my shorts and, grumbling, I continue home. Watching the flowery Communion girls, I get to the staircase that I use to cut through the block to my building over on 4th. But as I start up the stairs, I notice something out of the corner of my eye. It's a black Corolla that looks astoundingly similar to the car that just ran me down. But that can't be. Cars that hit pedestrians and flee the scene don't just flee eighty feet up the street and park...do they?

The Corolla is lurching spastically back and forth, struggling to fit into a parking spot that isn't even that small, and I'm overcome with curiosity. So I head back down the stairs and walk toward the car. And during this short journey, something sickeningly momentous occurs...I cross the border from Venice Beach into Santa Monica.

To the untrained eye, you'd never realize that you've stepped into a different town. This is especially true since the border of Venice Beach and Santa Monica inexplicably happens in the middle of the block. The sudden leap of addresses to a new random number is the only visible clue, yet these two towns are worlds apart.

They say that the people in Sweden hate Denmark, and people in Malaysia hate Singapore, when they don't seem all that different to me. On the other hand, I live a few yards from the border of Santa Monica and it might as well be another planet. While Venice Beach is a dirty, crime-ridden, scrappy beach town, Santa Monica is an uptight, over-regulated fortress of spite where all familiar stereotypes are fused into a wild menagerie of new unrecognizable beasts. Bustling with Communist landowners, right-wing weed dealers, and surgically-mutilated health freaks, Santa Monica feels morally superior to Venice Beach, while Venice Beach thinks of Santa Monica as trying way too hard and painfully unconvincing.

Santa Monica is its own incorporated city while Venice was forcibly seized by the growing metropolis of Los Angeles decades ago. Now in sunny Santa Monica, I approach the unwashed Corolla as the door swings open and the driver spills out. She's a drooping, messy woman with wild hair, juggling a backpack, her keys, a fistful of crumpled papers and a pair of oversized blue sunglasses. She hurries away from the car, mumbling to herself, and then flinches at the sound of my voice as I step closer and say "Excuse me..."

3

"Yeah?" she snaps. This woman is jittery as hell and her skin's covered with sickly pink blotches, just like the crystal meth addicts who loiter outside the St. Joseph's Halfway House on the corner of my street.

"Was that you who just turned onto 3rd from Rose?" I ask the twitching woman.

"Yeah," she grumbles, jerking her neck.

"You just hit me with your car."

Her face contorts with a defiant sneer. "Fuck you!" she snarls, "I don't care! I'm tired! I just came from the airport."

A stunned chuckle escapes my mouth. "Whoa, sorry," I reply, "Wrong answer. You ask me if I'm okay, and you tell me that you're sorry. And then I go home."

"Don't tell me what to do, you stupid fucking asshole!" the woman explodes as she winds up and swings a wild punch with her fistful of keys. I block her fist with my elbow and everything the woman is carrying spills from her shaky hands.

"Fuck!" she yells, bending over to pick up her junk. "You fucking asshole," she keeps repeating as she fumbles with the keys and drops everything again.

"Lady, you're crazy," I inform her as I back away, "You should watch it before you kill somebody." Then I turn and I leave.

A few steps later, an unseen hand yanks my shirt from behind and I hear the woman yelling more obscenities at my back. I pull free from her clutches and turn to face her. She throws her fist at me again and I duck back. Clutched in her fist is her pair of oversized blue sunglasses. "You broke my fucking sunglasses!" she yells.

"No, I didn't."

"Look!" she shrieks, pointing to a tiny scratch on one lens of the clownish blue goggles.

"I didn't do that," I tell her. Not waiting for a response, I walk away.

"No one else could ever be admitted here, because this gate was made just for you." – Kafka

11:52am - Between the punch-swinging spot and the corner of 3rd and Marine: Tugging at my shirt, the woman yells, "These glasses cost two-hundred-and-seventy-five bucks!" "That's insane," I reply. This is Venice Beach, you can buy all the ugly blue sunglasses you want for about five bucks down on the boardwalk.

11:56am – Enraged driver follows close behind as I walk up the hill on Marine Avenue. The hill is so steep that she is spewing obscenities at my ass.

12:00pm – The corner of 4th and Marine: Sad realization that I cannot go home with this crazy woman following me. Wild-haired nut is now yelling that if I don't give her three hundred dollars, she will kill me. I continue walking.

12:03pm – Walking down hill on 4th Street: Angry screaming driver begins to attract attention from beachgoers and tourists. Middle-aged couple crosses the street to avoid her. The crazed driver screams at two gawking teenaged girls,

"What the fuck are you looking at?!" Girls giggle and scamper away.

12:07pm – Nearing bottom of hill on 4th Street: I'm now standing across the street from my apartment building. Driver continues following me with a steady stream of profanity-laced threats. Yearning for the stage of my life before the screaming nut lady, I turn to face her with a plea for reason, and finally get a good look at her. The woman's sunken red eyes burn with lunatic zeal and she seems about fifty, but you can never tell a speed freak's age. Her frizzy, matted hair is a sickening fusion of brown and pink. She's dressed in rags, with a stained denim jacket and a long skirt held together with shabby patches.

I brace myself then say, "Okay, listen to me. Your road-rage, or whatever drugs you're on, are making you completely insane. Go home and sleep it off."

"Fuck you!" she shouts, "I want my money!"

"You just hit me with your car and I'm not giving you anything."

"Oh yeah?" she replies, "Then I'm gonna tell the police that you assaulted me and they'll make you fucking pay!"

I sigh tiredly, then turn and keep walking.

12:11pm – Approaching the corner of 4th and Rose: Thinking of ways to shake the insane screaming woman, I look at the laundromat across the street, weighing the possibilities. The usual crowd of lunatics is hovering by the laundromat door, so I decide against this plan of action and along walk Rose Avenue.

The store at 5th and Rose is your basic carniceria, as found on almost every corner of Los Angeles. A Mexican-deli-slash-liquor-store, this one is actually owned by a Persian fella named Farhad but still sells "Bimbo's Fried Bread", "Lucky Goose Enchilada Sauce" and other obscure brands from south of the border. This store made its acting debut back in 1976, when it portrayed an "ambulance company" in an odd movie called MOTHER, JUGS AND SPEED, starring Raquel Welch as "Jugs", that we rent sometimes to see what the neighborhood looked like during our nation's bicentennial.

With no better plan of action, I walk toward the store. "Where the hell do you think you're going?!" my stalker yells. A young mom with a stroller goes wide around the shrieking nut. Then it happens, an ordinary occurrence yet one that's about to change everything.

Tamara walks out of the store.

"Oh my god, are you okay?" That's it. That's all Tam says. And the crazy lady shoves me aside and lunges at my girlfriend.

Tam had been out looking at used cars, and she stopped for a Sunday paper on her way home. She comes out of the store and sees what she thinks is a demented homeless woman attacking me.

The woman grabs Tam's arm and yells, "Who are you?! Do you know this fucking asshole?!" Tam yanks her arm free and the woman hisses at her like the Bride of Frankenstein. As the lunatic driver moves toward Tam again, I shove myself between them and yell in the nut's face, "Get the hell away from her, NOW!"

The madwoman shrinks back a little and says, "You're assaulting me." My growing frustration brings on a mild stammering seizure then I say, "Go away."

The nut lady turns back to Tam, who's become the new focus of her furious spew. She snarls, "I'll have you thrown in jail, you bitch." Ignoring the crazed woman, Tam and I slip into the little zone unique to us. *Tam – What's going on? Me – This wackjob hit me with her car, now she's following me screaming that I have to give her hundreds of dollars. Tam – Oh Christ.* The woman dives at Tam again, but Tam turns sharply to her and yells "Back off!" And the woman jumps back.

You see, Tam's no slouch. In fact, she's the most capable person I know. She's a smart, sexy executive at an interactive company and she's produced a couple independent films. People often say that Tamara looks like the actress Sarah Jessica Parker. This generally drives her crazy but, to be honest, she does kind of look like Sarah Jessica Parker. Sometimes we get whisked past long lines at Hollywood clubs because the doormen think Tam actually is Sarah Jessica Parker. On several occasions, she's even forged autographs to prolong the illusion and get us in the door.

The woman keeps yelling at Tam, but Tam doesn't react. Instead, she calmly says to me, "Get in the car," and I suddenly notice Tam's crappy black Mustang parked a few feet away. We walk to the car and Tam asks me, "Are you hurt?"

"Not really," I reply, "She just sideswiped me and knocked me down a little."

As Tam opens the car door, the enraged woman slams her hands down on the trunk and howls, "You're not going anywhere, bitch!" Unruffled, Tam looks back and asks, "Could you get away from my car, please?"

The woman replies, "I'm going to make you miserable for the rest of your fucking life!" I'm staring at the crazy woman, astonished. As unnerving as her attacks on me were, suddenly switching gears to assail Tam is even more disturbing. I step away from Tam's Mustang, hoping to lead the nut away. But the woman is so absorbed in threatening Tam that she doesn't notice me go. So I walk back and announce, "Hey lady, yo. I'm leaving."

The woman still doesn't notice as I walk away the second time. I turn back and yell "Hey!" The woman finally sees that I'm leaving and hits a new level of berserk, bolting after me with a shrill war-cry. As the driver grabs my shirt, I yell to Tam, "Go!" Tam backs out of the parking spot, then hits the brakes and says, "Get in!"

Now that the nut has developed a violent fixation on my girlfriend, my primary goal is to get Tam away from there safely. "Just go! I'll deal with her!" I shout. So Tam drives out of the parking lot, onto 5th Street, and disappears behind the store. Tam needs about four minutes to get home, so I'll just let the crazy lady yell at me a little longer, then ditch her somehow. That's the plan, anyway. I look back at the nut, and my jaw drops open.

The crazed driver is standing there with a pen and a scrap of paper, talking to herself while scribbling down Tam's license plate number. "What are you doing?" I ask.

"I'm calling the police and telling them that fucking bitch just assaulted me!"

"You're crazy. She didn't do anything to you."

The woman twitches and growls, "I'm gonna find her. And you're gonna give me three hundred dollars!" She waves the scrap of paper in my face, ranting about how she's going to "get" Tamara. And I've completely had it. My hand flies forward and, with one fast fluid movement, I snatch the scrap of paper from the woman's fist.

"You just assaulted me! Again!" the woman yells as she slaps the side of my head. She claws at my hand, trying to retrieve the scrap of paper. Stepping back, I rip the paper to shreds and stuff it in my pocket. The woman screams "Give me that!" as she reaches for my crotch, but she suddenly stops her attack, distracted by the people who have gathered to watch. We've attracted a small audience, who stand at a safe distance observing the freakish sideshow.

The woman's blazing eyes bug out as she cries, "Did you see that?! This asshole just assaulted me! And that was the third or fourth time!"

I inch back toward 5th Street as the woman yells, "Help! Help! I've been assaulted!" The shocked tourists now provide a handy, serendipitous moment to the events so far.

They all laugh at her.

A few isolated giggles suddenly explode into a big group belly laugh and the crazy lady goes apoplectic, gagging for a second before she starts screaming again. Only now she's screaming at them. As the woman hurls random obscenities at the onlookers, I see my chance. I turn and run, hauling ass onto 5th Street and into the alley behind the store. I have no idea where I'm going but I know the woman will come after me in a few seconds. The alley intersects with another one that runs up the hill. I run up that alley, then hop over a short picket fence into somebody's yard. I squeeze through the narrow space between two bungalows, coming back onto 5th where I duck behind some bushes and desperately try to figure out what to do.

I know the insane driver is still stalking me. I can't go home and risk leading her to Tam. Then it hits me, a dull flicker in my tired little brain, "I know! I'll go to Liz's!"

My pal Liz is a very Venice Beach sort of soul, deeply spiritual yet a complete maniac. Her latest obsession is an extreme form of Chi Gong that builds mental and physical strength through meditation while beating yourself with bricks. Incredibly, it actually seems to work. That is, if you don't mind grotesque rectangular bruises on your sculpted abs.

Liz has many great qualities but her sense of humor is without equal. Frequently disturbing, most times I simply stand back and admire it. Liz once had a cookout for her many friends in drug "recovery" and made a special piñata for the occasion. As they swung the stick, Liz announced that she'd tossed in some Xanax tablets with the candy. The piñata bursts and there's a riotous scramble for the drugs, at which point Liz whips out her camera. Soon, she's shoving photos in her guests' faces while cackling, "Look at you! You're clawing in the dirt for drugs!"

As I hide in the bushes, I remind myself that my favorite thing about Liz is that she's not remotely put off by incidents like this. In fact, she thrives on them. Liz has the added benefit of living just two blocks away from where I'm crouched in the shrubs. I scan the street for my stalker, and then leap from the bushes and run like crazy to the tiny secluded house where Liz lives with her boyfriend Gary, a Japanese dude who gives massages and advanced astrological readings for a living. I barge into Liz's house, slam the door and duck down to hide.

"Hi Steve," Liz says without blinking. I tell Liz about the rampaging psycho who's stalking me. "Great, thanks. Lead her here," Liz replies.

"Well, I didn't want her to find Tam," I reply, "Where's Gary?"

"He went to Monterey Park for some Chinese roots. He's making a salve for his friend who stepped on a nail and got an infection."

"Christ, you people ever hear of a 'doctor'?" I ask, looking out the window. Liz walks to my side and looks too, "I can't believe you'd bring her here." Liz pushes me aside and walks outside, scanning the street, "Well, where is she? I want to see her." Liz shrugs and comes back in, "I have a hundred things to do today and I don't feel like doing any of them. You want a drink?"

"I should get back to work."

"Steve, the movie's not going anywhere. You just got hit by a car. Take a break." Liz pulls the vodka from the freezer. She makes me describe every detail of the crazed driver, over and over. Liz reserves a special scorn for crystal-meth addicts, and delights in hearing about the road rage woman's amphetamine-riddled blotches and twitchy mannerisms. As annoyed as I am by her twisted glee, Liz manages to wear me down. We're veterans of this fucked-up neighborhood and it does become pretty funny after a while.

But that's only because I have no idea what's going on at that exact moment.

trigger creeps in love...

"The two officers were standing there and, as if it were a matter of course, chased K. back into his room." – Kafka

Tamara is having an unusually motivated Sunday, first looking at used cars and now assembling piles of old clothes to take to the Salvation Army, when she's interrupted by violent pounding on the front door. "Santa Monica Police!" a voice outside shouts, "Open this door now!"

Tam opens the door and sees Officer Jeffrey Hink, a short man in a uniform that looks a size too big. "Are you Pamela?!" Hink yells.

"No," Tam replies.

Hink steps closer, "Do you drive a red four-door car?!"

"No. My car's right there," Tam says, stepping forward to point out her Mustang in the lot. That's when she sees the second cop with his gun aimed at her head. This second policeman is Officer Anthony Pitt of the Santa Monica PD. "Get back!" Pitt roars, "We're coming in!" Pitt leaps forward dramatically, holding his gun with both hands. "Down on the floor!" Pitt yells to Tam.

Tam stumbles back, away from Pitt's gun, and drops onto the sofa. She sits there, eyes wide, but this is only partly due to the gun aimed at her face. Pitt's bikecop uniform, with its tight spandex shorts and clinging knit shirt, makes his gut bulge out obscenely while simultaneously creating the impression that he has no penis.

Officer Hink empties a trashbag of Tam's old clothes onto the carpet, as Pitt shouts, "I said on the floor!" Tam is afraid to move and Pitt presses his gun to her head.

"What's this?!" Hink yells, looking down at the clothes.

"They're clothes I'm taking to the Salvation Army," Tam replies.

"Uh-huh," Hink grunts. He turns sharply, knocking the cable box off the television. As the cable box crashes to the floor, Hink points to the editing system. "And what's that?!" he yells with an excited tone like he's found the source of all crime.

"It's an editing system," Tam meekly answers.

Amy, our blonde next-door neighbor, rushes in to see what's making the violent noise. Hink swings his gun at her. "Back away now!" he yells, making Amy yelp and run away.

"Why are you here?!" Tam asks.

"Shut up! We ask the questions!" Pitt yells.

Outside, our neighbors have come out from their apartments to see what's going on. Dave the Actor yells, "Somebody call the police!" Amy squeals "They are the police!" from behind her half-open door.

Hearing the neighbors outside, Hink and Pitt react as if they're under siege, rushing to the doorway and yelling for everyone to return to their homes. None of the neighbors move. They simply stare at the cops, confused. Dave the Actor yells, "Tam, are you okay?! What's going on?" Officer Pitt yells to Dave that he's going to arrest him, so Dave steps back and watches from his doorway.

Tam gets up from the sofa, shaking and confused. Hink and Pitt see her and pounce. "On the floor!" Pitt yells, swinging his gun, while Hink grabs Tam's neck and forces her down to the carpet. Digging his knee into Tam's back, Hink roughly handcuffs her. "What are you doing?!" Tam yells as Hink grabs her arms and yanks her to her feet.

Pitt gets in Tam's face and shouts, "Do you want us to arrest you right now?!" Hink jumps in, "Or should we come to your office and arrest you there?! Then all of your co-workers will see you taken away in handcuffs!"

Pitt bellows, "If we arrest you now, there's no judge to set your bail. You'll have to spend the night in jail!"

"Arrest me for what?" Tam asks.

"Do you have a boyfriend?!" Pitt asks.

My god, Tam thinks, staring in horror at Pitt, if this bozo asks me out, I'm calling the ACLU. "Would you please tell me what this is about?" she asks.

Thrusting a vindictive finger at Tam, Hink yells, "You drove the getaway vehicle in a felony strongarm robbery!"

Pitt adds, "Now give us the name of the scumbag who committed the strongarm robbery and maybe we'll ask the judge to go easy on you!"

"There must be some mistake," Tam says, "Did you say you're looking for a red car?"

"We're looking for your boyfriend!" Pitt shouts. Hink finds a stray sneaker on the floor, "Is this his sneaker?!"

"My boyfriend hasn't committed any robberies, and my car's not red."

"Shut up!" Pitt yells, and then Hink continues, "We're going to do you a huge favor and give you a chance to save yourself."

"From what?" Tam asks.

Hink shoves Tam against the wall and removes the handcuffs, telling her, "I'm leaving my card. If your boyfriend doesn't turn himself in, we'll be back." Pitt aims his gun at Tam once more, "And if we come back, you're in serious shit, honey. You should thank us for not hauling your ass off to jail right now!"

Hink scribbles on his business card, then drops it onto the sofa. Guns drawn, Pitt and Hink tensely hop to the doorway. Pitt warns Tam, "If you step outside before we're

17

done, you will be arrested!" Then Pitt yells outside, "We're coming out!" Pitt rushes out of the apartment with Hink on his tail.

Rubbing her wrists, Tam looks outside, where two police cars block the alley and a gray-haired cop with a sagging paunch stands by the Mustang. Storming the alley, Pitt and Hink order our neighbors to stay back, while a stout Asian woman with a huge camera takes photographs of Tam's car.

*The Layman's Handbook for Those Falsely Accused of Felonies, page 31...**Physical evidence** is in the eye of the beholder. To an especially hellbent prosecutor, your physical evidence may actually exist only in theory...*

Walking home from Liz's, I remember that I still have the ripped-up scraps of paper in my pocket. I pull them out and toss them into a trashcan at the curb.

Our building seems quiet as I head up the stairs. Then Amy from next door runs at me screaming, "Where have you been?!" I see Tam through our open doorway. She's on the sofa and looks like she's been attacked. "Oh my god, what happened?! Was that crazy woman here?!"

"It was the police!" Amy squeaks.

"Why were the police here?" I ask.

"To arrest you," Tam says as she hands me Officer Hink's card, on which he's written 'FELONY STRONGARM ROBBERY.'

"Cops carry business cards? How civilized," I say as I look at the mess on the floor. I bend to untangle the cable box from some old sweaters and put it back on the TV. Tam informs me, "That insane homeless bitch reported a felony strongarm robbery and told the cops that I drove the getaway car."

"But that's ridiculous," I say. Tam's more shaken than I've ever seen her. "What the hell did they do to you?" I ask. Tam doesn't respond so Amy gives me an overexcited re-enactment of the blue knights storming our tiny apartment. Shocked, I reach for the phone and call the Santa Monica Police Station.

I ask to speak with Officer Hink, and the Mickey Mouse voice on the other end of the phone informs me that this is Officer Hink. "There's been a big mistake," I announce, "I'm coming in there right now."

"Um...okay," he says.

"I'll be there in five minutes."

Hink asks in a shaky voice, "Did, um...did you take a piece of paper?"

"What?" I ask.

"A piece of paper," Hink says.

"Oh...yeah."

"Um, what did you do with it?" Hink asks.

"I ripped it up and threw it in a trashcan," I tell him.

"Could you get it back? That would really help."

"Fine, I'll find it in the trash and I'll be right there." I hang up the phone and look at Tam, who's still dazed on the sofa. "Are you okay?" I ask her. She nods slightly and I walk to the door. Tam breaks her grim silence, "Wait!"

I look back, "What?"

"I'm coming with you."

We drive to 5th Street to retrieve the scraps of paper. I hop out of the car and see what I hadn't noticed before. The entire block is lined with identical, recycling-style trashcans. "Which one is it?" Tam asks.

"Shit..." I reply

I walk along the curb. "It's this one," I say as I pull up the lid and look inside. But I'm wrong. As I look at the trashcans up and down the street, Tam yells from the car, "If you think I'm digging through all these trashcans to look for a piece of paper, then that car did something to your head when it hit you. What's on the paper, anyway?"

"Nothing. Just the first two digits of your license plate number." Tam waits in the car, annoyed, while I try to retrace my steps in my head. Finally, utilizing the clever plan of looking in every trashcan along the street, I find the stained scraps of paper and we're on our way.

The Santa Monica Police Station is deserted. Its vacuum-like stillness is creepy. The police station lies in a wide, municipal complex that also includes the Santa Monica City Hall and Civic Auditorium. Its flatness is overwhelming. We start up the long path, our voices dulled by the nuclear-winter acoustics of this flat, lifesucking expanse.

The police station is undergoing a massive renovation and, as we approach it, we can't find an entrance. We walk up a flimsy wooden ramp, then under scaffolds draped with dirty plastic sheets. Soon we see a big hole blasted through the wall, covered with more plastic sheets. Above the hole is a battered piece of cardboard with the word 'ENTRANCE' written in sloppy handwriting. I reach for the plastic sheet and turn to Tam, who looks very nervous. I tell her, "You don't have to do this. I'll just go."

"What if they arrest you?"

"I don't know. What if they arrest you?" I reply.

"I haven't done anything," Tam says.

"Neither have I. This is crazy. I'm straightening it out right now." I pull the plastic sheet aside and step into the police station. Tam follows me, but we pause just inside the hole, alarmed.

"Are you sure this is the right place?" Tam asks, "It looks like a bomb went off in here." We stand there, afraid to move in the dark, dirty hallway under the flickering lights that buzz like locusts. The floor tiles have been ripped up and tossed into sloppy heaps. Broken furniture is piled everywhere. Crusted plastic sheets hang from the ceiling, pulsing with sickly fluorescent light.

In the eerie distance, I see a grim yellow square of light. Slowly making our way through the apocalyptic mess, we approach the smeared window. There's a man behind the glass. I look at his badge and realize that this is Officer Hink, the undersized punk who shoved my girlfriend around. Nonetheless, I put on my friendliest smile and introduce myself.

Hink smiles nervously and thanks me for coming in. I tell Hink that I don't know what he thinks happened but I was struck by a car while crossing the street. Hink says that's fine and there's really no need to get into it. I don't know what to make of this, so I repeat what I said, that I was hit by a car at the corner of 3rd and Rose. Hink asks if I brought the piece of paper with me, and I say yes, pulling the ragged scraps from my pocket. I slide them through the slot in the bulletproof glass. Hink looks at the scraps of paper then pushes them to the side. He looks like he doesn't know what to do.

"Do I need to make a statement or something?" I ask, but Hink waves his hand and says, "Oh no, there's no need for that."

"Okay, then...what?" I ask. Hink sits awkwardly, avoiding eye contact with me. He tells me to wait there and disappears behind the cubicle walls. I look at Tam and she shrugs.

More minutes pass. I glance around the deserted bombed-out hallway, getting a little nervous. "Why don't I need to make a statement?" I wonder aloud.

The Layman's Handbook for Those Falsely Accused of Felonies, page 11...Beware when a **police officer** *tells you that you have nothing to worry about. He's probably lying or, at best, wrong...*

A deep, jarring buzz shakes the laminated wood door and Hink steps into the hall. He pauses uncomfortably. "Why don't we go over here?" he suggests, leading us around a corner into another devastated stretch of hallway much like the one we came from. Clusters of cables hang from holes in the dropped ceiling. The fluorescent lights flicker more violently here, casting spastic dancing shadows on all the dusty surfaces.

A long trophy case lines one wall. The glass is caked with dirt, obscuring the sinister objects inside. In front of the trophy case are three orange pressed-fiberglass chairs, like in a seedy bus station. Hink asks me to sit down.

I cautiously sit on the dirty chair. Hink sits down next to me, and Tam sits on my other side. These chairs are connected at the seat so we're uneasily close to each other. Hink pats my knee and begins spouting a clumsy speech about the letter of the law versus the spirit of the law. I try to pay attention but there's something off-kilter about Hink's anxious sincerity. This cop is vastly at odds with the brutal little tough guy described by Tam and Amy Nextdoor. Maybe he only beats up girls.

"Listen," Hink says, "I've spoken to this woman, and she's behaved very badly."

"She hit me with her car," I remind him.

"Yes, and she's very sorry," Hink tells me.

"Sorry? You said she accused me of felony strongarm robbery."

"Yes, but obviously that didn't happen," he says, "Remember what I said about the spirit of the law." Hink then tells me that I have nothing to worry about because he'll take care of it. I ask Hink about what the enraged driver did - hitting me with her car, stalking me, attacking Tam, and falsely accusing me of crimes - and how that fits into the spirit of the law. Hink nods and glances around, then tells me that what she did violated both the letter and the spirit of the law, and for my own protection, as well as to set things right, I should file a complaint against the woman.

"Okay, great. Let's do it," I reply.

Hink gets flustered. "Oh no!" he blurts out, "You can't do that here."

"Why not? This is the police station, isn't it?"

"Yes, but this is Santa Monica. When you got hit by that car, technically you were in Los Angeles. You have to file your complaint in Los Angeles."

"But the bogus robbery this woman reported happened in Los Angeles too. That store at 5th and Rose is in L.A., not Santa Monica."

"Yes," Hink agrees.

"And you guys got involved in that," I say.

"Yes," Hink nervously says.

"So why can't I give my complaint to you like she did?" I ask.

"Because you can't," he squawks, jumping up from the chair, "You have to go to Pacific Station."

I start to stand. A deep buzzing noise erupts in the flickering shadows. A dark door is thrown open and an Asian woman with a big camera leaps in front of me and flashes off a blinding photo. Hink thanks me for coming in. Still blinded, I ask, "Are you sure this is all okay?"

"Absolutely," Hink says, "I'll take care of everything."

As Tam and I start to leave down the dark hallway, I realize that Hink hasn't acknowledged Tamara in any way since we arrived. Far from simply avoiding eye contact, it's more like he genuinely can't see her. I chalk this up to embarrassment from his earlier treatment of her and decide that it's best to just let it go.

We walk toward the big hole in the wall when I remember something and turn back. I call out to Hink as he slinks away. Hink flinches at the sound of his name, and then pauses before slowly turning around. Before I say anything, Hink yammers out the address of Pacific Station and turns to go. "Wait, that's not it!" I say and Hink squeamishly turns to face us again. I tell him that I don't know the woman's name or license plate number, and he must since he spoke to her. Hink simply stands there with his mouth hanging open. Then Hink tells me to give his name to the officer at Pacific Station and he'll take care of it. So rattled by my request that he forgets his handy business cards, Hink quickly scrawls his name on a tiny tablet, rips off the page and hands it to me. Hink yammers that it was nice meeting me and hurries back toward the bulletproof window.

Back in the car, I'm wondering if the diarrheic knots in my stomach stem from a subconscious fear that I've committed some capital crime without realizing it, like in Stalin's Soviet Union. But as we drive out of Santa Monica, my queasiness fades. Maybe it was just brought on by the flickering fluorescent lights, I tell myself.

We arrive at Pacific Station, which seems deserted as well but lacks the catastrophic devastation of the previous police station. As we enter the silent lobby, Tam and I immediately notice lots of colorful posters covering the municipal-tile walls. All of this civic artwork is designed in a clunky style as if drawn by a kindergarten class, yet these posters contain messages about how we citizens can successfully co-exist with the Los Angeles Police Department. I pause, staring at a childlike poster that tells us not to park in a red zone because it could interfere with police activity. Do small children really need to know this? Does the police poster division think drivers are so dense that they must be approached on a nursery school level? Or is the LAPD Poster Unit actually made up of children happily drawing these instructive scenes?

We move past the posters and find the cop at the desk, who's almost as wide as he is tall. He smiles and gestures for us to wait while he gets off the phone. I look back at the weird posters. Maybe the posters are drawn this way because that's how the cops themselves like them. *"Oh Sarge, isn't it darling? Just like it was drawn by a five-year-old!"*

The musclebound box of a guy behind the desk is Officer Beale. Beale hangs up the phone and gives me a bright smile. "Hey there! What happened to you?" he asks. I tell him that I was sideswiped by a car while crossing the street. "Oh no!" Officer Beale says. He steps out from behind the desk and puts his firm hand on my shoulder, very concerned. Officer Beale asks if I want to see a doctor and I tell him that I'm not that hurt. "Well, let's have a look at that leg," Beale says, crouching down and pulling up the leg of my shorts. "This leg?" he asks, looking up. Officer Beale is feeling my leg, working his hand a bit higher than the spot where the car hit me. He smiles up at me and pays me a compliment for keeping fit. I thank him, gently pulling my leg away from his hand.

Beale walks back behind the desk and starts filling out a report. I begin to tell him the whole story. Beale is riveted to my tale, jotting it all down with a wide smile. Like Officer Hink, Beale doesn't seem to notice Tamara at all. I keep glancing over at Tam, just to make sure she's still there. Beale asks if I got the license plate number of the car and I tell him about Officer Hink. I begin to tell Beale about the angry stalking and the bogus strongarm robbery but Beale raises his hand, stopping me. "Let's just keep it to where you got hit by the car and the driver left the scene. Anything you were falsely accused of, we can forget about."

Beale writes Hink's badge number on the report, then rips off my pink copy of the report and hands it to me with a beaming smile. I'm suddenly exhausted. It's been a long day and I'm pretty sure Officer Beale just winked at me. I want to go home. Beale steps out from the desk, grasps my shoulder and tells me to call him if there's anything I'd like to talk about. Beale says nothing to Tam and we leave, silently staring at the kiddie posters on our way out.

Back home, our worried neighbors stop by to ask about the day's police activity, so we tell them the whole story. Our neighbors are disgusted as they hear about the Santa Monica police and the crazed road-rage woman. The funny thing is, we're all talking about it in the past tense, as if it were over, when in fact this little German Expressionist nightmare is just getting started.

Officer Beale had mentioned that, due to the enormous volume of complaints, it would probably be a week or so before I heard from anyone. However, on Tuesday morning when I stop editing long enough to check the answering machine, I find a message from Detective Bender of Pacific Division. "How prompt," I say. I'm actually impressed, which frankly, makes me an utter moron. So, like Heidi skipping through the Alps, happily unaware that she's ten seconds away from getting gang-raped by the entire Austrian cavalry, I pick up the phone and call.

"Bender," says the gravel-scratched female voice.

"Detective Bender, hi. My name's Steve Bevilacqua. You called me about a complaint I filed."

"Oh you," she grumbles.

"Thanks for getting back to me so quickly," I say.

"You should go to prison for what you did!" Detective Bender sharply announces.

"Huh?"

"You heard me, scumbag," the voice growls.

"Um, I think there's been a mistake. I'm the guy who got hit by the car."

"Oh please, I wish she had killed you with her car. That's what garbage like you deserves!"

"Whoa! What? I'm sorry, I don't understand. Did you talk to Officer Hink?" I ask.

"Yeah, I talked to Hink. And you're lucky."

"Lucky...how?" I ask.

"You're lucky you're not going to prison! That's what usually happens to muggers," Bender sneers.

"I didn't mug anybody. A car ran me down in the street and the driver took off."

"You have no grounds for a complaint!" Bender yells.

"Why not?"

"If you make me investigate this bullshit complaint, I'll make you so fucking sorry! Now drop it or I'll personally see to it that you go to prison for years! You should be charged with felony assault and robbery for punching that woman and stealing her bag!"

"I didn't steal her bag, and I didn't punch her, either."

"So consider yourself lucky that the Santa Monica D.A. has thrown out the complaint against you," Bender barks.

"Well, that complaint never happened, but I guess that's good," I say.

"Good?! Listen asshole, I could make this a lot worse for you!"

"The complaint against me is really dropped?" I ask.

"Yes! Now will you drop this complaint of yours?!"

"Okay, I guess. But shouldn't that driver have to go to traffic school or something? She's pretty dangerous."

"I'm warning you," Bender snarls, "You make me investigate this and you'll regret it."

"Okay. But you know, I didn't attack anybody."

"Goodbye!" Bender yells as she slams down the phone. I sit there trying to fathom what just happened. What was Detective Bender talking about? Did she talk to Hink and if so, what the hell did he tell her? But still, I admire Bender's commitment to pursue her calling while maintaining a sunny, almost giggly, demeanor. She would've made a good nun.

Before I can move, the phone rings again.

"Hello?"

"Can I speak to Stephen Beh...Belav..." The voice mangles my name like a telemarketer until I cut him off, "Yeah, that's me. What do you want?" But this is no telemarketer, it's Officer Hink. I tell Hink that I just got off the phone with Detective Bender and he innocently replies "Oh?"

I ask Hink if he'd spoken with Bender and he says, "No...I mean, yes, actually."

"What did you say to her?" I ask.

"That's not important," he replies.

"You sure? Because that wasn't entirely pleasant."

"Um, listen, the reason I'm calling is..." His voice trails off uncomfortably.

"Yeah?"

"I spoke with the driver of the vehicle and, uh, she's very sorry. She feels badly about the whole incident now."

"Okay," I say.

"The complaint against you has been dropped," Hink tells me, "And now I would personally appreciate it if you would drop your complaint against this woman."

"Well, shouldn't she get a ticket or something for running down a pedestrian? She could kill somebody."

"You weren't badly injured," Hink says.

"I know, I never said I was," I tell him.

"Then just be thankful you weren't hurt or even killed. You're very lucky," he announces, and being called 'lucky' by the second law enforcement officer this morning is beginning to irritate me. I ask Hink, "You don't think some road-rage warning is in order?"

"She's very sorry!" Hink whines, his voice cracking slightly, "Now I think it's best if you just walk away from it, okay?! You should drop your complaint against her, because the complaint against you has been dropped."

"So the complaint against me is definitely dropped?" I ask.

"Yes!" Hink assures me.

"Alright, if that's what you think is best. I pretty much just told Detective Bender that, anyway," I inform him.

"Good," Hink sighs. But my conversation with Bender was so jarring that I'm curious, so I ask Hink, "What did you tell Detective Bender about what happened on Sunday?"

"Well...that doesn't matter now," Hink stammers.

"Why not?" I ask.

"Because you've agreed to drop your complaint," he says.

"But-"

"I have to go. I'm on duty." Hink hangs up on me. I sit there, completely confused. A dial tone starts ringing through the receiver. Well, at least it's over, I tell myself.

It must be over. Officer Hink said so.

fly, monkeys, fly...

The next day, life returns to its regular chaos of editing round the clock. I haven't earned a dime in almost a year as I've struggled to make the movie, and my life is beginning to implode. The events of that grisly Sunday quickly fade into a Venice summer tale to be told alongside stories of German tourists in obscene speedos asking locals where they can find the lifeguards from *BAYWATCH*.

A few weeks later, it's Friday evening and, aside from eating an occasional sandwich over the sink, I've been sitting at this editing system for the past eight hundred and twenty three hours. Our neighborhood's annual summer invasion of tourists is in full swing outside my window, and I'm assembling a scene where young drunk guys play Risk and joke about how their lives are falling apart.

Tam gets home from work and tells me about a barbecue someone from her office is having. I'm only half-listening so she swats the back of my head and says, "It's Friday night. Take a break. We have to go to this thing."

"Fine, but I haven't checked the mail all week. Let me do that."

I head to the mailbox and find the usual junk. Then I pause. Hiding among the cell phone offers and carpet cleaning flyers is a letter from the Santa Monica City Attorney.

The other mail spills from my hand as I open the letter. "Dear Mr. Bevilaque," it reads, officially misspelling my name, "You are hereby ordered to appear in Department S of the Municipal Court of Santa Monica on August 9th at 8:30 am. The following charges have been filed against you..." The letter is signed by "Noreen McDonough, Deputy City Attorney".

I stagger back to the apartment. What the hell happened? What did Hink and Bender do? Tam sees the letter in my hand. "What's that?" she asks.

"I've been screwed," I inform her.

I examine the letter more closely and learn that I've been charged with a violation of 'Section 242', which means nothing to me. The letter then proclaims that "Bevilaque" also committed a violation of 'Penal Code 243' which seems to have something to do with a "violent assault". I've also been accused of a violation of Section 594 in which "Bevilaque did maliciously deface with graffitti (sic) or other inscribed matreiel (sic) and/or did otherwise destroy real property." I have no idea what any of this means. All I can tell from this letter is that these people can't spell for shit.

Impotent in my inability to understand the strange language of the letter, I read it again, trying to make some connection between its foreign code and what actually occurred on that

Sunday. Tam is furious. She snatches the letter out of my hand and drags me to the cookout, but by the time we get there, the beer's gone and I'm downright shellshocked.

Early Saturday morning, the editing system sits dark and dead as I stare blankly at my invitation to the dance. One strange thing about this letter is that while I was originally accused of felonies, all of these charges seem to be misdemeanors. I don't know what to make of this. I've never been charged with anything before. I've never even been inside a courtroom. Lacking any better ideas, I call every single person I know and leave a bunch of messages. The first person to call me back is Rob D-, a video game producer whose girlfriend is a pal of Tam's.

Rob D- tells me to call his buddy Curt, who's a corporate lawyer. I've met Curt a few times and he's an insufferable prick, but I call him anyway. Curt grows outraged as he hears the story and, surprisingly, offers to help.

*The Layman's Handbook for Those Falsely Accused of Felonies, page 25...Always get a **lawyer** who knows the area of law that you need him to know. If not, the consequences may be devastating...*

Curt looks up my charges and their corresponding sentences, then informs me that I'm facing three years in prison. However, like everything Curt tells me, this isn't entirely correct. I'm actually looking at two years in prison, a distinction that, given the circumstances, I find somewhat meaningless. I ask Curt why I'm not being charged with the original felonies of strongarm robbery and assault, but he doesn't know. However, I have since learned why.

The Layman's Handbook for Those Falsely Accused of Felonies, page 17...You generally won't be charged with a felony unless you've been arrested for it, because the first thing a District

Attorney does when taking a felony case to trial is to ask for your **arrest record**...

If Officer Hink was trying to screw me, he missed slightly because he never actually arrested me. I walked in there on my own, and Hink gave me his little speech, then he shook my hand and sent me home, which apparently has created the need for this very long list of misdemeanors. However, as Curt tells me, one of my charges was passed under a brand new law called Prop 22, which was designed to curb gang activity. If I'm found guilty of this charge, it comes with a mandatory six-month prison sentence. My complete lack of any gang affiliation won't matter at all, at least not to the court. Hink's diatribe about the "letter of the law vs. the spirit of the law" is growing more ironic by the minute. I tell Curt that this can't be true, but he tells me that it is true, I'm going up the river on some instantly-abused new gang statute.

While my situation rapidly grows worse, Curt tells me that what I need to do is call the LAPD Detective who handled my hit-and-run complaint against the driver. Curt instructs me to tell her what's happened and ask for her help. I tell Curt that, based on my conversation with Detective Bender, I don't think this is a very good idea. "She called me things like 'asshole' and wasn't particularly helpful," I explain.

Now Curt gets snippy, telling me that I don't know the legal system like he does. "What harm can it do?" he scornfully snorts, and he sharply refuses to do anything to help me until I talk to Detective Bender again. Like a fool, I agree to this.

Monday rolls around, and I call Pacific Station. "Bender," growls the two-pack-a-day voice.

"Detective Bender, hi. My name's Steve Bevilacqua. I spoke to you back in May about a hit-and-run complaint I filed. I'm the pedestrian who was hit by a car."

"Yeah, I remember you."

"Good, because I really need your help."

"You're the asshole who attacked that woman," Bender replies.

"What? No, I was hit by a car while crossing the street."

"That case is closed. The D.A. rejected it," she tells me.

"You asked me to drop my complaint," I remind her.

"Dropped? Yeah, that's right. It was dropped," Bender says.

"I need your help. I'd like to have my complaint investigated."

"It was investigated!" she barks.

"I thought you just said it was dropped. Or rejected," I say.

"Are you looking for trouble, you little shit?! That case was investigated!"

"But you never took a statement from me, or even asked me what happened."

"I did take a statement from you!" Bender yells.

"Um...no, you didn't," I cautiously tell her.

"Do you want me to come find you?! Because I promise you'll regret it."

"No, please. I'm not trying to make trouble."

"I'm busy!" she snaps.

"I understand that, and I really appreciate you taking the time to talk to me-"

"There's nothing to talk about!" she yells, cutting me off.

"You told me that the complaint against me in Santa Monica had been thrown out, and you advised me to drop my complaint."

"Yeah, so?" she growls.

"But the complaint against me wasn't thrown out."

"I never said it was! That case is closed and I'm not going to re-open it!"

"I'm sorry, but that is what you told me. Listen, I'm sure you're swamped with cases, but I was hoping you could help me out."

"You're a fucking liar!" she yells.

Okay, clearly this isn't going well. I am quickly losing control of my conversation with Detective Bender, which would be assuming that I had any control over it in the first place, which isn't remotely true. Nonetheless, thinking that the worst that could happen would be for things to remain as they are, I attempt to forge ahead, "I think there's been a misunderstanding and I apologize. But I'm in trouble here. I was hit by a car and now I've been charged with things that never happened. You told me they dropped the complaint, and I should forget about it, so I did. But now it's come back."

"I never told you they dropped that complaint! And I think you're getting exactly what you deserve for assaulting that poor woman."

"I didn't assault anybody. Why do you think that? You never even asked me what happened."

"You didn't get hit by a car. You mugged that woman and I think you're lucky." There it is again. Why is it every time I speak with a law enforcement official, they keep insisting that I'm 'lucky'?

"I'm sorry," I tell Bender, "But right now I don't feel very lucky. I'm facing charges for something I didn't do. For god's sake, how 'lucky' would you feel if this were happening to you?"

There's silence. I'm confused. I'm wondering if Bender's still on the other end of the phone. I begin to say "Hello?" when Bender's voice booms through the receiver, "IS THAT A THREAT?!"

I now have absolutely no idea what's going on. "Is what a threat?" I ask.

Bender explodes, "Are you threatening me, asshole?!"

"What? I'm not threatening you," I say.

"You are threatening me!" Bender shouts, "You just threatened to hit me with your car!"

"No, I didn't," I tell her.

"Yes, you did! Do you know what happens when you threaten a Los Angeles police detective?! Do you have any idea what kind of shit you're in now?!"

"But I didn't threaten you."

"You did! You threatened to run me over with your car, just like what happened to you!"

"Wait a minute. You just said that I didn't get hit by the car, so how can I be threatening you with that?"

"I've got you now!" Bender yells, "Threatening a police detective! I'm gonna put you away for years, you piece of shit!"

"Whoa, wait! Please, Detective Bender, I did not threaten you," I plead with her.

"Yeah, you did. I felt very threatened," she growls menacingly through the receiver.

"I'm sorry. Nothing I said was intended to be a threat," I reply.

"Doesn't matter! You're in a shitload of trouble now! I'm making a report to my superiors that you threatened to kill me."

I yelp, "I didn't threaten to kill you!"

"Yeah? We'll see who they believe," Bender snarls, "I'm an LAPD detective and you're the lying scumbag who mugged that woman. I'm bringing charges against you, and you're going to prison for a long time."

"No, please, I'm very sorry," I stammer.

"Fuck you, asshole. I'm putting you away," Bender says with a chuckle, "And I know where to find you."

"Oh my god." Overcome with panic, I slam down the phone. This can't be happening. Actually, I'm not sure what is happening. All I know at this moment is that things just got a lot worse. A few minutes later, it's still sinking in and shows no signs of stopping.

Somehow, not only am I facing a prison sentence for something I didn't do, I'm now also facing a longer prison sentence for something I didn't say. I take a quick moment to observe how Curt's advice was easily the most disastrous advice possible. But there's no time to waste on that because I've got much bigger problems now.

I pace through the apartment, frantically trying to figure out what to do. If a simple phone call hoping to straighten it out can make it this much worse, there's no telling where this might go. My legs suddenly feel weak. I need to speak with somebody who knows what they're talking about.

"God damn it!" Tam announces, "I need you to finish the movie. I can't believe we're falling even further behind because of that lunatic who hit you with her car. I'm finding you a lawyer."

"I can't afford a lawyer," I sadly point out.

"I can't afford to have this movie unfinished much longer," Tam says, "And I can't afford to have you go to prison because then the movie will never get done."

"You're right. Let's find a lawyer."

"I'm on it," Tam replies.

Tamara's office is next to an auto shop for expensive foreign cars and the guys who work there rope her into a conversation every time she walks by. One of these guys is Jimmy H-, who looks like a wholesome Midwestern farmboy. Jimmy actually did grow up on a farm in the Midwest, but that's as far as the All-American facade holds true, because Jimmy is a violent drunken brawler who gets arrested almost every weekend. Apparently, he's been involved in some weird car destruction incidents as well.

Jimmy has a lawyer who handles his constant arrests and has managed to keep him from serving any real time despite the astounding volume of criminal charges. Jimmy tells Tam he'll refer me to his lawyer, so I swing by the auto shop to talk to him. As the mechanics hammer away on Alfa Romeos and other flashy sportscars, Jimmy tells me stories about his past, very distinctive stories, which kicks off a bizarre new trend in my life.

When you're falsely accused of a crime, strangers come forward to tell you secrets that they've kept hidden for years. They seem to figure that you're no threat so they might as well spill. What are you going to do about it? Nobody believes you. You're going down for something you didn't even do. In the coming months, when people hear my story, it happens. Someone will pull me aside and say, "I hit a homeless guy with my car once. I took off and they never caught me." You're never sure how to respond.

Do you say "Atta boy, tiger!" or just a simple "How interesting"? Eventually, I realize that people want you to congratulate them on their unpunished crimes. But this disturbing trend builds and soon people are confiding to me about the house they burnt down or the time they totalled a block's worth of parked cars, and then waiting for me to pat them on the back.

I suppose everyone gets away with something at some point but I never suspected the degree of criminal secrets in otherwise unassuming people. I break my share of small laws but I never accidentally killed someone back in high school, and there are far more people out there who have than you'd ever suspect. And they all got away with it, yet I'm going to jail for something that never happened. Not only that, now I'm the great confessor for everyone's dark guilty secrets. This is turning out to be one excellent summer.

Jimmy tells me about his lawyer. His name's Gavin Dodd and he's in Century City. The guy must be good, Jimmy's only done a few days in the hole and he's always guilty. So I call Dodd and make an appointment. Tam offers to come along.

Bucking all expectations, Tam had recently succeeded in selling her dismal lemon of a car. A cadaverous young German appeared at our door, announcing that he's here to apply to a "Hollywood film school" and needs a car. The German sees the editing system sprawled across the living room and runs to my side. Watching the scenes, the German excitedly begins barking insane suggestions like "Show more feet!" I start to disagree, but I see the look on Tam's face and shift gears mid-sentence. "That's brilliant!" I exclaim, and the German informs me that he's going to be the next Orson Welles.

We take the German to look at the Mustang. Tam gets in, reaching over to open the passenger door before the German notices that the outside handle doesn't work. I distract the German by informing him that Orson Welles shot *TOUCH OF EVIL* right here in Venice Beach, not in Mexico like most people think. Tam turns the key, but the engine won't start. As the car makes some emphysema-inspired noises, I distract the German by telling him that Roger Corman shot many of his 60's biker movies like *THE WILD ANGELS* in this neighborhood. The car still won't start, so I tell the German that the movie *MOTHER, JUGS AND SPEED* was shot on our corner and flash Tam a look informing her that I can't keep this up much longer. The Mustang coughs to life and the starry-eyed creep actually buys it, as we thank god for foreign tourists.

So the 'getaway vehicle' described to the police is now being driven by some skeletal German and Tam has bought a spiffy used Saab convertible that is, ironically, much closer to the road-rage nut's description of the getaway vehicle than Tam's former car. The crazy lady reported that the strongarm felons fled the scene in a red foreign car when Tam's Mustang was black and American, so Tam's accidentally corrected her mistakes by buying the red Saab.

We're getting blown to hell on the freeway with the top down, but neither of us has ever owned a convertible before and that top is staying down until the novelty wears off. We drive through the stunted skyscrapers of Century City and find the office of Gavin Dodd.

Gavin Dodd is precisely groomed. His silver suit is shiny but not totally awful, and it perfectly matches his meticulous silver hair-helmet. Dodd's an overly tanned, barrel-chested bulldog, the kind who gets ferociously obsessed when clenching his teeth on a knotted sock. Dodd is puzzled as he reads my charges, so I tell him the whole story from the screeching tires to Detective Bender's threats. Dodd loudly announces that in his thirty years of practicing law, this is the most absurd thing he's ever heard, which marks the first of countless times that I will hear this. Every lawyer in the coming year reacts exactly the same way, "In my X years of practicing law, this is the most ridiculous thing I've ever heard." It gets old. On the other hand, it's a great way of learning how long a lawyer's been practicing without having to ask.

Dodd is outraged that the driver who hit me is getting away with this. Dodd thinks that the cops are morons, and he thinks Noreen McDonough must be an idiot.

Then comes the bad news. Dodd starts rattling off the long list of things that I've done wrong. Not criminal, just wrong. "You should never have talked to the police!" Dodd barks.

"But why not?" I ask, "I didn't do anything."

Dodd roars, "Never talk to the police!" Dodd yells that I shouldn't have found that scrap of paper in the trash and taken it to the station. "I was just trying to help," I tell him.

"Never cooperate with the police!" Dodd yells, "They'll just try to fuck you! Which is exactly what they've done." Dodd's face grows scarlet as he clamps his teeth on my case like it's the knotted sock. Meanwhile, the color is draining from my face. Dodd notices my distress and asks what's wrong.

"This is insane," I tell him, "I like to think that cops are good. Sure, there are bad ones but, for the most part, I really want to believe that they're good while criminals and lawyers – no offense – are bad."

Dodd flashes his blinding smile, "I love you, kid! You're so fucking innocent. And I don't just mean of these bullshit charges." He bellows a big bulldog laugh then continues, "Now here's the problem. Since you were dumb enough to try to do the right thing, you're definitely going to trial."

My stomach lurches, "What?! Why?"

"You should never have gone to that police station," he says, "And you definitely shouldn't have taken that ripped-up paper to those pricks. You screwed yourself there. Now you're going to have to go on trial. Did you give the cops a statement?"

I think for a second, "No, I didn't."

"Good!" he yells.

"Well, I tried to, but they said it didn't matter."

Dodd roars with laughter, "Well at least you've got that going for you."

"How so? I didn't do anything wrong," I say again.

"Who cares?!" Dodd yells, "That doesn't matter anymore. You're FUCKED! And you walked right into it. In a weird way, it's a shame you weren't hurt when that car nailed you, because for some reason they've decided to protect this bitch driver and railroad your ass into prison."

"Yeah. Why is that?" I ask.

"No idea," Dodd says, "Why does a dog eat its own puke? You can't waste your life trying to figure out these assholes. I can't wait to get these motherfuckers on the stand."

I'm impressed by Dodd's bellicose style. The problem is that his rancorous outrage is making me sick to my stomach. The more he yells about it, the worse I feel.

I'm about to throw up. I have to get out, now. I excuse myself and run to the bathroom, but I just stand at the toilet. Away from the wrath of Dodd, my frantic urge to puke quiets down. I go to the sink and splash water on my face. I look at myself in the mirror. This sucks, and it's getting worse every minute. I take a few deep breaths and return to the conference room.

Dodd is now pacing around the room, furiously erupting. I tense up again at the sight of him, but I'm determined to hang on. Dodd sees me, "How you doing, kid?"

"I'm okay," I tell him. "Good!" he bellows, pounding my back. I sit down as Dodd resumes his march around the table. "So how're you feeling about this?" he asks.

"Well, basically you're telling me that I'm screwed," I reply.

"Yep! But the good news is, a lawyer on heroin could get you off of these bullshit charges," he announces.

My voice quivers slightly as I ask, "How about you? Can you get me off of this?"

"Yeah, kid. No problem. They'll regret the day they decided to take a hit-and-run pedestrian and listen to the bullshit story of the fucking driver. The wrong person's been charged here, dammit!" He's arguing the case right now, and it sounds pretty good. He slams his hands on the table, "Have you ever been arrested before?"

"No, I wasn't even arrested with this," I say.

"And you're a pretty well behaved guy?" Dodd asks.

"Yeah," I reply, "I jaywalk sometimes. I don't rob liquor stores or anything."

"Good!" Dodd starts pacing again, "How about mundane shit? You got DUI's or anything?"

"Nope," I tell him.

"Excellent!" he yells, "But since you've obviously never been through this before, this is gonna be news to you."

"What?" I ask.

"This trial's going to cost you twelve thousand dollars."

My stomach almost empties on the conference table, "What?!"

Tam jumps in, "Is that for the trial, or the pre-trial?"

Dodd shakes his head, "There is no pre-trial. He took that paper to the station and he talked to the asshole cops. Listen, your boy here meant well but he's screwed. He's going to trial."

"I don't have twelve thousand dollars," I tell him, "Shit, right now I don't have anything."

"Well, you better find it," Dodd says, "Because that's what any decent lawyer in this city is going to charge you for this trial."

I'm getting clammy, as the idea of going to prison on false charges because I can't afford a lawyer sets up shop in my gut. "What if I can't find it?" I ask.

"Listen kid, I don't mean to scare you but these charges do come with some prison time. Most judges would let you go with something other than prison, but..." He looks at my letter, "I think this one comes with a mandatory sentence. The judge won't have any say."

Tam says, "The gang one." Dodd winks at her in the way men of his generation do, men who still use the word 'tomato' when describing a woman. "Yeah, the gang one," he says, "And that's total bullshit. I mean, shit, look at you kid. Do they really expect us to believe that you're in a fucking gang?"

I mutter, "But I don't have the-"

"We'll find the money," Tam interrupts me, "But what then?"

Dodd looks at my letter, "Hmm, August 9th is your court date, that's when they'll set the trial. You guys go get twelve thousand dollars. I'll hand this over to my associate and he'll take you through the trial."

As I deflate in the chair, Tam sits up sharply, "Why your associate? Why don't you do it?"

"Oh believe me, normally I would," Dodd says, "With a case like this, I like to set things right. But tomorrow I leave for

Bali. I've chartered a boat. I'm taking my wife, my kids, her kids. I'll be gone for six weeks and that's your trial time right there. But don't worry. My associate's a good man. He'll get you off this, no problem. I'd introduce you to him now but he just left for the day."

Tam says, "But it's only 2:00."

Dodd shrugs, "Yeah, his first marriage is breaking up. It's a mess, ugly as hell and hitting him hard. But he'll do a great job, I promise."

Tam asks, "Will you be involved at all?"

"Sure, I'll just be off the coast of Bali. And some other islands."

The conference room is starting to spin. I jump to my feet. "I need to think about this," I tell Dodd, "I'll call you later today."

Dodd slaps my back and says, "I like you, kid, and I'll take care of this for you. But I was actually going to take off right after seeing you. Got to pack." Dodd writes on his card, "This is my number at home. Call me."

damascus...

Back in the convertible with the wind forcing us to yell, Tam and I assess the situation. My first-ever meeting with a criminal defense attorney has made me physically ill. Beyond that, I don't know what to think because I've been so disastrously wrong at every turn. I'm almost afraid to think anything.

Tam likes Dodd but she's annoyed that he won't be handling it himself. "Who is he passing it off to?" she yells, "And if he's handing it to an associate, why can't it be a woman? I think that'd be smarter. A female attorney would help defuse the fact that you're a man."

"Where the hell am I supposed to get twelve grand to pay this guy?!" I yell, "And why is he so certain that there's going to be a trial? They can't prove these charges, they never happened." A new dagger of tension hits my gut, "We didn't even talk about Bender's threats. What if she tries to railroad me too? Will that be another twelve thousand? How much are we ultimately going to have to pay this guy, and what happens if he turns on us?"

"You think he would?" Tam asks.

"You saw him. You want to be on the wrong side of that maniac?"

"Alright, I'm thinking," Tam says.

"Isn't the lawyer supposed to make things less stressful? Isn't that what you pay him for? Face it, on any normal day, I'd actually pay that guy to go away." A colossal wave of anxiety crashes on me and I explode in a frustrated scream, "Shit!"

"Calm down," Tam yells, then it hits her, "Oh my god! What's wrong with me? I know what to do!"

"What?" I moan.

"I'll call Blodg," she announces.

The Layman's Handbook for Those Falsely Accused of Felonies, page 4...When falsely accused, be sure to keep an open mind at all times. Help may be found in the most unlikely of places...

Blodg is one swinging cat. He's been bouncing around L.A. for decades. Back in the 60's, Blodg used to host a local TV dance show called *GROOVY!* Every afternoon on the Santa Monica Pier, there was Blodg with no shirt while a bunch of bikini girls danced and some pop group like The Boxtops sang their latest single. The title was a colossal understatement. This was beyond groovy.

Blodg was also an actor, guest-starring as a dreamy-eyed gunslinger on a lot of TV westerns. Then he went on to write a novel and a few movies about tough cops with mismatched partners.

But more than anything, Blodg's lasting achievement happened in 1970 when he starred in the film masterpiece *BEYOND THE VALLEY OF THE DOLLS*, which as the credits announce is "NOT a sequel to *VALLEY OF THE DOLLS*" but an entirely original film that just happens to contain the title of the old film in this new, longer title. Directed by Russ Meyer so it takes place in a world where all women have implausibly gigantic breasts, *BEYOND THE VALLEY OF THE DOLLS* soars into a realm outside the normal criteria of film judgment and stands alone as one of the most amazing movies ever made. Critics generally hate it although, incredibly, it was actually written by future-famous-critic Roger Ebert.

In the film, Blodg plays Lance Rocke, the porn-star stud. When Tam and I first moved in together, I had to clue her in to some of the stranger things that I do. "First," I said, "three or four times a year, I rent a big pile of Elvis movies and stay up all night watching them." Then, pulling out my very own widescreen copy, I announced, "And this is *BEYOND THE VALLEY OF THE DOLLS*. I've seen this movie two hundred times and I'll probably watch it a few hundred more before I die."

Tam wanted to see it, so we watched the movie together. Tam kept asking novice questions. Granted, the movie is rather hard to follow at first due to its choppy, LSD-inspired editing. But when Lance Rocke bursts onto the scene and starts charming the big-breasted babes with suave lines like "Hey, what's not to dig?" Tam blurted out, "Oh my god! That's Mike Blodgett!" I patted her on the knee and said in an extremely patronizing tone, "No, that's Lance Rocke and he's my hero. Just watch the movie."

Tam then said, "No, the actor, that's Mike Blodgett. He's a friend of my family's from Minnesota." I ignored her, my eyes glued to my favorite psychedelic 'happening'. A few seconds later, it sunk in. My jaw dropped and I turned to her, pointing at the swinging love-fest on the screen, "Whoa, wait a minute! You know this guy?"

"Sure, that's Blodg," Tam said.

"Oh my god!" I yelled, impressed beyond measure.

Blodg loves Tam and he's extremely protective of her. When Tam first introduced us, Blodg kept sizing me up to see if I was good enough for her, but there in the presence of groovin' Lance Rocke, I just kept giggling.

These days, Blodg spends twenty-four hours a day on his cell phone in his car. Sometimes I wonder if Blodg ever actually arrives anywhere, or if he's just been driving around lost for the last six months. His wavy blonde hair has been replaced with steely gray but Blodg remains a total ladykiller. He still talks like he's in *BEYOND THE VALLEY OF THE DOLLS* yet somehow makes it work because women drool over him to this day.

Marching steadily forward while keeping one foot firmly planted in 1969, Tam and I are often called on to help Blodg maneuver newfangled contraptions like the 'Internet'. But in so many ways, Blodg really is my hero. I told him this once but he was only half-listening because to get Blodg's full attention, you really need to be a woman. He didn't even turn. He just sort of patted me on the head and said, "Swinging, kid. I like you too."

Tam dials her phone, yelling over the wind, "With all his stories of booze, drugs and brawls, Blodg must know a lawyer...Blodg? It's Tamara."

"Hey doll!" Blodg yells back, "How are ya?"

"Good," Tam yells.

"How's that boyfriend of yours treating you?" Blodg asks.

"He's in a little trouble, actually. He's been accused of something he didn't do," Tam tells him.

"The law?" he asks.

"Yes, Blodg, the law," Tam says with a grin.

Blodg laughs, "That little boyscout-looking fucker? What could they accuse him of?"

"It's a long story. He got hit by a car."

"Shit, is he okay?" Blodg asks.

"Yeah, he's fine," Tam replies.

"What the hell is he charged with? Getting hit by a car is still legal in this state."

"He's charged with assault and robbery," Tam tells him.

"How's that?"

"The driver said that after she hit him, he attacked her."

"They believed that?" Blodg asks.

"Apparently. It's pretty bad, he's looking at some prison time."

"You need to talk to Phil," Blodg says.

"Blodg, I love you. Who's Phil?"

"Phil's my criminal defense guy," he tells Tam. You see, in all things that Blodg does, even the most ordinary interactions, he needs to personalize the experience. Blodg doesn't simply buy a soda, he has a "soda guy". I'm sure psychiatrists have a word for this, but right now I just need a lawyer. I jump in, "What's he saying? Does he have a lawyer guy?"

Tam nods, "Phil."

"Phil who?!" I ask.

Tam slaps the air by my head, "Shut up, let me handle this."

Blodg explains that, whenever he's in trouble, he always goes to Phil. Blodg even keeps Phil on perpetual retainer, just in case. Because you never know with Blodg.

Tam gets off the phone, "His name's Phil Damascus. I'm calling him." Tam dials the phone. She introduces herself and mentions Blodg. "He can see us right away," she says.

Since Damascus was recommended by Blodg, I'm expecting someone louder and slicker than the fiery bulldog Dodd. But right from the start, Phil Damascus is not at all what I'm anticipating, which only reinforces my impotent anxiety. His office is not in Beverly Hills or any of the expected flashy spots. It's in a nondescript area of West L.A., more functional than showy, in a simple office building that's fifteen stories tall.

We go to the moderately-placed ninth floor, where the receptionist asks us to have a seat. My efforts to remain calm have completely failed. Clutching my court papers, I'm bouncing my right leg without realizing it. Tam grabs my knee and sharply whispers for me to stop.

I look around the reception area. While Dodd's office was all chrome and glass, here the oak-paneled walls are covered with English hunting prints that show packs of dogs leaping over rustic fences, murderously hounding down a poor little fox. I focus on one painting, trying to escape into it. Given what's happening, you'd think I'd feel like that fox. But I don't. For some reason, I feel more like the fence.

A young woman leads us to an office. It's not even a corner office. This isn't Blodg's style at all, I think as Phil Damascus stands up to greet us. He's in his late forties but looks younger, in good shape but not very tall. Phil's vaguely Mediterranean face has a well-scrubbed All-American look, Greece by way of the Pacific Palisades. Phil's a true Pali guy, a lifer. He even went to Pali High back in the days when French sociologists were studying it because of its world-record student mortality rate. But the kids who survived high school apparently held up okay.

With a friendly smile and a calm respectable tone of voice, Phil ushers us to two chairs at his desk. Tam handles the small talk since I'm currently reduced to a big, jittery, stomach cramp of a man. I'm staring at Phil's subdued banker's suit and the pictures of his wife and daughters on his desk. Phil notices my state but doesn't seem too judgmental about it. He's obviously seen people in this condition before. Phil keeps his eyes directed at Tam but periodically glances my way, I guess to see if I'm going to projectile vomit on his family.

Phil tells Tam about some of his past clients. He's handled a lot of celebrity drug-and-alcohol-related cases. Phil describes each case skillfully, with the utmost discretion yet revealing enough information so that we can follow. Phil represented a famous movie director when he was arrested for driving drunk and possessing "hashish", as the papers called it.

"Where the hell do you buy hash these days?" Tam asks.

"I didn't ask," Phil calmly replies.

Phil tells us about a few more showbiz drug boys, and I suddenly speak up. "You should hang their pictures in here," I say, gesturing at the walls, "Like in a deli." Phil looks at me, surprised, and smiles cautiously.

Despite my churning stomach, I'm dying to hear more about Phil's Hollywood clients, but he switches gears. Concerned that he's coming off like some celebrity DUI lightweight, Phil brings up some of his more serious cases, including major death penalty trials.

"Alright, as awful as this is, I don't think I can get the death penalty for it," I say, suddenly feeling something rising up my throat. I instantly shut up, gag a little and take a deep breath.

Phil is exceedingly civilized, describing capital crimes in a flatly detached manner. It's hard to believe that this guy and Gavin Dodd do the same thing. Dodd's ferocious style is more obviously what you'd expect. Damascus is harder to gauge. My stomach feels stabilized and it's time to join in the conversation for real, "Aside from the A-list fuck-ups, your clients sound like a pretty treacherous bunch."

"Some of them have been," Phil replies.

"And you stay mellow and matter-of-fact about it, huh?"

Phil nods, "I find it's usually best to stay focused on the facts and not get emotional until it can be put to good use."

"You're not like that other lawyer we just talked to," I tell him.

"Oh no?" Phil asks.

"No. How's your track record?" I ask.

"Above average."

Tam jumps in, "According to Blodg, your success rate is incredibly high." Phil gives her a humble smile.

"Wow, you're modest, too," I say, "You're nothing like that other guy. But is quiet modesty the way to go with this kind of thing? So far, it seems like a game where the loudest person wins."

Phil looks at me uncertainly. Just as he's not what I expected, I don't think I'm what he expected either. I change the subject to give us more time to form an opinion of each other. "Tell me about Blodg and all his scrapes with the law."

Phil smiles, "Blodg will have to tell you about those."

"He already has. Now I want the truth. And don't get me wrong, I love Blodg."

Phil leans forward, "Tell me something."

"Sure, what?"

"What in god's name are you accused of?"

I start telling the story. Phil's eyes grow wide with astonishment as my tale proceeds. Soon he stops me, "Wait, I'm sorry..."

"What?" I ask.

"I usually hear these stories from the driver who fled the scene. How does this lead to you getting charged with crimes?"

"I'm getting there..." I tell Phil about the crazy lady attacking Tam at the store, and Tam jumps in to describe the cops storming the apartment. By this point, Phil's mouth is hanging open. Then I tell Phil about how I immediately called Officer Hink and went to the police station. Now his mouth closes. We're back on the part of the map he understands.

Phil asks to see my court papers. He reads my charges, shaking his head. "I've got to tell you," he says, "in my twenty-two years of practice, I've never heard of anything as bizarre as this."

"What the hell did I do wrong?" I ask, "I went to the police immediately and did everything they said."

"You just answered your own question," Phil says, "You went to the police. I'll bet they said they needed your help, and that's how they got you to trust them."

"Well, yeah. Then they said it would help if I dropped my complaint against the driver."

Phil asks, "You filed a complaint against her?"

"Yeah, but I dropped it," I tell him. Phil lifts a curious eyebrow at me, so I tell him about Hink advising me to file a complaint but making me go to Pacific Station to do it. My nausea starts to return as Phil begins scribbling notes on a legal pad. I suddenly remember Detective Bender and her threats to bring more false charges against me. "Oh, there's something I forgot," I say.

Phil looks at me gravely, "You have to tell me everything."

"Sorry, there's a lot to this story, if you haven't noticed." Phil's new expression looks like he expects to find the smoking gun that will make sense of this mess. Sadly, he's wrong. "Was it something you did?" he asks.

"Not exactly," I say and I mention Detective Bender. Phil's face turns grim. "Bender?" he asks.

"Yeah," I say.

"Pacific Division?"

"Yeah."

"Real surly and nasty?" Phil asks.

"Yep, that's her."

"Oh no," Phil sighs, "Did she do...that 'lucky' thing?"

"Wow! How did you know?"

"And she twisted it around and ended up threatening you?"

"Yes! Exactly! How the hell do you know that?"

"This is bad," Phil says. My face sinks as he continues, "I've dealt with Bender before."

"How bad is it? Wait, you mean she's done this to other people?"

"Bender's a real piece of work. But she usually pulls that trick on suspects, not victims. She was investigating your complaint, right?"

I nod nervously, "Does it work?"

"Sometimes," Phil says, "You don't really seem the type to make terrorist threats against a police detective. That's what she said, right?"

"Threatening to kill her, yeah."

"Hopefully no one's going to want a big drawn-out trial over that, but I guess we'll see."

Frustration digs its claws into my gut. "Fuck!" I yell, "Am I going to prison for this?! I didn't do anything!"

"Hopefully not," Phil replies. He looks down at my charges with an awkward grimace.

"You're about to tell me about the mandatory sentence."

"Oh, you know about that, huh?" Phil says. I'm feeling very nauseated again. Phil looks at me and sighs. "Listen to me," he says, "You seem like a nice guy who's in way over his head. I'll take care of this for you...if you promise me something."

"What?" I timidly ask. Phil seems genuinely concerned but I'm waiting for the catch. He leans forward and looks me in the eye, "You have to promise me that you will never talk to a police officer again, especially if they tell you to trust them. Even more so if they ask for your help."

"Really?" I ask.

"Yes, really," Phil says, "Now repeat after me..."

"What?"

"I am asserting," he says. Confused, I just stare at him. "Say it," he orders, so I say it, "I am asserting..."

"My right to remain silent..." Phil waits for me to repeat it.

"Until I speak to an attorney," he says, then I say it too.

"Good!" Phil announces, "If you promise to say that every time you're with a cop, I promise I'll always take care of you."

"But won't that make me seem guilty?" I ask.

"As opposed to what?" Phil replies, "The only way this could've happened is if they'd already made up their minds before they even met you. These cops just took you, the guy who was run down by a car, and fixed things to send you to prison. Don't worry about seeming guilty. That's not how these people think. That's how normal people think."

"What do we do about Detective Bender?"

"Nothing," he says.

"What?" I ask, my heart jumping.

"Nothing for now. We wait to see if she goes ahead with her threats."

"She sounded pretty serious," I point out.

"Yes, that's from years of practice." Phil holds up my charges, "You've got enough to worry about here. If Bender has enough free time to railroad some hit-and-run victim, then I'll get into it. I know her superior. His name's Richter, Sergeant Richter."

Surprised, Tam asks, "You know him?"

"Like...well?" I add.

"I've dealt with Richter on a few cases over the years. He's a decent enough guy. She's claiming you threatened to kill her?"

"Run her over with my car, actually," I sigh, "This is all so fucking wrong."

"Don't think about that," Phil tells me.

"I'm being forced to think about it," I snap.

"What do you want?" Phil asks patronizingly, "Do you want a perfect world, or do you want to stay out of prison?"

"Stop grinning at me like I'm some Pollyanna fucking idiot."

"Just remember why you're here," Phil says, "Let's talk about what's next."

"What is next?" I ask.

Phil replies, "Like I said, until Bender makes the first move, we shouldn't do anything about that. Your court date is August 9th..."

"You think I'm an idiot now, don't you?"

"No," Phil says, "You're just someone who's never had to think about these things before, which is actually a good thing. And don't worry about what I think. Worry about yourself."

I switch gears, "You seem to know people. How about this Noreen What's-her-name, you know her"?

"Oh, I've known Noreen for years. I used to work in the Santa Monica City Attorney's office."

"Whoa, you're good," I tell him, "So what's Noreen like?"

"Let's just hope she'll be reasonable," he says, forcing a smile.

"And what happens if she isn't reasonable?" I anxiously ask.

"Don't jump ahead," Phil says.

"Aw Christ, come on! What happens if she isn't reasonable?!"

"Don't jump ahead," Phil calmly insists, "Or I'll think you're an idiot."

"I don't care what you think. You just said not to."

"Good. I'll call Noreen tomorrow," Phil replies.

"What's this going to cost?" I ask with dread.

"For the pre-trial, my fee is five thousand dollars," he says.

"Fuck," I gasp.

"And if you go to trial, it will be more. I know it's a lot. I think you should talk to other attorneys and compare their fees. That's generally the going rate for any decent trial lawyer."

I say to Tam, "Dodd's twelve thousand."

"That's because he's going right to trial," Tam points out.

"I don't have it," I confess. With the tone of an undertaker, Phil says, "Then I don't know what to tell you."

Tam grabs my arm, "We'll figure it out."

I sigh, then ask, "Do you take credit cards?"

"Yes, I do," he says.

"Well, it's a start." I tell Phil that once I've figured out the money, I'll be in touch. Phil walks us to the elevator, then goes back to his office. The second he's gone, the tidal wave of stress crashes over me again.

"I think that's our lawyer," Tam says.

"I think I'm about to puke," I inform her.

swami...

When I am pushed to extreme limits of stress, I become grimly quiet. It's happening now, as we drive away from Phil's office. Tam notices my near-catatonic state. "What?" she asks, but I don't respond. I'm wishing this snowballing fiasco would reveal the depths of its potential damage. Once the nightmare has boundaries, I'll stand up to it better.

Tam invades my silence, "We have to go with him. He knows everybody involved."

"That other guy seemed tougher," I respond.

"Great," Tam says, "So we'll have Dodd running around, pissing people off. Then things will really go your way."

"Yeah, but he took it so personally. I kind of liked that."

"You're crazy. I like Damascus," she says.

"He does know Blodg," I say, thinking out loud.

"He also used to work in the Santa Monica City Attorney's office. He even knows Bender's boss." When Tam is pushed toward her stress limit, she becomes fiercely focused, which is also happening now. "Dodd's going straight to trial, which I think is a little rash," she yells over the wind, "Dodd's also going to the South Pacific tomorrow and leaving you with some lackey in the middle of a nervous breakdown."

"I'm so far in debt right now, I'm never getting out. Where am I supposed to get five grand?"

"You'll have to borrow it from somebody," Tam tells me.

"Who?" I yell.

"I don't know," she says, "Can't you get any more credit cards?"

"I can try," I glumly respond. At this moment, I have sixteen credit cards, all maxed out with enormous sums. Tam starts rattling off names of people I could ask for money. She mentions my parents, but this is a bad idea. My elderly parents are happily sheltered in the suburbs of Philadelphia, and they don't handle the pressures of the outside world particularly well. This stress of this nonsense might kill them. Nice old folks in Philly shouldn't be ushered that much closer into the ground because some pockmarked crystal-meth fiend in Los Angeles can't control her road rage. "Not a chance," I tell Tam.

Tam continues listing names and I keep saying no. She mentions my buddy Stu F- and I pause, considering it. "He's a maybe. I don't think he's got thousands to spare, but maybe he could cough up a little." Maybe if we gather the money from a variety of sources, it won't be too much skin off anyone's back. Rationalizing faster than the speed of sound, Tam decides that Stu F- would be downright furious if we didn't ask him. I think of my old college roommate, Ken S-, who's a lawyer in D.C. Ken's one of my favorite people on earth because, for some reason, every word that comes out of my mouth frightens him irrationally. "Aw Christ, he's going to wig," I say.

"Call him!" Tam snaps at me.

That night, we're brainstorming for ways to raise defense funds. Liz stops by and joins the effort with her trademark unnerving enthusiasm. I'm afraid to even imagine what kind of twisted bake sale Liz will dream up, but I figure we're in enough trouble already, so I tell her not to worry about it.

The door swings open and Allie, our commando-hippie pal, barges into the apartment. Allie's a deceptively angelic-looking blonde who grew up following the Grateful Dead around the country. The first time I met Al, she had one of her irritating hippie friends in a headlock. He'd stolen drug money from her, and then justified it by explaining that his sacred animal is the crow, so thievery is his natural karma. "Fuck your sacred animal!" Allie yelled as she beat the tie-dyed freak into a puddle of goo. I knew immediately that Al and I were going to be friends.

Allie once joined a cult, bursting with glee over this "exciting new direction in her life". This was a notorious cult that never lets anyone escape, yet they sent Al packing after three days. "Well, fuck them if they're so afraid of a few simple questions," Allie announced on her arrival back home.

The real reason I want Al here is her vast experience with the criminal justice system. Allie once faced federal drug trafficking charges after a backpacking jaunt through Mexico. Hitchhiking home, she got a ride in a car crammed with illegal drugs and some "really nice dealers" as she called them. The car was stopped at the border, the drugs were discovered and everybody got hauled to jail. Even though the drugs weren't hers, Allie remained upbeat and stoic as she fought major drug smuggling charges. "Oh face it, I knew damn well what was in that car," she told me.

And she was acquitted.

I ask Allie for advice. "First off, my charges were federal and yours aren't," she says with some strange misguided pride. Then I ask her how she got the money to pay for her big federal trial. "Oh, some rich loser who was in love with me forked over forty grand for me to beat that rap," she tells me, "You got anybody with a hopeless crush on you?"

"Nobody with five grand," I shrug.

"What about that scary drag queen who stalked you a few years ago?" Liz excitedly asks.

"I don't know what he does for a living," I tell her, "I think he sells wigs. And you're not helping."

"Well, whatever you do, never sleep with them or they stop the cash flow like that," Allie snaps her fingers.

"Thanks Al, I'll try to remember that."

Allie punches my shoulder. "Don't worry, bucko," she says, "We'll beat this."

Liz and Allie are now trying to outdo each other by telling tales of people they know who've gotten away with enormous crimes. The door flies open again and in pops Gwen, our actress friend. Gwen knows nothing about my charges, so while Tam, Allie and Liz all start telling the story at the same time, I go into the bedroom and call Gavin Dodd at home.

Dodd is on a packing rampage. I ask him about Phil Damascus. "Never heard of him!" Dodd bellows, "I wish you'd let me handle this!"

"You're going on a cruise."

"It's not exactly a cruise," he replies.

"That's not the point," I say.

"My associate could handle this," Dodd insists.

"The one dealing with the ugly divorce?" I ask.

"Yeah, he is pretty fucked up these days, now that you mention it."

"I think I'm going with this other guy," I tell him.

"I hate to see them doing this to you, kid. Let me give you some advice..." I grab a pen as Dodd starts spouting, "No moral turpitude! Whatever you do, do NOT agree to any deal that involves moral turpitude!"

"Okay!" I yell back, writing down what Dodd says, but with no clue what any of it means.

"And no expungement!" Dodd yells, "Don't agree to anything like that!"

"Wait! Isn't that a good thing?" I ask.

"Aw shit, kid, just trust me," Dodd says, "Hopefully this lawyer knows what the fuck he's doing because you sure as hell don't. But I like you. I wish you were my client. For Christ's sake, you're innocent. How often does that happen?"

"I don't know," I say.

"Didn't need an answer on that. Now listen to me..." Dodd barks more advice through the phone. None of it makes sense and I can barely hear it anyway, because Dodd has people yelling all around him as his family packs for their big, loud vacation.

Dodd comes to terms with my choice of lawyer. "I'm sure he's fine," he yells, "Now kid, if you run into trouble and want to talk, definitely try to get me on the phone. To be honest, I don't know how you're gonna do it since I'll be on the boat. But call my office, maybe they'll be able to help you." I thank him, and wish him bon voyage. "No problem, kid," he yells, "Good luck with these assholes. You're gonna need it."

"One cannot pay Evil in installments...yet one always keeps trying to." – Kafka

Next to my desk, I keep a small "designated trashcan" where I toss all credit card offers that come in the mail. While making the movie, every time we ran out of funds, I'd pour out the contents of this trashcan, find the best offers, get some new plastic and keep going. This dubious plan has left me wallowing in fiscal oblivion, but it's time to dump out the trashcan again. Late that night, I'm examining the fine print with bleary eyes.

The next morning, I call and line up two more credit cards to cover Damascus' five grand, kicking myself for thinking I could swing this ruinous financial situation for a few months longer with villainous road-rage psychos and the City of Santa Monica lurking outside the door. I call Damascus' office and give his billing department the new credit card information, experiencing once again the indescribable joy of getting new credit cards and maxing them out in less than half an hour.

I need to call Stu and Ken to ask to borrow some money, but the thought of it makes me cringe. I've never borrowed money from friends in my entire poverty-riddled adult life, so I procrastinate online, looking for ways to raise some money. I click on an ad that takes me to the eWin Internet search engine with its blazing banners screaming that I can win a million dollars by clicking onto their ham-handed news stories. In sheer desperation, I begin clicking on every headline from the Middle East to some singer's nervous breakdown because every story I call up and don't read gets me another five (count 'em, five!) chances at winning this mythical million dollars.

To further pad my total chances, I hit every section of this magical site, which soon leads me to the amazing eWin horoscope. As my legal proceedings grow more entangled and costly, I start keeping notes while continuing to click all over this goofy lottery site trying to bag some cash. These two birds meet their one stone as I develop the habit of printing out my eWin horoscope and writing my legal notes on the page below. In the coming months, the eWin horoscopes prove to be a prescient fountain of insight on my case, while providing a handy source of paper on which to keep my dismal journal of this hellbent trip. And all this time, I'm racking up scores of "chances" to win the big bucks.

Let's see what my eWin horoscope says for today, July 28th: *"This is a time for grand celebrations, Cancer! Keep that smile on your face!"* Wow, it's as if they're watching me right now. But enough otherworldly wisdom, it's time to beg for cash.

Stu F- is an advanced computer systems guy in Boston. He works for a major mutual fund company but exactly what he does is somewhat of a mystery because all we ever talk about is his lovelife. Stu has made a career out of dating, overanalyzing the tiniest inferences of every word and glance. Romantically, Stu is the king of the pre-emptive strike.

Stu F- constantly asks for my advice on his relationship labyrinth, which is absurd because that's one of the very few things I've never had to think about. I've had girlfriends and I've had no-strings sex, but I don't think I've ever been on a traditional "date" in my life. Then I met Tam and I haven't looked back. As far as relationship timetables and what-means-what, I haven't got a clue. But to Stu, my lack of awareness makes me a frustratingly model example of both sex and relationships.

The second Stu picks up the phone, he launches into the latest news about the three girls he's currently dating. Number One is too young, far younger than I'd ever deal with. "She actually told me I remind her of her dad," Stu says.

"Were you in bed at the time?" I ask facetiously.

"As a matter of fact, yes. But we weren't having sex."

"Aw Jesus," I groan, "That's twisted. Move on."

Never one to listen to me, Stu continues, "She didn't mean it like that. We were talking about music."

"Doesn't matter, I feel unclean just hearing about it."

Stu then tells me about Bachelorette Number Two, who is age-appropriate but lives in New York. Stu debates with himself whether Boston to Manhattan constitutes a "long distance relationship". He feels guilty because he doesn't see much future with this woman. After five more minutes of Stu's solo debate, I cut him off.

"How's the sex?" I ask.

"Excellent," he tells me. So I tell Stu to continue seeing this woman just for sex, knowing damn well it will push him over the guilt cliff and he'll break up with her, thus sparing me from having to listen to this the next time we talk.

We move on to Number Three, a painfully boring woman Stu met at the wedding of his old girlfriend, who devastated him by dumping him and marrying someone else. Stu doesn't even like this woman yet he's still dating her.

"You're a masochist. A monkey could tell you that you're only dating her because she's the last vestigial remains of Laura." Stu agrees, yet decides to go on seeing her so he can make himself, and me, miserable by discussing it for hours on end. I interrupt Stu's dating epic to tell him about my charges and he hits the roof.

"I warned you about this!" he yells. And it's true. For months now, Stu has been queasily fascinated by my surviving on the credit-cards-and-plain-rice plan while making the movie. Nonetheless, I counter with "There's no way you knew this was going to happen."

"Well, not this exact thing. How the hell could this happen?!"

"I have no idea," I tell him.

"Shit..." he replies.

I tell Stu about the five grand I need for the pre-trial, and the calamitous further thousands it will cost if I go to trial. "Oh, I forgot the best part," I add, "I've actually been charged with some anti-gang law that comes with a mandatory sentence."

"I'll give you eight grand," Stu says without missing a beat.

I almost drop the phone. "For what?" I ask.

"This is a big deal! You're destitute as it is. They're going to put you in prison. You've got to fight this and win, or your whole life is screwed."

"Jesus, how much money do you make?"

"I make a lot."

"I had no idea."

"It's really no problem," he says.

"In a way it is," I reply, "Because I could never take that much from you. Shit, I was just going to ask for a grand."

"Fine, you can have ten," he says.

"Jesus! Is this some kind of secret I'm not in on? Who else makes this kind of money? Oh, and by the way, this changes everything in terms of your dating."

Stu tells me that he knows I'm good for it, but I refuse to take that much. Stu yells at me to take the money and I still refuse. Stu announces that he's sending me a check.

"Don't send ten thousand dollars!" I yell at him, "Send me a check I can deposit without jumping off a building." I tell Stu that if he sends more than fifteen hundred, I'm ripping up the check. But I'm moved. What a guy. My new hero, despite his hapless love life. Nobody's ever done anything like this for me before. I thank Stu F- profusely until he gets sick of it and grumbles, "Aw hell, it's just fucking money." Ah, the rich and their capricious ways.

I call Tam to tell her about my conversation with Stu. "Who knew Stu was so flush?" I say, "We never talk about that kind of thing." Tam yells that I'm stupid and should have taken the whole ten grand, and I tell her to shut up.

I hesitate before calling Ken S-. I look at the phone, and then it rings. It's Phil Damascus. "Very happy to be on board," he calmly announces. Phil has called the Deputy City Attorney Noreen McDonough and requested a meeting for the three of us. He's also requested all the police paperwork, which should arrive soon. Done with Damascus, I brace myself and call Ken.

Ken S- is a reasonably relaxed guy with the rest of the world, saving his flailing neuroses for whenever I speak. I'll say "It's Tuesday," and Ken will explode, which I've always found endearing.

Before I can tell Ken about my legal troubles, it's time to hear the latest about Ken and his wife's ongoing efforts to have a baby. Lately, Ken's been asking for my advice on conception which, in a way, is as crazy as Stu F- asking for my advice on dating. I generally remind Ken that, not only am I not a doctor, I've spent most of my life trying to prevent that exact thing from happening.

However, Ken's not completely off the mark because, for some reason, young married couples tend to confide their reproductive secrets to me. While treacherously competitive with each other, these couples consider me so far out of the game that it's safe to spill and, as a result, I've picked up a bit of knowledge over the years.

Ken is stressing out over a recent miscarriage. I tell him that it's no big deal, lots of our mutual friends have experienced miscarriages, even the one who had three babies in five years.

"How do you know all this?!" Ken asks, reeling with frustration.

"Because I sneak through hospitals at night, disguised as a doctor, looking up the fertility records of people we went to college with. How do you think I know?! They tell me! Don't worry so much."

Ken starts telling me their latest reproductive strategy but I cut him short. "Listen, I'm in a little trouble, but I don't want you to overreact..."

"What kind of trouble?" Ken asks with his familiar tone of dread.

I tell Ken about the criminal charges and he erupts huge. I think this conversation's may need to be a two-parter, because Ken seems to be having some kind of seizure. I then tell Ken about Curt's attempt to help and the ensuing disaster with Bender. Ken gasps "Oh my god!" about fifteen times.

Ken is shocked that I talked to Curt at all and didn't immediately go to an experienced criminal defense attorney. "That's so like you," he bitterly spits. Ken demands to know the vitals on Damascus so he can look into his record. Ken's law firm has an L.A. office, so he's going to ask around there for any helpful advice. Ken yells that I have to fax him all the police reports. I tell Ken that I don't have the police reports yet and he moans "Oh my god!" some more.

Ken is foaming so drastically at this point, I decide that the further shock of asking him for money might make him sterile. I tell Ken that I'll call him back in a couple days when I know more. I feel awful. Usually when I bring Ken close to a massive aneurism, it's just for fun. This is for real, and it blows.

On Monday morning, I get a call from Phil Damascus as he drives back from an Orange County courthouse. My police reports have arrived, and he tells me to meet him in his office in an hour. When I tell Tam, she announces that she's coming too.

An hour later, we're sitting with Phil in his office. Since I have no experience with criminal court proceedings, Phil must explain everything as we go. He tells us that we're entering the "discovery" phase, during which the Santa Monica City Attorney must hand over all of their evidence. What none of us realize at this moment is that this is only the first of several discovery phases for my case, and that the real "discovery" for me will come in learning that fighting these false charges is to grow into a full-time job.

"First, I have some bad news," Phil informs me.

"What's that?" I ask.

"Noreen doesn't want to talk about this," he says, "She's certain they can get a conviction."

"For what?" I ask.

"The assault," Phil says.

"What assault?" Tam asks.

"I don't know, but she's very determined. She said no deals. She's going for prison time."

"You're kidding," I gulp.

"Unfortunately, no," Phil replies.

Tam is shocked, "My god, are you sure?"

"Well, not entirely," Phil admits, "With Noreen, sometimes..." Phil trails off, not finishing the thought.

"With Noreen, sometimes what?" I ask, growing nervous.

Phil sighs, "Noreen has certain issues...Things of a personal nature, that she must deal with..."

"What, like a medical condition?" I anxiously ask.

"Yes, you could say that," Phil says, "You have to understand that Noreen handles many cases at once, and on some days..."

"What?" I ask.

"There have been times when Noreen wasn't entirely sure which case I was referring to when we spoke. She sometimes...confuses things."

"How can that be?" I ask.

"It's just that some days, she's not as clear as on other days," Phil diplomatically explains.

"What the hell is wrong with her?" Tam asks sharply.

"It's a shame about Noreen. Each day is a struggle," Phil tells us.

"Well, that's moving and all," I reply, "But I'm not going to prison because she's confused. I didn't do anything."

"We need to look at these," Phil says, holding up a large brown envelope.

"Why doesn't she want to talk? She really wants to put me in prison?" I ask.

"We'll get to that," Phil somberly replies, "But first, we have to deal with these police reports."

discover this...

*The Layman's Handbook for Those Falsely Accused of Felonies, page 29...As though torn from life's pages, your **police report** provides a thrilling narrative of what occurred on the day you got cornholed. Relish the lies that led to your false charges. Relive the magic, in hopes of triggering the fatal stroke that will solve your current dilemma...*

Phil hands us copies of the police report. Certain sensitive bits of information have been concealed with black rectangles like on Japanese pornography, but I finally learn the identity of the woman who hit me with her car. Her name is Lauren Louise Toomey. She was born on December 13th and she is 43 years old.

I hear a deep sigh come from Tamara as she settles in to read.

The SANTA MONICA POLICE DEPARTMENT: CRIME REPORT boldly announces that a ROBBERY/ STRONGARM took place on 5/7 in "Rpt. Dst 2C." It further informs us that this is a "CRIME".

I come to the box where the "Trademarks of Suspect(s)" are revealed. It says "SUSPECT SLAPS SUNGLASSES OFF VICTIM, TAKES RECEIPT, STEALS PEN, FLEES." Confused, I break the silence by quietly asking, "What the hell does that mean?" Phil doesn't look up. "Just keep reading," he says. I turn the page and get to the account of Sunday's events as spun by Officer Hink into a police-issue dictaphone on Monday, May 8th.

"5/7 at approximately 1613 hours, I recieved (sic) a radio call of a (sic) assault which had just occured (sic) at 3rd and Marine. I drove to victim's house and spoke LAUREN LOUISE TOOMEY. She told me that she had just returned from San Francisco where she had been taking her medical board examination for general opthalmology (sic). TOOMEY told me that she had had about 3 hours of sleep in the last week and, as a result, she was tired. Upon arrival in Los Angeles, her luggage was lost..."

I stop reading, "She's a doctor?"

"A medical student, it seems," Phil replies, still not looking up, "Sleep deprived and frustrated, by her own admission."

Tam flips back to page one. "But she's in her 40's. She hasn't finished medical school yet?"

Stunned, I ask again, "She's a doctor?"

Neither Tam nor Phil responds as they sink deeper into the police report. Phil intently reads the account of the 'incident' and says, "The amazing thing is how many laws this woman admits to breaking."

"She's a doctor?!" I yell.

Phil finally looks at me, "Yeah, so?"

"Well, unless the Hippocratic Oath has been radically altered since the last time I checked, what kind of doctor does that?! She hit me with her car, gave me the finger and took off! She didn't even ask if I was hurt!"

Tam replies, "She's an ophthalmologist. If you had been hurt, what could she do? Test you for glaucoma?"

"That's not the point!" I yell, "She stalked me through the streets like some deranged drug addict."

"Exactly," Tam says with a shrug as she continues reading, "The last thing I'd want is that nut's medical opinion."

"I'm calling the medical board," I announce.

Phil looks at me and says, "I think that is a wise and responsible course of action. However, unless you finish reading this report, you may be calling them from prison."

I stop short, "Why? Does this get worse?"

Phil gives me his mortician half-smile, "It definitely gets more bizarre. Keep reading."

I move further into Hink's recounting of the incident. "As Toomey executed her right hand turn, a male later identified as STEPHEN RICARD (sic) BEVILAQUE (sic) was walking east across 3rd Street. Toomey told me that she did not yield to Bevilaque (sic) and as she drove away, she "flipped off" Bevilaque (sic)...

The Layman's Handbook to Those Falsely Accused of Felonies, page 30...Correct spelling is a luxury for those not falsely accused. Don't drive yourself crazy. Disregard the continual misspellings of the police and officers of the court. That is, unless their misspellings create, or add to, your false charges, which does occasionally happen...

I look at Phil, "Didn't the cops notice something wrong with this story?"

Phil nods, "You mean that this woman just admitted running you down with her car, flashing her middle finger at you, and leaving the scene?"

"Yeah, something like that," I say.

Hink's epic narrative continues, "Bevilaque struck Toomey in the face, snatching the sunglasses off Toomey's head and smashing them on the ground."

"I didn't do that! She swung at me!" I protest. Phil calmly sighs, "At the rate you're going, this could take a really long time."

I return to the gripping tale, "Toomey apologized to Bevilaque, five or six times. Victim Toomey was now very afraid of further attack." The report describes Toomey as so paralyzed with fear that she "follows Bevilaque through the streets, apologizing further, continuing to the store at 5th and Rose, where a female white with brown curly hair and a slim build exits store."

Now it's Tam's turn to yell, "This woman is clearly insane! Do you know how much this red cost me?!" She points at her hair to make her case.

"Maybe she's colorblind," I say, hoping to soothe, "After all, she said your car was red when it was black." Phil gives me an admonishing stare. "Ssh. We're reading now," I tell Tam.

The report describes how Toomey was "standing behind the vehicle, but not with the intent of blocking the vehicle," which makes me ask, "So when she screamed 'You're not going anywhere, bitch!' what did she mean?" Phil gives me another stern look and I keep reading.

Now it gets really good. "In fear for her life at the hands of suspect and his female accomplice, victim Toomey did not know what to do." Desperate to escape, she starts writing down Tamara's license plate number and I snatch the paper from her hand. Tam drives away from the store, and I run away through the alley. But then, somehow "Bevilaque grabs gold pen from Toomey's hand." Next, defying the laws of physics and nature, "Bevilaque leaves scene in female's car, driving through alley as Toomey gave chase."

"Okay, may I speak?" I ask Phil, who gently nods. "This makes no sense," I say, "How many times did I leave the scene? I left on foot, not in the car. And I never touched her pen, even if it was made of gold. What the hell is going on here?"

"Can't you tell?" Phil asks.

"No, I can't, so please tell me."

"You didn't even read to the end, when the cops have to explain how she's still in possession of the pen you allegedly stole. After you leave the store, it says here that 'Toomey retrieved the gold pen.'"

"According to this story, I leave the scene twice. Once on foot and after that, in Tam's car. I don't get it."

Tam chimes in, "I'm kind of curious myself. And how bad is this?"

"One thing at a time," Phil tells her.

"Fine, start with the pen," I say.

"Well, it's hard to charge you with robbery if you haven't taken anything. And even if you admitted taking a piece of paper, that's not actually a robbery since you ripped it up in front of her. Robbery only occurs if you take something with the intention of keeping it. So she added that you stole a pen, a valuable pen made of gold. A pen that this Toomey woman somehow retrieved. I wouldn't be surprised if the cops noticed it in her possession and had to slip in the retrieval part toward the end of the story."

I sigh, "I'm so fucking lost, I'm not even sure how pissed off to be."

"You're a clever guy," Phil says, "Can't you see the pattern through this whole story?"

"No," I admit, "This story makes no sense at all."

"One reason for that is every time this woman accidentally volunteers that she's broken a law, the cops fix it for her."

"What do you mean?" I ask, as conspiracy gears start to grind in my head.

Phil points out various statements in the report. "Here the woman freely confesses that she ran you down, gave you the finger and fled the scene. Then the story goes back and repeats itself, only adding more words. In this case, it adds that she knows it was wrong to leave the scene of the accident, but justifies it by claiming that you irately showed her your middle finger and she was in fear of bodily harm."

"But I didn't give her the finger. She gave me the finger," I point out, "I was busy falling on my ass."

Phil keeps going, "And here...Toomey initially claims that she blocked Tamara's car from leaving. But then it goes back and adds that she stood behind the car, but not with the intention of preventing it from leaving. It's against the law to hold someone against their will in a parking lot, just like it's against the law to stalk you through the streets, assaulting you."

"They were coaching her?" Tam asks.

"Yes, but they didn't do a very good job of it," Phil points out, "They try to explain Toomey stalking you through the streets because she was so afraid."

"That's just dumb," I say, "And why do I have to leave the store twice?"

"I think Toomey originally told the cops that you left on foot. Then somebody realized that it's hard to justify accusing Tam of driving a 'getaway vehicle' if you didn't actually arrive or depart in it. So they fixed the story."

"But they didn't fix it. They just tacked things on to suit them."

"There are two things going on in this report," Phil explains, "One, they're trying to cover for all of the illegal things this woman did. Two, they're trying to pump up everything you did and turn it into a crime they can put you away for."

"Why fix the story?" I ask, "Are all police reports like this?"

"I've never seen anything like this," Phil replies.

"So why did they do it?" I ask.

"Cops hate people like you," Phil tells me.

"How come?"

"Because you're not afraid of them."

"Why should I be afraid of them?" I ask.

"I think they're trying to show you why with this inane police report," Phil informs me.

"But why? What did I do to them?"

"For one," Phil says, "You went to the police station of your own accord."

"Wouldn't they like that about me?" I ask.

"No."

"I was just trying to help," I tell him.

"Exactly," Phil says, "And while you were there, were you like this?"

"Like what?"

"This," he gestures at me, "Smiling, helpful, casual. Not threatening and not groveling. Dealing with them eye-to-eye as if they're just like anyone else."

"Well, yeah, probably," I admit.

"They hate that. Cops like people who are afraid of them, and people they have something to hold against. Then they don't have to worry too much about how they act themselves. Cops don't really like innocent people because it takes away their leverage." Phil gestures at me again, "Friendly and forthcoming, like this, they don't like at all."

"That's crazy," I say.

"Then how do you explain this?" Phil shakes the report.

"I can't. But that still doesn't explain why I'd actually get charged on the basis of such an idiotic story. Does this nutcase driver know somebody in the City Attorney's Office?"

"I don't know about that," Phil tells me.

"No, she's probably screaming at the City Attorney like she screamed at you," Tam says, "And they're just trying to get her to shut up."

"That's more likely," Phil says.

"I can't believe they'd press these bullshit charges simply because some road-rage maniac is bitching at them," I say.

"None of this matters," Phil announces, "One, you've been charged so there's no going back. Two, we're dealing with Noreen McDonough here. And three, there's more to this report. You haven't even reached the bad parts yet."

"Which are?" I ask, sinking with dread.

"For starters," Phil says, turning the page, "Here the police have you freely confessing that you committed a felony strongarm robbery."

"What?!" I jump in my seat, "I never said that."

"You think they only put words in the driver's mouth?" Phil asks, pointing out this section of the report. I stare down at my copy, dumbfounded. The cops didn't put too many words in my mouth, only enough to screw me. "Bevilaque acknowledged his part in the attack and in the robbery."

"I never acknowledged anything!" I yell, "I didn't give them a statement at all. I asked if they wanted one and they said it wasn't necessary."

Phil shrugs, "Obviously, it wasn't necessary because they just made one up for you."

I'm crumbling in my chair, "Why the hell would I admit hitting her when I didn't hit her?"

"This happens all the time. Hink didn't take a statement so he just filled in the blanks when he made the report. And while Hink's storytelling is extremely dubious, there is one gigantic problem in this report," Phil informs us, "Right here..." We crane our necks to see what he's pointing out. Cringing, I ask, "What's that?"

Phil looks grim, "The part where it says there are photographs of this woman's injuries."

Tam and I are quietly stunned for a moment. "But I never touched her," I say.

"She didn't have injuries," Tam says, "I was there."

"Well, they took pictures of something," Phil replies.

"Oh my god. Did that crazy bitch go home and smack herself up to show the police and fuck me over?" I ask.

Phil states with confidence, "Things like that have been known to happen."

"This is insane!" Tam announces.

"Nonetheless, right now I'd say those photographs are your biggest problem," Phil tells us.

"Photographs?" I mumble as I stagger to the elevator, fucked into a stupor by the expert police work of Officer Hink.

Back at home, I call Ken S- in D.C. and tell him about the police report. I also ask him to lend me some money. Ken says he'll kick in fifteen hundred but he wants to see the police report. "I'm a lawyer," he reminds me. "Yeah, but you're a bankruptcy lawyer, which means I may be needing you soon, but I don't know what you can do about this demented police report." Ken yells at me to let him see the report.

"I don't want you to overreact," I tell him.

"I won't overreact!" Ken yells, "Fax me the fucking police report!"

An hour later, I get a call. I hear no voice, just some gurgling noises. "You read the report, huh?" I say. Gagging with outrage, Ken explodes about the idiot cops and this ridiculous story. After I've talked Ken down from his neurological tree, he mutters something about passing the report around his office to see if his fellow attorneys have any ideas.

The next day, I get a check from Stu F-. Instead of the agreed upon fifteen hundred, he's sent a check for three grand. I call Stu and tell him that it's too much but he yells at me to shut up and cash the check.

Two days after that, Ken calls to tell me that my police report is making a huge splash in his office. He gave the report to a few colleagues, who found it so hilarious that they passed it on to their friends. No one can believe it. Now strangers from other law firms are calling Ken to ask if they can read the report. I ask Ken if any of these lawyers want to help me out, but he tells me no. It's just something they laugh about by the coffee machine.

Phil calls with news from court. Soon I'm in his office, telling him about the cult following my police report is developing in our nation's capital. "It's like the Rocky Horror Picture Show of police reports," I proudly inform Phil.

"Noreen still doesn't want to talk," Phil tells me, "She's taking a hard line with this one."

"Has she read the report?" I ask.

"I'd like to think so, but you never know with Noreen," Phil says.

"Then why is she taking such a hard line with this?"

"Hard to say. Mostly luck of the draw. I have to admit, this is a strange one to take a stand on, because the story in the report is so dubious. Then again, there are those mysterious photos."

"So what do we do?"

"Your new court date is August 18th. I have an idea I'd like to swing by you."

"Is it something else horrible?" I ask.

"No," Phil says.

"Swing away."

"I find it's generally smartest to tackle these situations by finding their pre-existing strengths. Now these charges don't fit your personality at all. But Noreen doesn't know that, and she's refusing to talk to you. So we look for another way."

"Like what?"

"You're an articulate guy. Let's take advantage of that. If Noreen doesn't want to talk, then write to her. It's hard to argue with a letter, and this way, you can tell her what really happened."

"I'm not a lawyer," I say, unconvinced.

"Exactly. I want it in your words," Phil tells me.

"You'll look at it first, before giving it to her, right?"

"Of course," he replies, "What are you worried about?"

"Ever since that car hit me, people have twisted everything I've said and done, trying to wring out the technicalities that will send me to prison. I don't want to accidentally write the one word that enables the death penalty."

"That won't happen," Phil assures me.

"How do you know?"

"Because I'm here now," he says.

I sigh. "Alright. If you say so."

I think there's more to this than Phil's telling me, but I shake off those doubts. By the time I reach the car, I am bolstered with renewed enthusiasm. I hurry home, eager to address these absurd accusations. "Of course this will work!" I convince myself, "I'll just tell Noreen what really happened."

The editing system sits quiet and forgotten as I jump into this exciting new task. "Dear Noreen..." I begin to amicably explain how the story this Toomey woman tells is extremely implausible. You don't even need to read between the lines to see that she's lying. Her inconsistencies and internal contradictions speak for themselves.

I stop writing as doubts start to gnaw at my affable prose. Composing this letter soon becomes a skittish dance through a minefield, like writing a cheerful thank-you note for the kitchen appliance that burned down your house. I decide to try again later.

As this situation proceeds, it's starting to eat away at me. I'm having nightmares, and they're growing increasingly strange. Most of them start with the loud screech of tires then leap into phantasmagoric totalitarian scenarios. I jump awake a lot during the night. Tam doesn't notice this and I don't tell her about it.

So as August rolls along, a meteor shower twinkles in the sky above Los Angeles and I struggle to write my love letter to Noreen, for whom "each day is a struggle." As usual, my eWin horoscope says it all...

My eWin horoscope for August 14th – Too much of a good thing floods your life, Cancer. Try to enjoy it.

theme park of death...

The groovy Commie teens are twisting away on the beach, when a sinister shadow crosses the sand. "NO MORE DANCING!" the voice booms from above. The giant dictator is upset! The kids tremble as the mighty fist slams down. "Who dares question the reports of my police?! HA! Bring this missive of subversion to me!"

The next morning, I'm still struggling to get my letter to Noreen just right. Somehow the first fifteen tries didn't work, mostly because in the police report's unfathomable cavalcade of lies and nonsense, it's hard to find the right place to start.

Crumpled yellow legal pad pages with scribbled notes are scattered by my feet as I delete the latest version on the computer and start again. As with every aborted draft so far, I introduce myself and then begin the Herculean task of presenting all the errors and obvious fabrications in Toomey's tale.

I point out to Noreen, in my friendliest possible tone, that initially I'm simply accused of chipping Toomey's sunglasses, but as her tale swells to grotesque proportions, I am accused of violently assaulting her numerous times as she yells apologies, and then of stealing a pen made of gold. I humbly suggest to Noreen that these are inventions added after the fact to make for more exciting reading.

Every attempt to make sense of the police report gets hopelessly muddled from the sheer volume of improbable events. However, Attempt 24 succeeds in staying on track to the end. I rub my eyes, exhausted, and send the letter off to Phil to see what he thinks. Then I remember Detective Bender and her threats to bring more false charges against me. I sit there, glumly anticipating doing this all again with Bender's spurious claims.

Soon the phone rings. "Steve, it's Phil. You need to make a few changes to this."

"Shoot..."

"First, the Toomey woman should not be referred to as the 'screaming nutcase' or even 'the driver who hit me with her car'. Instead, she's to be known as the 'complaining witness'."

"Fine," I say, "I'll play their little word game for now."

"And don't make reference to any 'lies' told by Toomey or Officer Hink. Do not use the word 'lie' at all."

"You sure?"

"Yes," Phil instructs me, "Call them 'misstatements'."

"Alright. Is that it?"

"One more thing. Don't use the word 'cockamamie'."

"Why not?"

"Just don't."

That evening, I get an e-mail from Phil informing me that "the comments, as amended, are fine" and setting a time to discuss my impending new court date.

"What time should I get to the courthouse?" I ask Phil from my regular seat in his office.

"Oh, you don't need to be there at all. In fact, I'd prefer it if you didn't come."

"Why?"

"I'd like to keep things simple at this point."

"What's going to happen?"

"Very little, and nothing you need to be there for. They'll call your name and I'll talk to Noreen. I'll give her your comments about the police reports and we'll take it from there."

"That sounds too simple," I say.

"Nothing's too simple, especially with this case," Phil tells me, "But I'm hoping they finally take a good look at the complaint and your charges, and just dismiss the whole thing."

"But you said Noreen didn't want to talk," I point out.

"Well, maybe tomorrow she will."

The next morning, I'm back editing the movie. With Phil in court, this is a great chance to catch up a little, which of course isn't happening because I can't concentrate. I'm sitting there, watching the same footage over and over as I try to visualize what's happening in the courthouse. Just before noon, the phone rings. "What happened?!" I eagerly ask, but Phil simply tells me to meet him in his office at 4:00.

"So I gave Noreen your comments," Phil says.

"Cool! What now?"

"Well, I'm still hoping for dismissal. But right now, I'm really just hoping that Noreen reads the comments."

"You don't sound too optimistic. What happened?"

"This wasn't a good day for Noreen," Phil informs me.

"Is this about her 'condition' again?" I ask him.

"Yes, you could say that. Noreen was not responsive. She's clinging to her 'no deals' stance."

"Even for the charge with the mandatory sentence?"

Phil looks down, "She seems determined and confident regarding prison time."

"What aren't you telling me?"

"I'm still trying to gauge Noreen on this. I'll be honest with you, I'm reasonably certain that she hasn't read the police report at all."

"Then why the hell do you think she'll read my letter?"

"Because she should," Phil says, frustrated.

"There's still something you're not telling me."

Phil reluctantly informs me, "Noreen mentioned something about additional charges if you don't cooperate."

"By 'cooperate', do you mean hop on the bus to prison?" Phil shrugs and half-nods, so I ask, "What else could they charge me with?"

"I don't think she was talking about you," he replies.

It takes a second to sink in. "Oh my god, Tam?!" I yell. Phil replies with an uncomfortable nod.

Starting to panic, I ask, "But what could they charge Tam with?"

"I'm not sure," Phil says, "Noreen doesn't know any specifics of the police report. She simply mentioned charging the woman who drove the getaway vehicle if you don't comply with their wishes."

"She's using threats against my girlfriend to leverage their case and put me in prison?"

"It would seem so," Phil somberly nods.

"So this write-a-letter-to-Noreen-and-straighten-it-all-out plan was a bit unrealistic, wouldn't you say?"

"You have a new court date one week from tomorrow. I'll approach Noreen again and see if she's more informed about your case."

"They're really blackmailing me with charging Tam?" Phil replies with a grim nod. "What nasty motherfuckers," I say, "Which reminds me, what about Detective Bender and her threats. Have you looked into that?"

Phil nods, "I have a call in to Sergeant Richter, and I'm sure we'll speak soon."

"So you'll talk about my new false charges?"

"No," Phil tells me, "Well, probably not." My confused mouth opens but Phil grins confidently and continues, "We'll chat about his daughters, and our mutual acquaintances. So, in the next few weeks, if Bender decides to make her opening strike against you, I'll be in a good position to defuse her bomb."

I smile at Phil, impressed, "You're a deceptively snarky son of a bitch, and I like you."

I arrive home and find a message on the answering machine from a non-profit organization. I've worked for non-profits a lot, which has apparently put my name on many lists. A man named Norman W- from the "Sunny Day Foundation" wants me to edit a video. I ignore the message and sit down at my own editing system.

I'm feeling besieged by these sinister forces, and I can't focus on the movie at all. The shrill roar of summer tourists outside my window only adds to my embattled state. What if I really have to go to prison? What if these people make good on their threats to go after Tam? It was bad enough when the crazy woman attacked Tam and the police brutalized her. Now the courts are gearing up to harass her. The technicalities and momentum of this unstoppable mess seem orchestrated by some demon hand.

Wait a minute! That's it! I need to turn this nightmare around, and what better way than to spend a day or two helping out some worthwhile charitable cause? I'm going to stem the evil tide with some good karma. I leap to the phone and call Mr. W- at the Sunny Day Foundation.

The pattern of my involvement with non-profit organizations is painfully predictable. An organization calls and offers me a job for peanuts, describing their heart-wrenching cause. I jump in, all inspired, and within minutes they announce that they don't have any money to pay me at all, while shoving pictures of miserable handicapped people in my face to make sure I stay committed to the cause. Soon, they begin asking for more time and effort until it becomes a full-time-plus slave job, and I try to extricate myself from their bloodsucking web. Then the non-profit folks get indignant and often angry, with bitter proclamations of "I thought you really cared!" and "Boy, were we wrong about you!" I point out the hundreds of hours I've put in for free and they respond like I've just whipped out my penis and pissed on an amputee, until I yell, "Fuck you and your sanctimonious fucking cause!" and I'm done. Then the Thrift Shop for the Blind calls and we start the process all over again.

On the phone, Mr. W- tells me about his non-profit organization, which provides fun activities for sick children. Sunny Day's distinction is that these kids are beyond all medical hope and have been sent home from the hospital to die. There's the Make-A-Wish Foundation and then there are these guys, who are more like the Last Wish Foundation. "How noble!" I think as I gush to Mr. W- about his worthy cause.

Norman W- needs me to edit a video of a Sunny Day trip to Disneyland. "Sounds good," I tell Norman and the next morning I go to an industrial concrete-block building in Marina del Rey where I find Norman, a gigantic man with a very gentle voice.

The soft-spoken talking bear leads me through the cramped office and hands me a soda. Soon I'm sitting in a tiny windowless room with an editing system, a caffeine-free soda, and a chance to do some good. I'm stoked. Let's turn the karma tide around!

I begin watching the footage of a group of frail children going on rides at Disneyland. Look how happy they are. I'm inspired! Behind them you can see the healthy kids, who are all whining, shoving and yelling at their parents. But not the Sunny Day kids. A hot dog, a balloon, plop them in a puke-covered teacup and they're ecstatic. This is awesome. My legal troubles and my unfinished movie retreat like tiny bumps in the road of life.

Norman sticks his giant head in the doorway and asks how I'm doing. He tells me he needs the edited video to have a section featuring each of the twelve kids so he can give their parents a copy. Norman gives me a list of names so I can slap on some simple graphics with each kid's name. I tell Norman how amazing it is to watch these kids be so excited, despite life dealing them such a horribly unfair hand. Norman says that it's true. It's been seven weeks since the Disneyland trip and he is still bolstered by the life-affirming attitude of the Sunny Day kids. I ask Norman if there's any soda with caffeine and he says no.

I hop back to work creating a laugh-filled frolic through the Magic Kingdom. Listening to the kids, I giggle along with their infectious high spirits. Something begins nibbling at the back of my brain, but I'm still glowing with joy watching the kids in line for Mr. Toad's Wild Ride. They bounce over to Space Mountain when Norman's "seven-weeks-ago" comment starts seeping through my head. Look at these amazing kids. They're smiling, they're laughing...They're DEAD!

Oh my god, it's true. These kids were sent home from the hospital with a few weeks to live and that was almost two months ago. I look at the list of names, remembering that Norman said he wants to give the tapes to the parents. He never mentioned the kids, because these happy laughing children are now all deceased.

Hours pass and I start to wilt. I kick myself back up, hoping to enthrall the parents with this memory of their poor departed children. Some employees of the Sunny Day Foundation stop in to watch the video as I work on it. They say things like "Oh look, it's David," then burst into tears and run from the room, leaving me to continue my fun-filled jaunt of dead kids on the rides of Tomorrowland.

I try to find footage of each child speaking into the camera. Little Jonathan says "This place is the best!" Anita squeals "Thank you!" while waiting to fly inside Dumbo. David smiles and yells "I love Star Tours! It makes me forget my Non-Hodgkins Lymphoma is terminal."

Wait! Shit! He didn't really say that, did he? The footage is working on me in strange ways. By lunchtime, I want to kill myself and I'm not even halfway done. While the kids are shaking Goofy's hand, I hear some adult voices just off-camera talking about how Brian's Leukemia ravaged his system far faster than the doctors expected. In the windowless gray room, I try to match the last names on the list with the kids I haven't identified yet. I swear these kids look sicker than when they first got to the park.

Norman pops in and tells me that it's eight o'clock. I've been at this for eleven hours straight. Norman asks if I'd like to come back and finish it up tomorrow and I snap, "No! I'll get this done tonight!" Norman goes home, leaving me with the laughing ghosts of cancer kids skipping around an imitation castle. By three in the morning, the tape is finished and my soul has been sucked from me. I stagger into the apartment, a dry husk of a man, and plop down on the sofa, staring blankly at nothing.

My eWin horoscope for August 27th – When did the walls start closing in around you? Arm yourself for a grueling battle...

On a blistering summer morning, Phil returns to court for our new rendezvous with Noreen. Again, he tells me that there's no need for me to be there since Noreen's condition may be acting up again and he may not make any progress on the case. However, he's hoping for the best.

I'm sweating at the editing system, unable to concentrate. Outside my window, the screaming, honking tourist flood has scaled to manic heights, threatening to explode before Labor Day defuses it. I finally get the call from Phil, and rush to his office.

"Has Noreen read my letter, or the police reports?" I nervously ask.

"It wouldn't appear so," Phil tells me.

"She still hasn't read the reports? How can Noreen make any decisions on a case she knows nothing about?"

Phil smiles and ignores the question. "This was a better day for Noreen," he informs me.

"Really? What happened?" I ask, awash in hope and enthusiasm.

"We had an interesting day in court. Your case was called and I approached. Then Noreen and I went into conference on the case, with each of us offering critiques and suggestions on how it might be resolved."

"Do me a favor. Tell me what happened in words that I'd use if I were describing it to you."

"We stepped aside to discuss your case," Phil says.

"Aside to where?" I ask.

"Out to the hallway."

"You went out to the hall? Isn't there a place for you to do this?"

"Yes, the hallway. That's what happens at court."

"You stand in the hall and try to figure things out?" I ask.

"Yes," Phil informs me.

"That's weird."

"Is it?"

"Yeah."

"Do you want to hear what happened or not?" Phil asks.

"Yes, please," I say.

"While Noreen still seems strangely confident in her ability to put you away, today was one of her better days so we could discuss your case. She's clinging to that gang statute."

"Why is that?"

"I don't know," Phil admits. He looks down, thinking, and something on his desk catches his eye. "Ooh," he says, "I wonder..."

"What?" I ask.

Phil shrugs it off, "Hopefully it won't matter. Let me finish." I nod, confused, as Phil forges ahead, "Since Noreen wasn't familiar with any details of the incident, I gently tried to bring her up to speed."

"Did you tell Noreen that before Toomey made up any of this robbery and assault crap, she hit me with her car?"

"Yes, I brought that up."

"And what did Noreen say?"

"She said 'Really?' and seemed a bit surprised. Then she bounced back with a tough kind of attitude. Her exact words were 'So? It's not like he was killed or anything.'"

"Isn't she sweet?" I say.

"As we proceeded, Noreen seemed confused by your case. I filled her in further regarding the events of that Sunday, which seemed to make her weary."

"Tire her out, excellent."

"Then something positive happened," Phil informs me.

"What?"

"Noreen suggested a civil compromise, in which we would pay for the cost to repair the chipped lens of Toomey's sunglasses, at which point Santa Monica will dismiss the case."

"Really? That's bullshit, I didn't break her stupid glasses but what the hell..."

"I thought that would be your reaction. However, I pointed out to Noreen that this proposal would have to be signed off by Toomey, and due to her manifest instability, there is no assurance that she would do so."

"You tell 'em, tiger, in your own highfalutin' way."

Phil continues, "I then asked what would happen if we propose this to Toomey and she turns it down. At this point, Noreen sighed with an air of resignation, rolled her eyes and said 'Then we'll just let it go.'"

"Really? This is good, right?"

"Yes, this is good."

"You rock, sir! So what now?"

Phil nods with authority, "Now I contact this Toomey person and see what she has to say."

doom's mascot...

The summer Olympics have begun, which means that Tamara is planted like a mighty oak in front of the TV for the next fifteen days. Tam is a pathetic Olympics junkie, helpless in her secretion of an insect-like glue that oozes from her pores and holds her to the sofa, captive to all the colorful athletic events. A few feet away from the TV sits the monstrous and ever-growing editing system. I'm editing around the clock, while Tam spends every second home from work yelling her head off at competitors from around the globe.

Despite the percentage of her life spent watching these games, Tam never seems to learn any more about their rules or the intricacies of how they're played. However, she immediately chooses her favorite contender in each event and cheers them on rabidly. Just as quickly, she viciously despises all rivals impeding her favorite's chance at Olympic glory. The TV attempts to guide Tam's allegiances with filmed pieces about the moving, sometimes tragic, lives of certain athletes. As often as not, Tam rejects these compelling backstories, opting instead to form her extreme opinion from a bit of offhanded trivia from the commentator. Tam shouts at the screen, "I don't care about her knee surgery, I want the South Korean who's back with her former coach!" I'm trying my hardest to ignore all of this while I piece together more of the movie.

It's been over a week since Phil told me about Noreen McDonough's proposal to pay for Lauren Toomey's sunglasses. While I hope this plan works, I'm still deeply troubled and puzzled over how any of this is happening. Currently, I'm trying to figure out Toomey's angle here. Why the hell would someone who's spent decades to become a doctor suddenly take on this strange sideline of attacking a perfect stranger, then screwing him over by lying to the police and pressing false charges? What bizarre mania propels this woman? Then again, maybe I'm answering my own question. Perhaps the reason she's still trying to become a doctor at her age is because she's crazy. None of this speculation helps with the mandatory prison sentence and I'm not getting any work done. Tam tells me to stop fretting over it, and to let Phil handle things. She's right, but it continues to chomp away on my brain.

While Tam gripes about the lame Olympic mascot, I grapple with another geyser of pus - paying back Stu and Ken for my legal fees. With my time eaten up by working for free, I'm not sure how to pull off this little fiscal miracle. Lacking any better ideas, I continue to spend a few minutes each day feverishly clicking away on the eWin website in hopes of winning those big bucks. I still print my eWin horoscope every day and use the sheet to scribble my notes on this legal odyssey. But one day, my copious scribbling requires a second sheet, and something dawns on me.

Lauren Toomey manipulated those lunkhead cops by claiming to be mortally afraid of me finding out her identity and where she lived. While I had no interest in learning any more about this deranged woman, her lies resulted in the realization of what she claimed to be her deepest fear. I was handed a Xeroxed pile containing all the details of her stupid life, and I've decided to put this information to good use.

I've ceased to expect any insight regarding my court case from the eWin horoscope. What a laughable conceit that now seems. Instead, I'll seek wisdom about this debacle in Lauren Toomey's eWin horoscope! And I get five more chances to win a million bucks!

As gleaned from the police report, Lauren Toomey was born on December 13th in a year before the TV had color. This makes her a Sagittarius. Knowing nothing about astrology, I have no idea what personality traits this should bestow on her. I suspect that Toomey's unhinged character would override any standard zodiacal parameters. It doesn't matter, I just need something else to write on as this damn fiasco grows longer and more complicated.

Lauren Toomey's eWin Sagittarius horoscope for September 6th - Remember that a smile is contagious! Your cheerful attitude is sure to help you find a date...

Phil has been in court in Long Beach all week, dealing with the trial of a lesbian who stabbed her lover to death. But I can't remain silent any longer...

Date: 09.06
Subject: the new plan
Hey Phil!
I hope things are going well with your trial. Any news
with Dr. Roadkill?
Steve
~~~~~~~~~~
Date: 09.06
Subject: Re: the new plan
Hi Steve:
I sent the good doctor a letter. Still waiting for her reply.
I'll keep you posted.
Phil

While yanking at my inner leash of reason, I still find my
subconscious hoping for the best. However, a resolution
doesn't seem likely given what's gone down so far. In fact, if
Toomey continues to be as hideously encouraged as she's
been, I now think she may try something more ambitious in
terms of slanderous accusations.

The Olympic speed-walking event creates a violent fervor in
Tam, during which time she should not be disturbed, but I
try to discuss my new fears with her during a sneaker ad.
"Talk to Phil," she says dismissively.

"I think Phil knows more than he's telling about why all this
is happening."

"Why's that?" Tam asks, her eyes locked on the TV.

"Well, for starters, he said so. He said it very pointedly,
while he was looking at something on his desk."

"What was he looking at?" Tam asks. While I try to
remember, I lose Tam to the archery highlights. "Oh, I

know!" I exclaim, "It was that letter from Noreen...the one with the charges written on it."

"Well, obviously," Tam absently replies, "if he were looking at the letter, I guess that would explain it."

"There's got to be slightly more to it than that. He didn't just look down and think, 'That's it! You were charged because you got this letter.' I think there's something else, some internal clue on that paper, that will tell us...something."

"Terrific, Encyclopedia Brown to the rescue."

"I'm going to look into this," I tell her.

But I don't look into it. Not yet, anyway. Because the editing system suddenly begins making a deep rumbling noise that stops my heart for a few beats. The sprawling machine is soon rattling, so I call Ian, my long-haired computer-whiz buddy from Singapore. Ian tells me that I need more memory and drive space. He'll bring over the components, and I can pay him later when I get some new credit cards. Ian tells me to keep plugging away and, if the system starts to shake, to whack it on the side with my palm.

It's taking way too long to edit this movie. Tamara is growing frustrated and angry as we start to miss the deadlines of the many film festivals we had planned on entering. But I keep at it, doggedly assembling our grungy modern-day beach party movie. Ian never shows up, and his recommended "banging" cure doesn't work for long before the system shuts down completely.

The next day, Ian arrives with the new drives and starts to implant them into the ever-growing expanse of cables and metal boxes that has completely engulfed our apartment.

Using the tiniest screwdriver in the world to magically bring the system back to life, Ian asks me about my impending mandatory prison sentence. I tell him about the new plan to avoid it, but I'm worried because I haven't heard anything from Phil. Connecting some cables, Ian says, "You know, if you go to prison in Singapore, you have to drink from the toilet. It's your only water source."

Lauren Toomey's Sagittarius eWin horoscope for September 21st - Isn't it nice to be loved and admired? You remain the center of attention...

Despite their track record, I feel the Internet swamis may have stumbled onto something here. How much is Toomey relishing the attention this is bringing her? "First those hunky cops listened to me, now I'm getting nice letters from a lawyer!" Could this be the poor wallflower's moment in the sun? Her chance to finally be noticed? Where might this lead? My mind becomes infected with the unshakable fear that, spurred on by her wild success so far, Lauren Toomey is going to accuse me of something else. Weeks have passed since Noreen suggested the extortion method of placating Toomey. I can't stand it anymore, so I call Phil, who asks me to come to his office.

Phil looks calmly fed up. "I've left more messages for Lauren Toomey but she hasn't responded. I thought perhaps she might have contacted Noreen to give her thoughts, but she has not, at least as far as I know."

"Have you seen Noreen?"

"I've been in Santa Monica twice in the last couple weeks. The first time, Noreen was out for the day. The second time, which was this morning, Noreen was in no shape to discuss your case."

117

"Oh, her 'condition' acting up again?"

"That's correct."

"That's a shame. But it's assuming a lot to leave the progress of this case in the hands of a mouth-foaming loon like Lauren Toomey. When's my next court date?"

"You don't actually have one. Noreen left that in the air, contingent on Toomey's response to her proposal."

"Is this 'proposal' going to work?" I ask uncomfortably.

"I hope so," Phil says.

"What can we do to speed this along?"

"Nothing. Only Noreen can do that," Phil informs me.

"But she's left it up to Toomey, who's oddly quiet and downright missing."

Phil sighs, "Yes, that's true."

"How much longer will I have this hanging over me like a guillotine?"

"Sadly, there's no set time-frame for this phase," Phil says.

"I'm facing a mandatory prison sentence for something that never happened, and now I'm floating off the grid and there's nothing I can do?"

Phil replies with a somber half-smile, "Hang in there."

Another gut-wrenching week goes by. My schoolgirl daydreams of closure for this nonsense are long gone, replaced with crashing anxiety. Each day, it becomes exponentially harder not to think about it. I had been fooled into thinking that some element of sanity had been injected to these proceedings by Phil, but now I'm realizing that this isn't the case. The original inexplicable forces that created this situation still seem to be in control.

Date 10.11
Subject: The best years of our lives
Hey Phil:
I'm dying here. Is there any news? I yearn for the former mess of my life, like a smallpox-afflicted Aztec yearns for the days when they'd just rip out his heart and chuck him down the stairs.
Steve

~~~~~~~~~

Date 10.11
Subject: Re: The best years of our lives
Hi Steve:
Still nothing. I'm at a loss to explain this, except that it's bureaucracy at its finest. Toomey's been silent and Noreen has been incapacitated every time I've tried to tackle the subject. Hopefully Noreen's condition will improve and we'll move forward soon. Again, sorry.
Phil

~~~~~~~~~

Date 10.11
Subject: Re: The best years of our lives
Hey Phil:
Can't help you with Noreen, but if you want to get Toomey's attention, you might want to try crossing the street while she's driving. Worked for me.
Steve

I find something else growing in my brain, something that makes me want to stab myself. As crazy as it is, I'm beginning to feel sorry for this Noreen McDonough, despite her being a major player in the crusade to wrongly imprison me. I'm not sure what 'condition' Noreen has, but from Phil's constant vague references to it, it's clearly some ailment that flares up unpredictably and affects her ability to physically and mentally perform her job. My guess is Multiple Sclerosis, and Tam agrees.

I'm painfully aware of how devastating MS can be. I know more than my share of people afflicted with it; two cousins, several friends, the young daughter of a high school buddy. From my experience, it seems to affect far more people than other "name" illnesses. I keep imagining poor Noreen shaking and quivering, struggling through the courthouse corridors, as she tries to rid the world of dangerous criminals. I feel bad for her, burdened with my stupid case while straining to do good, despite her tragic debilitating infirmity. This ludicrous business with me is probably just a misunderstanding, which she'll soon discover once she stops having horrible attacks of her MS.

I slap myself across the face, and I announce to myself that I can save the testimonials to poor Noreen until after she's realized the truth about what happened in May and set things right. I'm not allowing myself to be impressed by Noreen simply trying to do her job. Let's see if she can do her job well.

Aw hell, I can't help it. I still feel bad for Noreen.

Despite my original August court date, we're sinking into autumn with no end in sight. In fact, the truly gruesome parts have yet to begin...

it's a shame about noreen...

My eWin horoscope for October 19ᵗʰ – You're on the Love Roller Coaster today, Cancer! When you look back, you're likely to regret something you didn't do more than something you did...

Dig it! The Love Roller Coaster! I can feel the "love" blowing through my hair. But I'll give the Internet seers this, I've been regretting something I didn't do for months now. Not the actual lack of doing it, simply the part where I get charged with it.

I wake up constantly during the night, plagued by extremely disturbing Expressionist dreams. Set in colorless, dehumanizing places from German silent movies, these dreams are peopled with leering doctors, totalitarian goons, and deformed civil servants. While Tamara now thinks that Toomey is afraid to deal with Phil, I think differently. I'm growing more certain that an implacable sociopath like Toomey is delighted with the attention this is bringing her. It's her big chance for drama, because she probably doesn't get noticed very often. She definitely had that bitter edge on our first date. I'm also betting that Toomey is nothing but encouraged that her arbitrary wicked plan seems to be working. I'll bet she's daydreamed about doing something like this for years. This is her revenge for never being the popular girl in school. Never the one picked for volleyball. Never the one at the restaurant with some dreamy mystery stud.

"Look at me, so in demand!" she smiles in the mirror. She's probably scheming with her many cats right now, planning more stunts to bring her attention. At last, a chance to play the victim for an audience! She's developing a taste for it, and she wants more.

I try to stop myself from hoping too much, or from being too surprised when this all gets worse. If I'm prepared for some new grotesque turn of events, then I'll be better able to counter it. I'm growing my own invisible armor, ready to fight these people and their fatuous, vindictive madness. Day and night, I'm on guard because I'm convinced that Lauren Toomey is going to accuse me of something else. Her implausible terror-filled pleas to the police were obviously setting this up.

Phil and I continue our email relationship to discuss the thunderous silence from Toomey and Noreen McDonough. Then, on Friday, Phil calls me in for a quick meeting. Sitting across the desk from Phil, I can tell he's frustrated by this case, but trying not to let it show.

Phil has managed to procure a new court date for the following Tuesday. I ask if he's spoken to Noreen and he says no. I'm confused about how he placed me back on their grid without speaking with Noreen, but I don't ask because the answer will probably just perplex me further.

On Tuesday morning, I'm trying not to second-guess whatever's going down in the Santa Monica Courthouse, but big loud bells are going off in my head. Churning with dread, I'm trying to edit when I get the call. Phil doesn't sound happy but he won't discuss anything over the phone, so we set a time to meet that afternoon. Tam asks me if I want her to come. I tell her not to bother. However, fearing some new ruinous crackup on my part, she announces that she's coming.

Phil's standard calm demeanor seems to be requiring some effort, which gets me nervous right off the bat. Nonetheless, I put on my best smile and ask him, "So...how'd it go?" Phil grins uncomfortably.

"Well, we went to court..." Phil begins. He hesitates and I can already feel the internal bleeding of stress, "Come on, what happened?"

"I learned from the prosecutor that Lauren Toomey is not interested in a civil compromise."

My chest starts to tighten. "Alright. So then what?"

"Well, now you have some decisions to make."

"What kind of decisions?" I ask, "Did Noreen McDonough read my letter?"

"Mmm, it would appear not. My guess is no."

"Why not?" I ask.

Phil just shrugs and I'm struggling to follow this. I ask, "Noreen said that if Toomey was difficult about the civil offer, then she'd throw the whole thing out, right?"

"That is definitely what she led me to believe," Phil replies.

"That's great," I say. Phil just looks at me. "Why aren't you happy?" I ask him. Phil doesn't respond. I feel a nasty tingle like something large and horrible is about to land on me. Nonetheless, I press on, "So that...is what's going to happen, right?"

"No. Unfortunately, that no longer seems to be the case."

"Shit, I knew it," I throw my hands up.

Tam grabs my arm. She leans forward, concerned and not happy. "What exactly is the case?" she wants to know.

"It appears that Noreen spoke to this Toomey woman, and they discussed the offer to give her the appropriate blackmail money to sign off on these ridiculous charges."

"And?" Tam asks.

Phil hesitates, then announces, "Toomey's response was that she wants Steve to go to prison."

Even Tam looks nervous now. "For what?" she asks.

Phil sighs, "For the assault charge, the battery, and the robbery."

"But that's insane!" Tam yells, "He didn't do anything!"

"Why does it matter what Toomey says?" I ask, "This is Noreen's decision."

Phil grimly informs me, "Noreen seems all set. She's going to try to put you in prison for this."

My mouth drops open. I'm stunned. "For how long?" I ask.

"That's an entirely different conversation, one that we don't have time for right now," Phil remains composed.

"Did you remind Noreen of her initial plan to dismiss these charges if the civil compromise didn't work?"

"Of course I did," he says.

"And what was her response?" I ask.

Phil clears his throat. "It seems..." Phil pauses, but with the next couple years of my life on the line, I'm about to explode, "What?!"

"Apparently, Noreen has no recollection of that conversation. She denied ever discussing any kind of civil deal with me."

I'm at a total loss. "But that's crazy. How can that be? How could she forget?"

Tam's looking mighty pissed. "Are you serious?" she asks.

"Yes, I'm afraid I am," Phil tells us.

Despite being the seasoned pro, Phil seems extremely uneasy. It's cracking through his well-mannered persona like some hateful lava seeping up from the molten bowels of Santa Monica. I don't know what the expression on my face looks like, but Phil is avoiding looking at me.

Tam asks angrily, "How could she forget?!"

"Does this have something to do with this 'condition' of hers that you keep talking about?" I ask.

Looking down at some papers, Phil says, "Yes, I'm almost certain that this is a result of her condition."

"Well, I'm sorry," I tell him, "but I'm afraid this has gone too far. I can't believe I've been feeling sorry for this woman. How does her MS make her forget things that she says in court?"

Now it's Phil who looks confused, "MS?"

"Yeah," I say, "Multiple Sclerosis."

"I know what MS is. What are you talking about?"

"Noreen's MS," I say.

Phil stares at me like I've grown antennae, "Noreen McDonough doesn't have MS."

"Well, whatever she has. It sounded like MS the way you described it. What medical condition does she have?"

Phil's so thrown by this, a quick laugh escapes his lips. "She doesn't have any medical condition..."

Something drops in my stomach. "Then what are you always talking about?"

Phil says, "I don't know if-"

I cut him off, screaming, "What the fuck is wrong with her?!"

"She's an alcoholic!" Phil blurts out, then he stops short. His face turns red. I'm falling down the rabbithole now. I weakly gasp, "I'm sorry, did you just say..."

"Noreen doesn't have MS, she's a hopeless alcoholic." Phil sighs, and looks me in the eye. "Okay, listen. It's sort of a big open secret. We all just work around it. And sometimes it's more of a problem than...other times."

"You've got to be kidding," I say.

"I'm afraid I'm not."

I stammer, "But the way you talked about it..."

"I'm sorry. I didn't mean to mislead you."

"You obviously didn't mean to tell me the truth, either."

"I didn't think I'd have to." Phil admits. He looks embarrassed.

"How bad of an alcoholic is she?" Tam asks.

"I'd rather not discuss this," Phil says.

"Give me a ballpark," Tam insists.

"Oh, she's out of the park," he says.

"Holy shit!" Tam yells. Now she's furious. "Are you seriously telling us that the shots here are being called by an alcoholic who forgets entire conversations?!"

"Listen, I know you're upset..." Phil tries to keep us steady.

"To what degree does this affect her job?" Tam asks while I sit
there, stunned.

"Okay, stop," Phil says, "There are factors here that we can deal with, and factors that we can't change."

"Let's try changing this one," I yell, "Some pathetic morning drinker is leading a crusade to put me in prison for something I didn't do! How much of this is happening because we caught her on a bad day when she was hungover, or still drunk from the night before?!"

"With Noreen, I've found that timing is everything," he says.

"Stop being diplomatic about this! I'm about to strangle you!"

"Getting upset is not going to further any solution," Phil calmly says.

"Fine!" I bark, "Then all I want to discuss right now is how to use this in our favor. When we go to trial, how can Noreen's drinking help us win?"

"Are you crazy? They'd never let a lush like Noreen actually try a case-" Phil stops. He looks shocked. Then Phil clears his throat and says, "Noreen simply sets the calendar."

Phil's eyes leave mine. Clearly he feels bad about how I'm being treated, but he never thought that this one stupid case would call into question how his world works. And he's hoping that this conversation is not the thin end of a very big wedge. Meanwhile, I'm still trying to process this situation in my usual frame of reference, an illusory world where I attempt to find a cause-and-effect logic to events. "Do you think this Toomey woman knows those cops, or 'Last Call' McDonough?"

The guilty look on Phil's face melts away, replaced by the regular patronizing expression he wears when speaking to me. "I don't think so," he calmly responds.

"I'm trying to make sense out of this."

"Well, as explanations go, I think that's somewhat paranoid."

"Yeah," I say, "As opposed to the ludicrous false charges made by a wackjob being fully believed by the alcoholic City Attorney who's looking to put me in prison for two years while the local legal establishment looks the other way because it's easier for them."

Ah, success! I've made Phil uncomfortable again. He squirms a little. "Okay, fair enough," he concedes, "However, I don't think Toomey knows either the cops or Noreen. I think this is just one of those things that sometimes happens."

"How often is 'sometimes'?" I ask.

"I've already told you. I've never seen anything like this, and I've been practicing law here for over twenty years."

"So it never happens," I say, "Yet any attempt on my part to explain it makes me paranoid."

Tam jumps back in, "Can we get back on track here?"

"I don't like being called paranoid, especially when I'm the only one looking at this head-on, without the convenient filter of 'experience'."

Phil looks sincere, "You're right. I won't call you paranoid again. I think we should move forward," Phil says.

"I have another question," I say and Phil braces himself. Tam interrupts me, leaning closer to Phil, "You know, this is a lot to learn at one time."

But Phil's back in command. He says, in one unbroken line, "I'm sorry" to Tam and "What's your question?" to me.

"Why does Toomey get to decide if this moves forward? Isn't it Noreen's job to assess the credibility of the accusations?"

"Noreen's just doing her job the best way she knows how."

"That doesn't answer my question," I tell him.

Phil says, "I've known Noreen for years. I think it's a shame about Noreen. She has struggled with this condition for most of her life."

"That's very compassionate of you, but I'm getting fucked up the ass here, so why don't you try to explain it a different way."

"I don't have a different way," Phil admits.

"Is there anyone else we can appeal to? There's got to be more to the justice system than this one inept drunk," I suggest hopefully.

"I'm afraid right now, for you there isn't," Phil tells me.

"Why not?" I ask.

"Because that's what trials are for," he says.

The volcano in my stomach is about to blow again. "But this shouldn't even go to trial," I say.

"I agree. But it's their choice," he tells me.

"It's their choice, yet they've left it up to Lauren Toomey. How can Noreen McDonough not remember discussing that deal with you when she remembers discussing it with Toomey?"

"I don't know," Phil says, sounding frustrated about that himself.

I throw my hands in the air. "Okay, so as far as you know, Noreen hasn't read my letter, or the police reports, right?"

"That's correct," Phil replies.

"What the fuck...Are they so free from actual crimes that they can spend their time on imaginary ones?"

"Well, don't forget. There are those photographs of Toomey's injuries," Phil reminds me.

"She didn't have injuries," Tam says.

"Well, apparently there are pictures of them," Phil says.

Tam looks worried, and my attempts to understand this have left me floundering, "So you're saying they didn't read the police reports and they didn't read my comments, but they did look at the photos."

"Possibly," he says.

"That seems a little random, don't you think?" I say.

"If those photos are what I think they are, then right now that is as irrelevant as everything else you've been asking."

"Then why didn't they arrest me when I went into the station?" I ask.

"How should I know?" Phil says, "Why did these cops do any of the things they did? All I know is that Noreen is very determined to put you away."

"So there's no actual conspiracy," I say, "Noreen's simply a helpless gin-soaked pawn in Toomey's vindictive game?"

"Don't make yourself crazy over this," Phil tells me.

"I wouldn't be making myself anything over this if they weren't all working to defend Lauren Toomey's right to run down pedestrians with her car!"

"I agree, actually." Phil surprises me with some candor here. He continues, "I've never seen anything like this, and inside I'm quite disgusted. You're a nice guy, and you don't deserve any of this. However, what you have to remember is the fact that you're a nice guy is exactly how we can keep them from getting away with it. I think we should move on now, because we have a lot more to talk about."

"Well, what's next?" I ask.

"Your pre-trial is over," Phil explains, "And we move forward. Toomey's not going to get away with this. It's just going to happen in the next phase."

"The trial?" I ask with dread.

"Yes, your trial," he tells me.

I take a breath, trying to let it sink in. "Okay."

"There's just one thing," Phil adds.

"What's that?"

Phil looks grimly at me, "Your fees so far only cover the pre-trial motions. Now that we're going to trial..."

I groan, "Oh shit, I have to pay you more?"

"I'm afraid so," he says.

"How much more?"

"My fee for a trial is seventy-five-hundred dollars."

"Oh god..." The sheer bungee-less freefall sensation comes back, for the third time this meeting. "I don't have it," I mumble.

Tam chimes in, "We'll get it!"

I bark at her, "How?!"

Tam looks to Phil, "After we get the money, what happens then?"

"Well, we can set up some kind of plea bargain, or we can go to trial and ram it down their throats," he says.

"Can a plea bargain be considered part of the pre-trial?" Tam asks.

"We've tried that and Noreen keeps changing her mind," Phil says, "She's not discussing this anymore. Rightly or wrongly, Noreen has pushed your case forward to trial. I do feel that this is in spite of the facts of your case. However, that may not be true since Noreen's not actually aware of the facts of your case."

I blurt out, "Shouldn't she be aware of the facts of the case?"

Phil cuts this off, "Yes. Wrong things happen pretty frequently in this world. Now the key here is to get you past Noreen to the next City Attorney. But that brings us to the trial stage."

Tam asks, "So you're saying that it costs the same if we plea bargain or go to trial?"

"Yes," he says.

Tam exclaims, "Then I want a trial!"

I turn to her, "Okay, relax. You're jumping ahead here. I don't have the money for a trial." I look at Phil, "What happens if I plead guilty?"

"Why the hell would you plead guilty?" Phil asks.

Tam yells, "You're not pleading guilty! That sick bitch attacked me! I'm not letting her get away with it."

Phil smiles. He and Tam are on the same page here, and I am definitely not. Phil says, "If you plead guilty, you'll get screwed."

"Prison?" I ask.

"Who cares? You're not pleading guilty," Tam announces, "That's absurd."

"What are my other options?" I ask.

"There's always the public defender," Phil quietly says.

"What will happen then?" I ask.

"It's a risk," Phil informs me, "You might get lucky, you might get shafted."

I sigh, "Is there some option between 'lucky' or 'shafted'? How about 'fair'?"

"Oh...come on," Phil says, "If things were fair, you wouldn't be here at all."

"Right," I say.

"I'll tell you what, I'll talk to her again," Phil says, "You've got another court date on the 28th. I'll see how Noreen feels then. Maybe we'll catch her in a better frame of mind." I'm seizing up big-time but Tam grabs my arm and says to Phil, "If we need the money, we'll find it."

"Good," Phil says.

"But you'll make one more attempt to get this dismissed?" she asks.

"I'll do what I can," Phil assures us.

As we leave Phil's office, I find myself equally divided between the desire to die and the urge to kill.

beg...

The sacred stone colossus stands on the hill as the samurai forces decimate the feudal village. But one conquering warlord makes a fatal error. Striking a defiant stance, he laughs at the bleeding peasants, "You see?! I am stronger than your god!" **BAM!** *The immense stone foot comes down as the angry Japanese god wreaks his vengeance. Rivers of blood and guts flow toward the sea, while anguished warriors scream for mercy...*

I jump awake, but not as shaken as most mornings. I've had the angry-Japanese-giant-statue dream before, and I'm getting used to it. Other nights aren't nearly as good. The raging Asian colossus seems like a conga line through Candyland compared to what usually happens when I fall asleep these days.

I'm exhausted from thrashing through each night, plagued by dreams of Cubist-inspired, two-dimensional cops. As these months of legal peril drag on, my dream police grow more distorted, smudged in the soiled shades of an old silent movie. Their warped faces fire off what sounds like an extra guttural form of German, complete with subtitles. *"Ha! You see, Willem, he admits that he doesn't know the law, yet he claims to be innocent!"* *"Oof!"* his googly-eyed partner belches, then they both laugh like seagulls and move in for the kill.

The Layman's Handbook for Those Falsely Accused of Felonies, page 42...The sinister Puppet Masters of the mighty court allow you precious few times to speak. Indeed, only one such opportunity is mandated, when you are commanded to utter the few syllables of your **plea**. *You have meager options to choose from. Make sure you understand all possible interpretations of these simple words, as they will greatly affect your fate...*

I'm pacing through our cluttered apartment while Tam sits on the sofa and we discuss how I should plead. I don't know the first thing about "pleading" other than that it generally means begging, which I am more than happy to do to end this nightmare. "Pleading innocent" suddenly seems like a mixed metaphor. If I'm innocent, why the hell do I need to beg?

What kind of police record and punishment will I accept simply because I don't have the money or time to fight this any further? It's driving me crazy, trying to anticipate the ways in which cutting my losses now will come back and haunt me for the rest of my life. The larger problem is that I don't understand my charges, which are vague, arbitrary words loosely attached to a long, drawn-out incident, during most of which I was the one getting hit. Tam and I struggle through this over and over, only to end up frustrated and disheartened each time.

My eWin Cancer horoscope for October 26th – Being alone isn't always the same as being lonely...

Lauren Toomey's eWin Sagittarius horoscope for October 26th - Lucky Sag, with the Moon currently resting in your sign, you will receive a number of fortunate advantages...

"Call me crazy, but that bitch always gets a better horoscope than I do," I complain to Liz on the back patio of the Rose Café. But comparing horoscopes abruptly gets kicked aside when I drop the megaton bombshell regarding Noreen McDonough and her lack of Multiple Sclerosis. Liz is appalled, and launches into a tirade that's virulent even for Liz.

On most weekday afternoons, the back patio of the Rose Café is full of writers and other surly unemployed types. We generally keep to our small territorial groupings but, every so often, some matter is overheard that creates a more general discussion. This is one of those days. Soon the patio is buzzing with the shocking news about the stumbling alcoholic City Attorney in Santa Monica. Some of the other writers claim to have already heard rumors about this woman. Now the whole patio is disgusted, and joins Liz in hatching elaborate schemes to publicly expose this woman. I sit back, watching as the acrimony spreads like nerve gas through an extremely aloof crowd. Its speed and degree of impact are not lost on me.

Since this happy day, I've spoken with many local lawyers who are familiar with the Santa Monica Courthouse. They all snicker while saying something facetiously compassionate when asked about Noreen. Having enjoyed total life-immersion in the consequences of Noreen's "condition", I don't join in their snickering, which makes them suspicious of me. Like Phil, every one of them has at least one story about some guilty client who got off because Noreen was an incapacitated mess at a key moment. They all take advantage of it as much as they can. When they hear about me and my case, their reaction is generally along the lines of "I knew this would happen to somebody, someday." However, instead of feeling bad for me, they actually feel bad for Phil. To them, he's the one who got screwed in their much enjoyed loophole of how justice operates in Santa Monica. Petty Thefts, DUI's, domestic assaults, all kinds of charges have been mislaid and forgotten due to Noreen's slurred speech or wobbling hangovers. All except for mine. I'm not just going to prison, I'm going down in local lawyer history as the one time it backfired.

That night at home, Tam and I have yet another discussion about what to do if Phil can't get Noreen to agree to something reasonable. We also discuss what constitutes "reasonable" in a situation like this. My options are all so bleak that we get nowhere all over again. I've taken this as far as I can without coming up with a lot more cash. Tam thinks I should ask Stu F- for more money, but I can't because it's just too foul a proposition. Why should he pay through the nose because of some insidious med student and a revolting drunk? I tell Tam to forget that idea, which means we're back to credit cards.

I dump out the designated trashcan and dig out more credit card offers. My forehead gets clammy as I fill out the applications, because there's no way I'll ever be able to pay off these new debts. I've got most of the movie on these cards, as well as most of my expenses from the past year while I've worked my ass off with no income. My credit card balances are now mounting exponentially like some god-awful plastic tower in Middle-Earth about to crumble and crush the wee hobbits below. But expecting the worst in what legal peril lies ahead, I go ahead and mail the new crop of credit card applications.

I wonder how many people in America end up in prison simply because they can't afford to defend themselves. Guilt and innocence seem irrelevant in navigating this loathsome labyrinth. I'm trying to edit the movie when Phil calls. He wants to see me, so I head to his office and plop down in my regular chair.

I'm pale and shriveled from following my prospects to the same cliff, again and again. Phil is being extra conciliatory, with lots of gentle funeral director nodding. There's a queasy calm over us, stemming from the grim elephant in the room that if I can't conjure up another $7500, Phil's involvement in this case will soon come to an end. Tired and despondent, I jump on a new strategy. Remaining extremely calm, my new tact is to instill in Phil the fear of looking bad once I get reamed. I begin by telling Phil about the Rose Cafe's reaction to my big Noreen news, and how my case is becoming the talk of Venice Beach.

I can see it starting to erode Phil's calm façade. Phil tells me that Noreen won't succeed because she's incompetent, and because he won't let her succeed. I tell Phil that Noreen is going to succeed in bankrupting me. Then I tell him about my friends' ideas to contact various local columnists.

Phil clears his throat. This is definitely having some effect on him. Matching my deathly calm demeanor, Phil points out that he's certain my outgoing personality lends itself to spreading opinions in a very effective manner. I reply, "I think it's so forward-minded of Santa Monica to employ a twelve-step failure like Noreen in a position of major responsibility. It moves me so deeply that I feel obligated to announce their good deed to everyone I know."

Phil sighs. It's clear that he does not want to be connected to the guy who blows the whistle on morning cocktail hour at the Santa Monica Courthouse. The polite cat-and-mouse continues as Phil says that, for me, the stakes are very high and my every move must be well reasoned. I calmly announce to Phil that I'm not afraid of Noreen McDonough, Lauren Toomey, the Santa Monica Court, or even going to prison. I'm only afraid of my impending insolvency. My joining in Phil's hyper-civil game seems to work on him quite effectively. I decide to milk it because, until he gets used to it, it gives me the upper hand, or at least levels the playing field. I politely inform Phil that I think it will be best for all if I don't go to prison for this. With a reserved nod of his head, Phil says that he understands.

We move on to my favorite new hobby, pleading. I tell Phil that all attempts to sort this out have failed, and he suggests we try to think it through together. I tell Phil that, as agreeable as I generally try to be, I'm not pleading guilty to anything that involves using force against a woman. "It never happened, and fuck them for claiming that it did," I state. Phil nods and calmly says, "Okay."

I continue, "The destruction of property thing, fine. Who gives a shit? We're only talking about a piece of paper that she was using to threaten my girlfriend."

Phil asks, "What about the sunglasses?"

"Again, never happened," I say, "Let them try to prove it. And whatever injuries this woman inflicted on herself to frame me, bring it on. I'm not going to give in to this."

Phil's eyes light up. We seem to be in sync again. But I decide to test it. I ask him about the money, and what happens if we do indeed go to trial. "I understand your situation," he says, "But if this goes to trial, I really can't help you with the money. It's just the way things are." I nod glumly. Phil smiles, "I guarantee that it won't be money wasted. If they really insist on taking this thing to trial, it will be the biggest trial the City of Santa Monica has ever seen."

I ask, "Won't they try to sandbag me quickly, and be done with it?"

"That is exactly what they'll try to do. And I promise you they won't succeed with that. If your case means that much to them, then they're going to have to work for it. Harder than they'd ever imagine."

"Okay. Hey, one more thing...what does 'no contest' mean? I've seen that on TV."

"Let's not get into anything like that just yet," he says, "Right now there's no need to. Next week, I go back to Noreen and try one more time to straighten this out for you." Playing it cool with Phil is such a flimsy pose on my part that I can't believe it's not immediately recognized as such. Inside, I'm dangerously close to cracking.

It's November 4th - Election Day! I love voting. I even vote on Election Days when there's nothing to vote for. Tam and I wake up early and walk down to the Jewish Senior Citizen Center on the boardwalk. I love that our polling place is on the beach, and I love that it's commandeered by all these feisty old Jews. Just for kicks, I worked the polls there one Election Day, and I was immediately adopted by Hannah Singer and her gang of fellow octogenarians.

Hannah Singer is a hoot. She's the widow of the man who founded the International Ladies Garment Workers Union. Hannah also claims to be a card-carrying member of the Communist Party, which I didn't think was still possible. As

Tam and I walk in, Hannah and her buddies yell to me in their loud-deaf-old-folks' way. While I'm usually bouncing with excitement to vote, today my heart isn't in it and the old gang notices it right away. Hannah hands me a ballot and says, "Stevie, you look terrible! What's wrong?"

Extra-deaf Esther shouts, "Why the hell aren't you married?!" while Bea gushes to Tam, mistaking her for Sarah Jessica Parker, "I love your show! Such forward-thinking young women!"

"With the sex!" Esther yells.

As I hand in my ballot, Hannah clutches my hand with grave urgency. "They've gotten to you, haven't they?" she urgently asks. Not wanting to get into it with this crowd because it could take weeks, I simply reply, "Hannah, I'm just having a tough time these days." Hannah yanks me down for a hug. "Be strong and true," she whispers into my ear.

Tam leaves for work and I walk home, dispirited. I'm depressed by Election Day because, until I got hit by that car and sent on this sulphurous journey, I used to care about this stuff a lot. Now current events seem like some lofty luxury. In my current world, all I can think about is how I'm going to find another seven-grand-plus to keep my freedom campaign afloat.

I check the mail, and then stop dead...as something unspeakably horrible occurs. I receive a letter from a credit card company informing me that I have been "REJECTED". My heart skids. I've never seen a rejection letter from a credit card company before. I see another envelope amidst the junk mail and quickly rip it open. "Oh my god!" I gasp as I find a second rejection letter. Apparently, my debts are too large for these people to want to play with me any more. "Fuck!" I scream. I'm at a total loss as to how to react to this, so I decide to temporarily ignore it. That doesn't work at all, so I collapse onto a chair in shock. I have no idea how to continue living if I can't get any new credit cards.

I can't move.

sinkhole...

It's four in the morning, and my hand is cramping up from my frenzied writing. Earlier this evening, the trashcan of credit cards offers was poured onto the table again and I am now feverishly filling out every application in the pile. My pen runs out of ink and I throw it across the room, find another pen and keep going. By dawn, there's a pile of discarded envelopes at my feet and a stack of sealed applications ready to be mailed. I need those goddamn credit cards. One of these companies has got to be willing to let me dig deeper into my premature grave of debt.

As the Toomey incident drags along, the stress is beginning to take a major physical toll on me. I'm chronically exhausted, and I've developed a twitch in my left eye. Even Liz, who's generally irritated by my bouncy demeanor, finds the change in me disturbing. But the staggering mental effort required to not let this get to me, is what's getting to me.

Date: 11.13
Subject: SM court latest
Hi Steve,
Nothing but bad news on the case. I spoke with Noreen McDonough extensively this morning. The bottom line is that they will not drop any of the charges. I think it's time to circle the wagons.
Phil

Soon I'm in Phil's office, not letting on that I've reached the end of my credit and have no recourse to pay him for my trial. "Nothing but bad news on the case?" I laugh bitterly, "Big surprise there."

"Stop taking this personally," Phil tells me.

"Why shouldn't I take it personally?" I snap, "I don't see it happening to anybody else!"

Ignoring my foul temper, Phil flatly asks, "So, what are you going to do?" But I don't answer him. I'm starting to crack. The walls are closing in. Phil is talking about my upcoming trial date, but I'm not listening. There's an explosion building in my head, and here it comes. Now is when I start screaming.

I scream about these noxious fucking assholes who have nothing better to do with their lives than ruin me for no good reason. I scream that it's vicious and perverse, and that no lawyerly rationalizations can make it anything but wrong. I scream that I am taking it personally, "and no amount of smiling and nodding and making that patronizing fucking face at me is going to change that!"

Phil stops smiling, nodding and making the patronizing face. "I'll tell you this," he says, "There's no way I'm going to put you on the stand if you're going to act like this."

"Oh, fuck me! Why?! Because it turns out that there's a point where I actually get pissed off and start to yell?!"

"Don't do this," Phil warns me, "Because that's exactly how they'll win. If you start getting angry now, it will seem like they were right and you'll go down for this. You want them to win?"

"They've already won!" I yell, kicking his desk, "The very fact that this has happened at all, let alone gone this far, means I've already lost! Look what they've fucking put me through!" Shaking with rage and frustration, I jump to my feet and march for the door. With my hand on the knob, I hear Phil actually raise his voice, "Don't go! Please!"

I pause. Phil says, "Sit down."

"No," I growl.

"Okay, you're right!" he yells, "And I'm sorry. And there is a time for that kind of thing, it's just not now. So please, sit."

"Not until you tell me something," I say, standing my ground.

"What?" he asks.

"Drop the poker face and come down off your little game for one fucking second, and tell me what you actually think happened that day. Do you think I assaulted that woman? Is this some joke you play on everyone, pretending you believe them?"

148

Phil says, "I have very few innocent clients-"

"Ah!" I point at him, cutting him off, "That is <u>not</u> what I asked! I want you to tell me what you think happened that day."

"Fine," he sighs, "I genuinely believe...that you did not hit that woman. I also genuinely believe that somebody should hit her, because she's a dangerous, ignorant piece of shit who causes a lot of problems with her obnoxious behavior and her bizarre sense of entitlement. I know she's lying. I think everybody knows she's lying. And for some reason you just got fucked. So deal with it."

With the wind knocked out of my indignant sails, I think for a second, then say, "Okay...well, I guess I'll sit down, then."

As I return to my chair, Phil continues, "At least now I know that there's a limit to your affability. For your sake, that's a good thing. At the moment, it's a bad thing. You're a tough defendant, worse than most, because you're not used to having to defend yourself and it doesn't come easily to you. But you have a trial date now. So we need to talk about that."

I settle into the chair as Phil goes on, "I spoke with Noreen several times this morning. For some reason, she does have it in for you." I open my mouth to speak but Phil raises his hand and cuts me off, "And we're not going to get into the reasons for that now!"

I sigh, "Fine! Just tell me what she said."

Phil says, "We talked about the assault charges, and the entire incident. I reminded Noreen that Ms. Toomey sideswiped you with her car."

"And what did Noreen say?" I ask.

"She said 'So? He wasn't killed or anything.'"

"Isn't that what she said last time?" I ask.

"She doesn't remember the last time," Phil says, "I also pointed out that not only did you have the right of way as a pedestrian, but that Ms. Toomey, after hitting you with her car, flashed her middle finger at you and fled the scene."

"If Noreen didn't care that I got hit, I doubt she'd care much about that."

"Well, yes," Phil shrugs, "But since Ms. Toomey admitted giving you the finger in her statement to the police, she can't claim now that she didn't see you."

"But Noreen doesn't care about that either."

"No, which is weird, because it makes her case a lot harder for a jury to get behind."

"A jury?" That part hadn't dawned on me before. Phil nods, "I also pointed out to her that Ms. Toomey's complaint is full of obvious misstatements and what could easily be presented as deliberate lies."

"And what did Noreen do?" I ask, rather intrigued.

"She rolled her eyes, and announced that she was pursuing this to the fullest and there was nothing to talk about."

"And then?" I ask nervously.

"I brought up the notion of saving us all a lot of time by working out some type of plea bargain."

"And how did that go?"

"Noreen replied that the only arrangement she would entertain would be if you pled guilty to all of the charges."

I give a rancorous grunt, "What the hell kind of plea bargain is that? That's what I'd get if we went to trial and things went as badly as they could possibly go."

"Yes," Phil says.

"So, her only offer was for me to plead guilty to everything?" Phil nods. I let out an exasperated laugh and grumble, "Fine."

"What do you mean?" Phil exclaims, "There's no way I'm letting you give in to that."

"I think the old souse is being unreasonable. Is she always this inflexible?"

"Doesn't matter," Phil says.

"Was she hungover today?" I ask.

"Again, irrelevant. We're not getting into that. What did you mean by 'fine'?"

"I mean 'Fine! Fuck her!' This means war!"

"Good," Phil smiles.

"There's just one problem," I say.

"What's that?" Phil asks.

"I can't afford to go to trial," I tell him, "I don't have the money, and I can't get any more credit cards. I need a couple days to figure this out."

Back at the editing system, I can't get this nightmare out of my head. I fear my time with Phil is coming to an end. But public defenders simply perform triage because they're so overworked. If Noreen won't discuss a plea bargain, then there's little hope for me there. What kind of trial will I get with a public defender?

Option Two is pleading guilty like the drunken slag wants. I guess then I'd be handed my mandatory sentence, along with a lasting criminal record. I could always do like the real nuts do, and defend myself. I'm pretty sure I'd be screwed from the get-go there. The whole cracked system would band together to slam the insolent schmuck who thought he could speak for himself, and I see a noose in my future.

A dim lightbulb appears by my head and starts talking to me. "This desperate decision-making is aimed to find the quickest way to bring this nonsense to an end. And that's assuming a lot."

"What do you mean?" I ask the sinister lightbulb.

"Why would you even imagine it would end here? You have as little control in ending this as you had in starting it," the lightbulb sneers, "And after this part's done, there will be more charges for more make-believe crimes. And then that deranged shrew is going to sue you."

"Sue me for what?"

"Take your pick, she's nuts," the lightbulb replies.

Something in my gut tells me that the evil lightbulb is right. My initial hope to dismiss this notion as paranoid is immediately tossed out of my head since, throughout this debacle, my most paranoid fantasies have indeed turned out to be true. This could just be the beginning.

When Tam gets home, I tell her about my sordid revelation that these people are just getting warmed up and there's no telling where this will end. With a casual shrug, Tam agrees, "I've thought all along the dumb bitch is going to sue you."

"Yeah, if I'm convicted of the criminal charges, her lawsuit's a done deal. The only way to prevent that is to beat the criminal charges."

"You're right," Tam says.

"But I can't afford to fight the charges. And if I go with the public defender, my only options are possible acquittal, or two years in prison and then I get sued. This just gets worse and worse."

The local news is showing a massive sinkhole that opened up on a Woodland Hills street. Los Angeles is an area prone to sinkholes. The entire metropolis is built on unstable desert dirt, and under its sunny surface lies a vast network of leaky pipes, so it happens pretty frequently. An entire street will get sucked down into the darkness. Maybe someday God will send a sinkhole so big that it sucks this whole miserable city to the bowels of hell. Sinkholes are hungry beasts and, once they start, there's no stopping them. The problem is that you can never predict when they're going to occur, which is a shame. Because I wish the earth would swallow me right now. The phone rings and I absently answer it. It's my Mom.

I'm only half listening to Mom as I watch the sinkhole and wonder how to plead. She asks why I haven't called in so long, and I mumble that I've been busy. She asks when I'm coming home for Christmas, and I tell her I have no idea. She asks why, and I blurt out it's because I don't know when my trial will be over. And I stop dead.

My jaw drops open. The blood leaves my face. I cover the phone and yell "Fuck!" as loud as I can.

My parents are in their seventies. My Mom is a sweet, sheltered woman who went to a tiny convent school run by the nuns from The Sound of Music. The Von Trapp family even stayed there after they climbed that mountain and made it to America. My Mom possesses a deeply wonderful talent of finding the good in everything, no matter how hard she has to look. My Dad's a retired neurologist. He spent his entire adult life working fourteen hours a day, helping people with the most debilitating brain disorders. He also taught at one of the East Coast's best medical schools. Dad never really went for the flashy doctor lifestyle thing, and now he spends time with his grandchildren and consults for free for any acquaintance of anyone he knows, however intangibly, with a medical problem. He continues to help lots of people, for no reason other than the good of doing it.

These are the last people on earth who deserve to be confronted with the ongoing mess which stemmed from Lauren Toomey's uncontrollable road rage. But here it is. It slipped out and now I've got to tell them something. For a brief second, I consider concocting some stupid story to tell my folks. I immediately realize that I am way too exhausted to remember whatever I'll make up now on the spur of the moment. Aw, hell. Better just deal with it.

Mom's really upset. I am going to face it, but not this way. I tell her to put Dad on the phone. Dad gets on the phone, and I tell him the whole story. When I'm done my hideous tale, Dad's reaction surprises me. His immediate response is a very calm, "Mm-hmm, that happens a lot."

"What does?" I ask.

In his emotionless doctor-voice, Dad diagnoses, "This woman was returning from her medboard exams, and had clearly been on some type of amphetamine for the weeks prior."

"So you're saying it was because she was on drugs?"

"No, I'm saying it was because she went off the drugs," he says, "And subsequently reacted very badly. Was her behavior erratic?"

"To put it mildly. Yes."

"Was her skin blotchy?"

"Yes, terribly so," I tell him. To my unexpected relief, Dad is not overreacting. The medical school aspect of the story makes him react like an analytical professor giving an opinion. And I'm breathing much easier thanks to this small unforeseen miracle. Dad continues, "I've seen third-rate students do that countless times, abusing meds in hopes of improving their inferior performance. This woman has no business calling herself a doctor. So what are you going to do?"

I tell him I don't know, and promise to call him back. I can hear Mom worrying loudly in the background, and now this sucks that much more.

My eWin Cancer Horoscope for November 17th – Reality strikes like a slap across the face. It's in the universe's hands now, Crab. Financial matters seem extra daunting...

The twitch in my eye has grown stronger and more persistent. As I continue to avoid making the decision of how to plead, I find myself sinking into a strange surreal state of complete denial, like I'd been transformed into a giant bug but simply refuse to admit it. My brain is in overdrive twenty-four-seven trying to cloud the inescapable reality of the situation.

People are very fed up with me, and they snap at me constantly. Any compassion or empathy for my shitty situation is gone, and I find myself apologizing for everything. Apparently, right now I can offend someone simply by the look in my eye, which makes people imagine some insult I'm not even thinking. So now, I just automatically apologize for whatever it is they're pissed off about. But these apologies never appease the offended party. Then I find myself apologizing for the apologies, which were either unconvincing, or were actually apologizing for the wrong thing, as I'm taken to task for things both imagined and subtle to the point of absurdity. However, people feel no need to hold back their contempt for me, or edit anything they say, while I'm held accountable for "the look in my eye" and all the things it might possibly mean. I am a giant bug.

I've never been big on regret, but right now I regret everything I've ever done. Maybe that's the point of law enforcement in Santa Monica, to further the cause of regret in our lives. I regret everything from crossing the street, to ever moving out to this damn place, mostly because I have absolutely no idea what I'm supposed to do next. I don't really have any options, so running through the list is just a fanciful exercise in masturbation. The endgame is always the same, if I don't come up with a shitload of money, really fast, the City of Santa Monica is going to slam my ass into prison.

Tamara yells at me that I need to go talk to Phil again. I tell her I agree, and that I'm going to Phil's. Tam then yells, louder than before, that I need to go talk to Phil, as if I hadn't just agreed with her.

Once at Phil's, I notice that he's oozing scorn like everyone else. I'm tired of this, "Okay, in an effort to get you to stop looking at me like that, may I point out that you don't really know me, and you are seeing me at my absolute worst. I've never been this stressed out in my life."

"Alright," Phil says blankly.

"Well, that didn't work. You did say that you think I'm innocent, correct?"

"Yes," he replies.

"Then why do I have to keep apologizing to you, and to everyone?"

"It's just one of those things," Phil says, "People dump on you when you're down."

"Yeah. Ain't it swell?"

"Have you decided what you're going to do?" Phil asks.

"Not really," I tell him, "I don't have the money. I really can't continue to pursue this," I say.

Phil nods, "Well, if that's the case..."

"What happens if I get a public defender?" I ask.

"You think people are dumping on you now, wait til you have a public defender."

"Yeah, I figured as much," I sigh, "What happens if I'm found guilty?"

"Noreen says she wants to put you away."

"Super. Okay, what happens if I please 'no contest'?" I ask.

"Hard to say. Maybe jail time, definitely a hefty fine, extensive violence counseling, and I'll bet significant hours of community service as well."

"How badly can this hurt me in the future?" I ask.

"How should I know? Are you planning to run for elected office?"

"Thanks, you're tons of help."

"Well, what's your issue?" Phil asks.

"To be honest, it's just that...what's the big deal? If all this expense and effort is just to clear my name, I don't care that much. They can call me whatever they want to, a street felon, a wife-beater. That doesn't make it true. They can call me a fucking giraffe if they want to, it doesn't make me a giraffe."

"Yeah, so?" Phil replies.

"So I don't really care what they say about me, as long as it doesn't screw me up in the future."

"I think you need to fight it. I think this is eating you up a lot more than you're letting yourself admit."

"Oh gee, you think?" I say, "I just can't afford this."

"Listen, you need to figure out what is right for you. Nobody can decide this for you. But you need to decide fast. Your trial date is December 4th, and we need to be prepared so we can counter what they've got."

"What do you mean?" I ask.

"Their evidence," he replies, "Whatever it is they've trumped up to make them so cocksure about a conviction in this damn thing. I've been trying not to bring this up because you've aged about ten years since I met you. But think about it. There must be something."

"Shit..." I sigh. Phil is right. That would explain a lot. I promise him that I'll decide soon, and I go home. That night, I try discussing it with Tamara but this is wearing her down, and she keeps snapping at me. She now blames me for the whole ordeal, so I start apologizing again and Tam goes to bed, pissed-off.

At dawn I'm walking by the ocean. It's time to finally decide. I have to move forward. But who am I kidding? This sad delusion that I have any options is no longer sustainable. Financially, I can't swing the trial. There's just no way. I convince myself that if all this money is simply going to clear my name, then my name isn't worth it. Big deal. So they all get away with it. I'm going to cut my losses and move on. I have no choice. I'm pleading no contest.

That's it. I'm done. "No contest" it is. I'm going to cut this nightmare short, do whatever punishment these bastards think up, and be done with the whole thing. When Tam gets up, I tell her. She says maybe it's for the best, but she honestly doesn't know what to think anymore. Tam doesn't want to believe that I have no alternatives because it's too much of a drag, but she agrees that prolonging this any longer, just to prove the point that I'm innocent, only makes the whole thing more catastrophic for both of us.

As people check in, I tell them that I'm going to plead no contest. Liz thinks it's probably for the best, and that a criminal record is the coolest thing a dork like me could hope for. Blodg hits the roof. He tells me I'm a pussy for backing down, and he's probably right. But his reaction is nothing next to Stu F- and Ken S-, who have put up the money to get me this far. Stu is downright furious, yelling that I will regret this for the rest of my life. When Ken calls, I almost don't have the heart to tell him. But I do tell him, and he essentially has a stroke. I feel terrible for ever having allowed anyone to find out about this, because it's eating away at everyone who knows.

At the end of the day, I finally knuckle down and call Phil to tell him of my decision. He's extremely disappointed. I tell Phil that I can't spend my whole life trying to denounce one set of malicious lies. Phil asks if I'm absolutely positive that this is what I want to do. I tell him yes.

That night, I can't sleep. It's worse than ever, which puzzles me. I thought forcing the book shut on this ordeal would end it, and allow me to move on to more important things. I leave the bedroom and give myself a good talking to, sternly lecturing myself to get over it and move on. But the limitations of mere words are a two-way street. Just as them calling me a dangerous felon doesn't make me one, me telling myself that it's over doesn't mean that it's really over. But I stick to my guns because I just can't stand it anymore. This pointless bullshit has completely devoured my life.

The next morning I realize that, in all the diseased melodrama, I'd forgotten to call my parents back. I'm amazed that my Mom hadn't pestered my Dad into calling me. This demonstrates unusual and admirable restraint for those guys. So I call Dad.

I tell Dad that enough is enough. I've decided to cut my losses and plead no contest. He very calmly replies, "You can't do that."

I say, "Dad, I don't care about clearing my name anymore. It's a dubious victory, at best. I'm just going to do whatever they tell me to do and get it over with. It's not worth any more time, aggravation, and another seventy-five-hundred bucks that I don't have."

Dad quietly states, "That's understandable, but you can't plead no contest."

"Dad, I no longer care about having a criminal record. I'm fine with this decision."

"That's not why you can't plead no contest," he says.

"Then why?" I irritably ask.

"Because if you plead no contest, then this woman's going to do this same thing to somebody else."

Fuck! My whole brain jumps. I immediately know, deep down, that he's right. And damn him for knowing the one thing that would throw this whole nightmare back in my face. He's appealing to my innate sense of responsibility, which I always wish I didn't have. It takes a few seconds for me to respond.

Finally, I feel ready to counter. I say, "Yeah, so what?"

Dad replies, "Next time, she might do it to someone without the resolve to fight it off. Who knows, next time she might even kill somebody with her car. And if you don't do everything in your power to fight her attitude and behavior, then part of what happens will be on your head." Great, so now I'm Batman and Toomey's the Joker. Well, she's got the hair for it anyway. I'm stumped, because I know he's right. I sigh again, "So, I guess I'm not pleading no contest."

"You have to fight this, because not fighting it is wrong."

I sit down, trying to avoid it. I sigh, "Yeah, okay."

"Good. Keep me posted on how it goes," he says.

For the next two hours, I just sit in various parts of the apartment, trying not to face the inevitable. There's no use trying to get this genie back in the bottle, thanks to Dad. To procrastinate further, I go to check the mail, where I'm surprised to find two new credit cards! I guess that last batch of 16 applications did the trick. I knew there had to be some wicked financiers happy to hand me more rope to hang myself. The two credits cards that arrived are the extra sleazy kind with brutal terms, but still I take these cards as a sign from God that Dad is right. Okay, screw it. Let's go!

Dad calls back and offers to kick in some money. I call Stu F- and he kicks in some more. That, with my new lowlife credit cards, and I've pieced together Phil's fee. So I'll take on the extra debt, so be it! I feel inspired. I start to hear marching bands in my head. We're going to fight this, for all that is good about America. We're not going to let some twisted eye doctor and a nasty drunken civil servant abuse the system that I believe in! Because I'm going to fight it! In the name of all the insolvent underdogs and vulnerable pedestrians who are abused every day by people like Lauren Toomey, Noreen McDonough, the Los Angeles Police Department and the City Attorneys of Santa Monica, I'm going to fight this! They picked the wrong guy this time, and it's time they learned that.

Full of thunder, I call Tam. She reacts enthusiastically, and almost yells in triumph. Then she stops and asks, "Are you sure you want to put yourself through this?"

"Absolutely! Because it's the right fucking thing to do! My Dad is right. If she gets away with it this time, she'll just do it again to somebody else. I am her foe! And maybe there's a reason for all of this after all."

"Well, don't get too nuts about it," Tam tells me, "It's going to be a major pain in the ass."

"I have to do it," I say.

"Okay then, I'm with you," Tam replies.

Now I need to tell Phil. After my rock-solid pronouncement of the previous day, I feel like a fool, but soon I'm in his office again. Phil notices the change immediately. I tell him about the conversation with my Dad and announce that I want to fight it, because I'm obligated to. I blow out my inspiring hot-air some more, then add, "Oh, by the way, I've figured out the money, so we're cool there."

"Good. We have a lot to do."

"Now listen, I promise that I won't be the foulmouthed ranting Steve anymore."

"Good," Phil nods.

"You realize that's probably not true. I'm going to be totally stressed, but at least now it's with a purpose."

"Fair enough," Phil says.

"You have to remember that I've never done this before. I've never been accused of anything, and these people are ruthless lying assholes. So bear with me," I tell him.

"All the way, buddy."

It turns out that Phil is busy with another trial this week. However, his other client wasn't falsely accused, he actually killed someone. Phil's just trying to keep the guy off death row. We're also coming up on Thanksgiving so Phil and I make a plan to meet on Monday after the holiday. By the time I leave, Phil is beaming. This odd little case has been gnawing at him more than he'd like to admit and he's pretty fired up, in his reserved way.

I walk to the elevator, feeling better than I've felt in months. My bouncy step is back and WE'RE GOING TO TRIAL!!!

While I expected this elation to be temporary, I thought it would at least last until I got to my car. As I unlock the car door, it hits me, "What the fuck?! I can't believe I'm going on trial! This is going to suck huge. But shit, what choice do I have?"

Aw fuck it, we're going to trial...

christmas in prison...

My eWin Cancer Horoscope for November 22nd - You are the centerpiece of your community, a source of pride and admiration. Open your doors and let them all in...

For weeks now, the gruesome specter of spending Christmas behind bars has been tunneling through my subconscious like an army of Marabunta ants. As the various possible outcomes for my case develop, I keep a running tally of the odds that I'll be waking up Christmas morning surrounded by several hundred of my closest inmate pals. This municipal deathmarch began in May, my first trial date was in August, it's now Thanksgiving and there's no set timeframe for my trial, resolution or sentencing.

I'm guessing that no matter how this winds up, whether I'm incarcerated for the two years that La McDonough dreams about, or if Phil can contain the damage to ninety days or so, the goons of Santa Monica will try to arrange it so I'm in the pen for Christmas. In fact, it almost seems like they're stalling for this exact reason.

But now it's Thanksgiving, which in Venice usually goes like this...Tamara and I realize that nobody we know has anywhere to go for Thanksgiving, so we announce that we're going to have a small get-together. Then Liz, Allie, and everyone we invite inform us that they can't make it. This is because they're too cool to say they're coming, or because they're holding out for a better offer, which they never receive because, come Thanksgiving, although only about three people have said yes, half of Venice shows up at our door. Thanksgiving is traditionally our wildest bash of the year, an enormous spectacle of drunken misfits that spills into the street and goes all night.

Every Thanksgiving afternoon, to take a break from cooking and football, I go for a walk and invite everyone in our neighborhood who might not have a place to go, because everybody should have somewhere to go on Thanksgiving. I know from experience that even the scariest crack addicts will be on their best behavior if they're invited somewhere on Thanksgiving. Last year, we had an interesting bunch. It was our regular gang, along with every weirdo they could find, as well as the Persian opium addict from downstairs with his six "cousins", the two psycho Section 8 ex-Navy Seals who live in the alley, and Stefan the gargantuan bodybuilder from Germany who had just moved in. It was a good year.

But none of that feel-good shit is happening this Thanksgiving. We're invited to Tam's boss's house, which is terrific because I don't feel like cooking. I also don't want a mob of drunken dipshits around the sprawling editing system in the living room. In the days leading up to Thanksgiving, all the Venice hipsters and freaks who are normally too cool to admit that they're coming, start calling us to whine that they have nowhere to go.

167

Tan thinks they're all going to show up anyway. I say screw 'em, who cares, we won't be here. Tam is shocked by my response. I am usually the Spirit of Thanksgiving incarnate, but thanks to the City of Santa Monica, I need a year off.

On Thanksgiving afternoon, I go for a walk. Unlike my traditional Thanksgiving walks to make sure nobody slips through the cracks, this year I'm just walking. Without meaning to, I find myself walking up 3rd Street and retracing my horrible trek from that Sunday in May. Once on the path, I can't stop. This is where Lauren Toomey was pulling my shirt and yelling obscenities. A chill runs through me, as that grisly morning washes over me with renewed clarity.

This is the spot, far from the scene of the accident, where Toomey first got the idea to lie to the police. Her shrill voice rings through my ears, *"Oh yeah? Then I'm gonna tell the police you assaulted me and they'll make you fucking pay!"* So much has happened since then - the guns, the bullying, the lies and the threats - that it's fogged the original experience in my mind. But now it's back. I remember it all. I was walking down the street, minding my own business, when some insane medical student ran me down and decided to ruin my life. Now it's time to fight back.

I look in the mirror as we get ready to leave. My skin is green and my left eye still twitches. I seem to have lost weight, and not in a good way. We have dinner at Tam's boss's house, where Thanksgiving is much more traditional. They have a centerpiece on the table. We've never done that.

*The Layman's Handbook for Those Falsely Accused of Felonies, page 72...Comprehensive preparation for your impending **trial** is highly recommended, although this is an arduous and often tedious process...*

"How does this work?" I ask Phil, "Start from the beginning."

"Well, now that we're going to trial, I'm requesting discovery on Toomey. Her background, criminal records and so forth."

"I wonder if she's got any drug convictions. She was wacked out of her head that day. Does this discovery include her driving record?"

"Only if it led to a crime," Phil tells me.

"How long are we looking at, trial-wise?" I ask.

"I am anticipating that your trial will take a week," Phil says, "I'm shooting for a week and a half, but I think I can guarantee you at least four days. If they're really serious about this, like they claim, then I'm going to hold them to that. I know these people. They're going to insist it's of grave importance, but only to the degree that it suits them. Then they'll argue that it's no big deal and wrong to waste their time with it. You should simply be punished so that they can move on. This has been very easy for them so far. Now they're going to have to work for it."

"They won't like that, will they?"

"Nope," he says.

"So what's our big opening number?" I ask.

"First comes jury selection," Phil tells me.

"Right, I get a jury. Cool."

"They're going to fight us on that, and everything else, so be ready."

"Oh, I'm ready," I tell him, "What happens after we have our jury?"

"The prosecution makes their opening statement, which is followed by our opening statement. Then the prosecution presents their case. They bring in their witnesses, their evidence..."

"You know, in baseball, we'd bat first," I point out, "It's their field."

"Exactly," Phil replies, "It's their field, and they make the rules. Besides, how can you defend yourself if they haven't accused you yet?"

"Good point."

"After we present our defense, then come closing arguments. The prosecution presents their summation and then we present ours. Then the prosecution can speak again."

"So they get the last word?"

"Not necessarily. We can speak again if we want to," Phil assures me.

"And then what?"

"We wait for the verdict," Phil says.

I'm squirming a little, "What do you think the outcome of this trial will be?"

"With this case, I have absolutely no idea," Phil admits, "The most important thing here is that you be yourself. They've never seen you, and I guarantee that they're not expecting you."

"Why's that?" I ask. Phil shrugs vaguely, so I move forward, "What about those cops?"

"They'll be called as witnesses," he says.

"But they didn't witness anything," I point out.

"The cops will simply repeat what's in their report and say it's all true," Phil tells me.

"But their report is full of lies, and statements attributed to me that I never said," I say anxiously.

"Yes, which is a huge problem," Phil says somberly.

"Shouldn't there be some kind of record of statements I allegedly made to the police?"

"What matters more is what they say in front of the jury."

"So we're just going to let them announce that I confessed to crimes that never happened? Wouldn't we want to disagree with that a little?"

Phil gives me another vague shrug, "I've found it's best with a jury not to argue with the cops too much. Calling their credibility into question usually backfires. We'll present our case, and hope for the best."

I'm getting uncomfortable, "They can't just tell this fairy tale of my many felonies without mentioning the things that Toomey did, most of which are worse than anything I'm accused of. They'll have to reveal her hitting me with her car and then stalking me."

"I doubt they intend to do that," Phil replies.

"But their story will have too many gaps. What are they going to say, that I appeared out of the blue, attacked her, then was magically transported to a mini-market a quarter mile away and attacked her again?"

"I think they're hoping the jury won't wonder too much beyond what they tell them."

"But that's nuts! If they leave out all the aggression of Lauren Toomey, the story will be impossible to follow."

"You should expect them to manipulate this story to justify sending you to prison," Phil says, "They will leave out all the parts where Toomey did anything illegal. It's up to us to introduce all of that. And trust me, they'll try to prevent us from doing so. You just need to stay calm."

Phil begins to instruct me on how to testify. He tells me to never be evasive, which I rarely am, so that's easy. But harder for me, according to Phil, is the far more important directive to keep my big mouth shut and answer only the most specific interpretation of the question. "Here's a good example," he says, "When a lawyer asks a defendant if he or she knows what time it is-"

"I know!" I excitedly say, "You're supposed to say 'yes' and not tell him the actual time."

"Yes, that's correct," Phil says.

"Dude, that's old. Even I know that one."

"Yes. However, you're also not supposed to interrupt your attorney while he's speaking. And you're never to call him 'dude'."

"Right, sorry. I should probably just let you direct this thing, right?"

"That would be preferable," Phil smiles.

"It's your show, bud. Do you think we'll run into any problems with my side of the story?"

"You're story is solid. It's Toomey's version that has problems, with her so afraid that she follows you, and other illogical claims, including what was stolen that would constitute the robbery."

"That's what I've been saying for months," I remind him.

"That's right. Now you need to let me say it, because the jury doesn't want to hear it from you. Juries don't like defendants who don't need their help."

"Got it."

Phil tells me that it helps to impress a jury if we look like we're taking this as seriously as possible, and he asks me if I'd be willing to make some audio-visual aids.

"Like at the science fair?" I eagerly ask.

"Exactly," Phil says.

"Hell, yeah. Consider it done." I ask what Phil would like, display-wise. He tells me that enlarged photographs of all the locations involved would help, adding, "Be sure and get photos of the 25 mile-per-hour speed limit signs on the street." Phil says that he'd love some big maps and diagrams for reference.

Back at home, I call Tam to see if she can get the Art Department at her company to help make our big science fair project. She calls back a minute later and says that they're thrilled to help.

Trial fever sweeps through the neighborhood. Liz calls to tell me that she's organizing a protest for the courthouse steps during my trial. I'm pretty certain Phil will have big problems with this plan, but I don't squash it yet.

I'm too fired up about my trial to concentrate on editing, so I bail on that for the rest of the day. I find myself wondering about our mad eye doctor, beyond our cherished relationship. What has she been up to since maliciously invading my life? I think it's time to investigate this loathsome monster a bit further. Let's see what mutant creatures inhabit Planet Toomey. Set phasers on 'cringe'.

I'm only at it for a couple minutes and WOW! I hit a friggin' goldmine of Toomey info. It appears that Toomey actually passed her medboard exams and is now a certified ophthalmologist. In fact, she's joined the clinic of a French-Canadian eye doctor pal in the suburb of Hacienda Heights.

Toomey and her new Canadian colleague have even put up a darling website for their practice...

wall-eye...

Nothing can quite prepare one for the stomach-churning spectacle known as Lauren Toomey's website. According to this site, our treacherous ophthalmologist claims to be a world-renowned expert in treating the conditions of strabismus and amblyopia, better known by their street-slang handle of "lazy eye."

When you click onto the site, you are instantly treated to sad, crossed-eyed babies helplessly floating over the screen. Wall-eyed senior citizens drift past, and then confused-looking soccer moms with massively misaligned eyes. The swirling images show lazy-eyed people from all walks of life, a veritable wall-eyed global village. You watch the disturbing armada of visual clichés, waiting for the cross-eyed nun, Italian gondolier and Masai warrior holding a spear to swing by.

Next comes a repellent collage of "before-and-after" photos that shows miserable lazy-eye sufferers transformed into theoretically happier straight-eyed people, except that these "after" photos were taken way too soon after whatever radically invasive surgery these poor people have just undergone. They're attempting to smile, despite their painfully bruised faces and swollen-shut eyes.

I'm not saying their wondrous procedures don't work, but in terms of promoting this surgery, this website is the marketing equivalent of the bombing of Hiroshima. The text doesn't help, either. Deciphering its obliquely coiled prose, you discover that Lauren Toomey and her French Canadian friend Odette are the self-proclaimed Masters of the Lazy-Eye Universe. They seem in awe of themselves and their infinitely valuable contributions to the world of medicine. The "Patient Testimonials" page is full of uplifting moments from formerly tragic cross-eyed lives:

"When I talked to people, they kept turning their heads to see if I was talking to someone behind them..."

"I was at the end of my rope...My lazy eye was getting LAZIER!"

The most jaw-dropping section of this digital delight is the "Doctor Profiles." Toomey's profile is ripe with grammar and punctuation errors, but nobody ever said she was a doctor of punctuation. Maybe Toomey doesn't know the difference between "you're" and "your", but this pales in the face of her momentous accomplishments. "Through her education and spanning into her career, Dr. Toomey has received very much recognition and won several awards for her endeavors into the field of medicine." The profile fails to mention which specific "awards" or what type of "recognition" she's received. I guess we're meant to take it on faith, like the fact that she has a valid driver's license. It also turns out that the mysteriously acclaimed Dr. Toomey actually attended some dubiously accredited medical school in the West Indies.

The biography of Lauren Toomey ends on a particularly sickening note. "In addition to her demanding medical career, Dr. Toomey enjoys performing in light opera productions of Gilbert and Sullivan." Great, just what the cross-eyed masses need, Toomey flitting around as Yum-Yum in The Mikado. There's a photo of Toomey next to her bio. She leans against a tree, wearing a kittenish smile, as if daydreaming about her next light opera role.

I sit there, dumbfounded, staring at the monitor. The repugnant enigma that is Lauren Toomey just gets stranger and stranger. So after running me down, lying to the police and setting in motion the malevolent gears that tyrannize my life, Toomey has become the Queen of Lazy-Eye in some Hacienda Heights strip mall.

*The Layman's Handbook for Those Falsely Accused of Felonies, page 54...Your **"zero-to-ten" day** is intended to prevent your court proceedings from becoming unfairly prolonged. However, it does not always have the desired effect...*

My new court date is tomorrow, and as always, I'm sitting in Phil's office. Phil's feeling confident but I'm tense as hell, expecting some new cheap trick to Shanghai my ass to the graybar hotel. "Why's that?" Phil asks.

"Because of all the lies and manipulation that brought us here in the first place. It still seems like there's some sinister plot at work. Things like this don't just happen by accident."

"Well, not usually," Phil says, "On the other hand, this entire process has been as anomalous as can be. You shouldn't worry too much." The look on my face points out the contradiction in what he just said, but he continues, "Seriously, I think we have them in checkmate. Toomey's lying, and she's crazy. Once I get her on the stand, she's going to blow it."

"How do you figure that?" I ask.

"Toomey's the kind of doctor juries usually hate. This isn't a doctor who's helping the sick. This is a doctor who's done some very shifty things, yet is insisting that you be sent to prison. They won't like that. I'll make sure of it. How are all the photos and trial-aids coming?" Phil asks.

"I took the pictures, now the graphic artists at Tam's office are working on everything."

"Good," Phil nods.

"So what time tomorrow?"

"Tomorrow's just the zero-to-ten day," Phil says, "You don't have to be there."

"What's that again?" I ask.

"There comes a time in every case when the City Attorneys must set a date to commence their prosecution, after which they have ten days to start the trial."

"What does that mean in the language of us vulgar civilians?"

"Your trial will begin seven-to-ten days from tomorrow."

"What happens if it doesn't start within the ten day limit?"

"The charges are dismissed," Phil says, "But that's never happened, at least in my experience. They'll squeeze you in somewhere."

"So I don't need to be there tomorrow?" I ask, confused.

"No, I think it will be quicker if you're not," Phil tells me, "Nothing much is going to happen. They'll call the case, we'll get our requested discovery, and then they'll put it on the calendar."

"Ah, the discovery. What's up with that?" I ask.

"Nothing yet," he says, "We requested it in November, but Noreen argued that she couldn't possibly have it ready for us until tomorrow."

"And we'll find out if Toomey has a record?"

"Yep."

"Is that for Santa Monica, or for every place she's ever lived?"

Phil says, "It should be her entire record, but..."

"Right," I grumble, "That will depend on how Happy Hour went for Noreen."

"I didn't say that," Phil chuckles.

"Okay. Well, good luck, soldier," I say, "I'll be waiting to hear from you."

Lauren Toomey's eWin Sagittarius Horoscope for December 4ᵗʰ –
As the Moon visits Pisces, people are more likely to be your friends
when they're out of uniform...

Phil's at the courthouse and I'm clicking away at the prize
website, scooping up more chances for my million bucks.
Yet Toomey's horoscope for today only adds to my paranoid
suspicions. I can't shake the feeling that there's some unholy
link between Toomey and those cops. *"Out of uniform?"*
Now I'm imagining Lauren Toomey behind the construction
trailers by the Santa Monica Police Station, performing
unspeakable sexual acts upon the entire force to further her
vindictive games.

My horoscope for today's court date is almost as disturbing:

My eWin Cancer Horoscope for December 4ᵗʰ – See people as their
animal counterparts, and treat them with all the respect they
deserve...

Hmm, maybe the *"treating them with respect"* part could start
by not seeing them as animals. Oh well, five more chances
for the big piles of cash that I fully expect to win any day
now.

One thing my horoscope failed to mention is the joyous
event that occurred last night. While gobbling pizza and
stressing out about this morning's playdate with Justice, a
filling in my tooth cracked and fell out, creating a throbbing
flashpoint of unbearable pain. I just can't get a fucking break
these days. So while waiting for Phil to report from court,
I'm scrambling to find a new dentist. Of course, I have no
money to pay this dentist, but he or she doesn't know that
yet.

Tam and I have been meaning to find a new dentist for some time, as our last one proved unworkable. He was a drill-happy son of a bitch, and his bills were staggeringly exorbitant, which he justified by self-righteously proclaiming that he spent two days a month working on the teeth of homeless people for free. This bombastic dickhead's office was in Santa Monica, so I guess I should have known. I'm writhing from the jackhammering torture when Phil calls. "You better get in here. I need to talk to you," he says.

I hang up the phone, yell "Shit!" to no one in particular, and head for the car, dreading the next twist in this hideous tale. Driving to Phil's office, I notice the first of this year's crop of L.A.'s sad Christmas decorations. They say more people commit suicide around Christmas than at any other time of the year. I wonder how many of them know Noreen McDonough.

Phil looks quietly upset. I was expecting no less than the worst, so I'm not remotely surprised. "Are you okay?" Phil asks, noticing my watering eyes.

"I'm fine," I say, "What happened?"

"It didn't go as I'd hoped. What's wrong with your mouth?" Phil asks, so I tell him about the cracked filling and my search for a new dentist. "That looks very painful," he says.

"Yes, but I'm refusing to acknowledge it. Like everything else in my life right now, I'm keeping it at bay by the sheer force of my will. By the time this is all over, I fully expect to be able to move objects with my mind."

Phil swings his briefcase onto the desk and opens it, "I have some Excedrin..."

"I've got half a Rite Aid down there," I tell him, "Oh what the hell, a couple more couldn't hurt." Phil gives me a few over-the-counter pills, and I slug them down. "So what's the damage?"

"Things in court today were especially bad," Phil informs me, "For starters, Noreen did not have our requested discovery on Lauren Toomey."

"Why not?" I ask, growing anxious.

"It was embarrassing," Phil says, "When I inquired about our discovery, Noreen sniped at me that of course she didn't have it because we'd never requested it. The judge told me that I must be mistaken, but then the judge reviewed our case, and he pointed out that it was Noreen herself who had set this date for our discovery back in November."

"Jesus, what's her deal?" And then, it dawns on me. I never do get used to the idea. "Oh, right...was she drunk?"

Phil takes a breath, "It was extremely awkward to be there with Noreen in this condition. She was wobbling on her feet and slurring her words. By the end, it was downright sad."

"Oh yeah, I forgot, poor Noreen," I grumble angrily.

"I'm as disgusted by this as you are," Phil tells me.

"Right, you just do it...in your way," I snipe, "What does this mean for me?"

Ignoring my irascible tone, Phil continues, "The judge asked whether we wanted to proceed without our requested discovery. As this regards Toomey's background, I felt it would be wise to wait until we can obtain it. Bottom line, your case is continued again, and your new zero-to-ten day is December 19th. This means your trial will start between the 26th and the 29th."

It takes a second to sink in. "Wait. So what you're telling me is that this thing has dragged on for months because of this pickled witch, which is fine, I don't want to be thought of as less than compassionate.   But now, Noreen McDonough wants to take my trial, which should have started in August, and actually begin...on the day after Christmas?"

"Yes," Phil says.

I yell, "Are you out of your fucking mind?!"

Phil remains calm, "I don't believe so."

"Did you agree to this?! Of all of these delays, how many have been caused by us? None! Which means that all five months worth of them have been because of Noreen. If I have to stick around here through Christmas when I haven't seen my family in a year, just because Noreen couldn't lay off the hooch this morning, that's it! I'm warning you now. Remember when I threatened to scream about this to the local media?"

"You weren't serious about that, were you?" Phil asks with an uneasy grin.

"I'll bet there's at least one hungry bloodsucking journalist out there who'd be very intrigued by the notion that the caseload in the Santa Monica Courthouse is being managed by a whiskey-swilling soaker while the rest of you guys look the other way and feel bad."

Disgruntled, Phil tells me, "There's no need for that."

"Don't underestimate the influence of an extremely agonizing hole in my mouth," I snarl at him.

Phil sighs and nods, "I'll get an extension until after the holidays."

"How hard will that be?" I ask.

"In light of your reaction to this, just assume it's a done deal," Phil says.

"I've heard that before. I'm not buying a plane ticket until I know that I'm free to go."

"Get your plane ticket," Phil says, "I'll take care of this. I promise."

lazy racist drunk...

The Layman's Handbook for Those Falsely Accused of Felonies,
page 43...There are some who believe that a **secret network** *exists*
among those who are falsely accused, but this has never been
proven...

Through a complex series of recommendations, Tamara
manages to find a dentist to fix my tooth, Dr. Casey S-. He's
in Brentwood and it's rumored that he once worked on
Elizabeth Taylor's teeth. I stumble into the dental office,
clutching my jaw in agony, and I'm whisked to a small
examination room, where a technician takes some X-rays.
Soon, a gray-haired man with the jazzy-Caucasian body
language of Bing Crosby walks in and introduces himself as
Dr. Casey. He glances at my X-rays and comments that my
tooth isn't so bad. I don't know what to make of this
because I'm used to my previous dentist who'd look into my
mouth and run screaming from the room.

"We won't even have to do much drilling," Dr. Casey says,
"It's a total fluke it hurts so much. Just one of those things, I

guess." Dr. Casey asks me about myself as he pulls out the Novocaine. I tell him about my half-finished movie, and how it's left me incredibly broke. Even though he's jabbing a needle into my gum, Dr. Casey's mellow vibe is making me comfortable, so I tell him that the other reason I'm strapped for cash right now is because of the false accusations of the maniac driver and the alcoholic City Attorney. Dr. Casey suddenly stops. His blinding smile dims and he looks down at me.

"Santa Monica?" he asks.

"Yeah," I reply with the tone of a question.

"Is there a woman named Noreen?"

"Yes. Why?"

Dr. Casey gets up from his seat. Glancing into the hall, he shuts the door, and I'm getting nervous. Dr. Casey asks me to tell him everything, so I do, although my tale gets a bit muffled as the Novocaine kicks in. Dr. Casey picks up the drill and moves into my mouth.

As he drills my tooth, Dr. Casey describes what happened to him at the hands of the Santa Monica City Attorney's Office. A few years ago, Dr. Casey took his family to the Santa Monica Mall where a man tried to abduct his five-year-old daughter. The little girl had wandered off, and the man was carrying her away when she started screaming. When Dr. Casey saw what was happening, he dashed through the food court to rescue his daughter from this creep. Dr. Casey got his daughter back and the police apprehended the would-be kidnapper.

However, once this incident was processed by the keen legal minds of the Santa Monica City Attorney's Office, the attempted kidnapper was charged with nothing. Dr. Casey, however, was charged with lots of things, including assault which, according to Noreen, occurred when Dr. Casey pulled his young daughter from the arms of the man who was trying to abduct her. Dr. Casey endured a long, expensive trial as the City of Santa Monica tried to prove that this jazzy dentist was a hardened felon.

Dr. Casey's bitter grudge against Noreen continues to this day, so he informs me that he's fixing my tooth for free. As he leaves, he pats me on the back and says, "Good luck, fella. You're gonna need it."

With the raw agony in my mouth quelled, I prepare to flee the state. Christmas in Philadelphia with my enormous family and hordes of friends, is rather overwhelming for Tam. Because of this, she only makes the trip with me every other year. This is her year to come, but it's been an extremely draining autumn for all of us, so Tam decides to stay in Venice Beach this year, which sucks.

My next court date is on December 19th, when I'll be on a plane. Phil wanted to meet one more time before I left, but he's held up in court and I'm running around like a holiday maniac, so it doesn't happen.

I arrive in Philadelphia for Christmas, where everybody tells me that I look tired. I decide to not tell anyone about my impending trial, because I don't want to spend the entire trip telling this damn story over and over. Instead, I opt for unilateral omission and watch Flyers games in bars with old buddies, which I always love. L.A. isn't much of a hockey town.

As my return to California approaches, I'm feeling rested and eager to take on Noreen, Toomey, and anybody else the City of Santa Monica wants to throw my way. I'm looking out the window at the trees in my parents' yard, as some delicate snowflakes start to flutter down from the heavens. "How lovely," I think. Then I remember that I'm in Philadelphia and big clanging bells go off in my head.

Philadelphia is not a place that handles snow well. An eighth of an inch and the whole city cracks. I turn on the TV and hear a newsman say, "Not since the big one of '54!" while the footage shows panicked runs on the supermarkets. "Shit!" I yell, lunging for the phone to try to get on the next flight out of the city. The first airline operator says that there's nothing she can do. I thank her, hang up, and repeatedly call back, working my way through their entire bank of employees until I reach someone who succeeds in squeezing me onto another flight. As I frantically pack, my Dad offers to take me to the airport. I say fine as long as he drives fast.

We're in the car, but Dad isn't driving very fast. The snow is coming down hard, and I know that if I don't get out of this city in the next couple hours, I'm going to be there for four or five more days while those bumbling stooges try to remember where they parked the snow plows last spring. "Uh, Dad, I know it's coming down pretty hard, but could you just floor it and put it in God's hands?" I ask.

"No!" he yells.

It seems to be business as usual at the Philadelphia Airport, which means that there are infinite lines of shellshocked people who've been waiting so long, they seem to be wearing clothes from a past era. Astoundingly enough, all goes well and three hours later, I'm sitting in a window seat on a plane. It looks like there's about six inches of snow on the tarmac. I'm foolishly thinking how well that went when the pilot makes an announcement that our flight has been delayed for twenty minutes. An air of anxiety thicker than the falling snow begins to spread through the fuselage. A half-hour later, the pilot announces that we'll be delayed another twenty-minutes. I start to feel trapped, but that's not unusual. To be in, or near, any part of the Philadelphia Airport is to feel trapped, so over the years I've grown used to it.

I stare out the window, watching the dancing snowflakes create a deep shroud on the runway as a garbled version of Tchaikovsky's Nutcracker sputters through the airplane's speakers. I see the ground crew trying to operate the snow plows. A baggage tram jackknifes wickedly, spilling all the luggage into the snow. I gaze with fascination at one dope who can't get his snowplow to drive in a straight line. He's circling wildly, over and over. My eyes grow wide with horror as I watch two snowplows crash into each other and the pilot interrupts the Nutcracker to tell us that our flight has just been cancelled.

Panic crashes through the aisle. People fight for their carry-on bags and shove to the door. I remain calm, slipping through the chaos. My zen-like resolve braces me as I step back into the screaming free-for-all in the terminal. A loud, menacing clock starts pounding in my skull.

The crowd is rushing like the Titanic's going down. "There's no room in the hotels!" a woman howls, waving her arms wildly. Looking out the window, I notice that all of the taxis are gone. In fact, there are no vehicles out there at all. It's deserted. A new, horrible fact sinks in. Nobody's making it to the airport. I can't take a cab back to my parents' house, and nobody can get down here to pick me up. I'm not only stuck in this city for the next three-to-five days, I'm trapped in this cold concrete building. There's only one thing to do...Get on a plane, any plane, now!

I look up at the row of monitors with dread. My tense eyes watch as every flight down the list changes from "delayed" to "canceled" and a man shouts, "They're closing the airport!" The din around me fades in my head as I get into the ticketing line, intently focused on getting the hell out of Philadelphia. After twenty minutes and what looks like two more inches of snow, I reach the front of the line. I tell the ticket agent that I'll fly anywhere south and figure out the rest of my way from there. With a forced smile plastered on her face, she replies that there's no way. All flights are either full or canceled.

Soon I'm standing in the middle of the panic with no real plan. I look up at the bank of monitors but every flight is canceled. The monitors themselves are going dark as the airport shuts down. Canceled, canceled, canceled, all down the list...except for one flight at the very bottom. My heart leaps! It's even going to Los Angeles! This flight is on the big fancy airline next to my small crappy one, but I immediately drag my bags into their ticket line.

I plod forward to the big airline's ticket counter, where a testy ticket agent named "Louis" sees that my ticket is from another airline and gives me a nasty stare. As I begin to beg Louis, a bullish woman with huge thighs and a chrome nametag that reads "Angela" stomps toward us, bellowing that passengers from other airlines are NOT getting on their flights. Louis looks at me forlornly and says, "Please don't try this." Angela stops behind Louis' back and yells "Did you HEAR me?!" Louis cringes and nods. He looks at me and declares, "I can't help you."

Back in the shrieking chaos, I am discouraged but refuse to give up. Through the noise, I hear worried voices behind me, and notice a frail elderly black woman with a boy about eight years old, standing meekly in the panic. The old woman is trying to figure out what to do about their flight to Detroit. She's very upset, and seems unfamiliar with the workings of the airport, so I ask if I can help. She starts telling me about her grandson's flight, then I interrupt her as I realize something, "Wait a minute. You're not flying with him?"

"No, he's going by himself," she replies, "His mother's supposed to meet him, but I'm afraid to put him on the plane if it's going to end up somewhere else, because he's all alone." She timidly looks up at the dying bank of monitors and says, "I don't know what to do."

"Aw jeez," I say, looking down at the kid, who's staring at the screaming travelers, petrified. I take the nervous woman and the boy to the ticketing line. When we reach the front, I leave my bags in my spot and walk the old lady and her grandson to the counter. I get my previous ticket agent again, whose phony smile drops as she sees me coming, "I've told you already, there's nothing I can do!"

"Wait, please!" I reply as I pull the old woman forward and explain her predicament. The ticket agents smiles sheepishly and says she'll take care of them. I return to the front of the line, where my bags have been kicked aside and a fat man in a bad suit stands defiantly. I take my bags and try to stand at the front of the line when the fat man shoves my back and snarls, "What are you doing?"

"I was here. I just helped that woman and her grandson."

The fat man barks, "Forget it! Back of the line!" The fat man turns, refusing to look at me. So I ignore him, too, and take my place at the front of the line when he shoves me again and yells, "I said back of the line!"

I'm about to confront the fat man when I hear a voice ask, "Excuse me, can I help you?" I turn to see a mustached man with an airline-issue tie. The surly fat man says "Yes!" and pushes past me, but the mustached guy points to me and smiles, "I meant him."

This airline employee, whose name tag reads "Randy", gives me a knowing smile and asks me how he can help. I point to the monitor and the one remaining flight, and ask Randy if he can get me on that plane because if he can't, I'm screwed. The fat man starts to yell at Randy, who ignores him. Randy asks me why I'm so screwed if I can't get on the plane, so I give him a very brief account of my insane legal predicament in Santa Monica. If I have to wait out the blizzard in Philly, I'll miss my trial date. And while I'm sure Phil can take care of this, there's no doubt in my mind that there still will be some horrible vindictive consequences, thanks to Noreen and her wicked cronies. Randy looks at me curiously, trying to read my face, and then he decides that I'm telling the truth.

"Okay," he says with a determined nod, "We don't usually do this, so don't tell anyone, but here..." Randy fills out a blood-red form, rips off a carbon, and slams a stapler to secure the form to my ticket, while instructing me to take this to the other airline's counter. Glancing around, he says, "Keep this quiet. You better hurry. Good luck."

"Sir, thank you!" I exclaim, and I rush back to the line for the big airline's counter. I end up with snippy Louis again, who stares amazed at the blood-red form stapled to my ticket. "How...did you get this?" he asks, almost afraid.

"A nice man over there did it. Can you put me on the plane?"

"No, seriously. How did you do this?" Louis seems uncomfortable even touching the form.

"The guy over there."

"What did you say to him?" Louis urgently hisses.

"I don't know, I think it was 'please'." I'm so close to success that I'm getting very tense. I see Angela marching closer, roaring that they're not taking stranded passengers from other airlines. She sees me with Louis and looks suspicious. Her giant thighs start crashing angrily toward us.

Louis is still puzzling over the magical red tag on my ticket, "I don't think a simple 'please' would get you one of these." Angela is almost upon us, staring me down and screaming, "There is NO WAY any passengers from other airlines are getting on our flights!"

This is it, make-or-break time, so I plead with Louis, "Aw shit, dude, I don't know! They say God loves an optimist. Can I get on the plane or not?!"

Louis sees Angela coming and quickly starts clicking the keyboard. He prints a boarding pass and hands it to me. "Listen, linger in the back as you board. Do *not* show this to any other passengers. Just get on the plane like you belong there." He grabs my bags and adds, "I'll take care of these. Go!"

I turn and run for the gate, confused as hell. I have no idea what that red form was, but Louis seemed awestruck by it. Did I just talk my way onto Air Force One? I slow down as I approach the gate, feeling like a spy. I'm starting to sweat. There are angry people yelling at the check-in gate. Keeping my eyes down, I hurry past the enraged crowd and flash my boarding pass at the flight attendant. She nods and sends me through. The shouting recedes behind me as I bolt down the gangway to the plane. I'm psyching myself up, ready to argue my way into that seat. I am not turning back! Bracing myself for a big confrontation with the flight attendants, I march through the deserted doorway. And then I stop dead.

This plane is empty.

A flight attendant appears and gestures for me to sit anywhere. I slowly walk through the rows of empty seats. I see an old woman who's so tiny that she's hidden by the seat cushions. Then I see a pale, skeletal man with slicked back hair. And that's it. We're the only passengers on this flight.

I hesitate before taking a seat, completely freaked out. Why was there such drama to get on this plane? Why was Angela screaming so murderously? But as we pull away from the gate, I get all fired up. I can't believe I'm getting out of Philadelphia when hundreds of other stranded passengers gave up. Maybe God does love an optimist, and that is what's going to get me through my Santa Monica legal nightmare. The ice-crusted plane is creeping toward the runway. "We're really taking off!" I think. The plane starts going faster, whirring and shaking, when the scariest thought slams into my brain. "Oh my god. Nobody knows that I'm on this plane. I didn't call Tam or my folks." I look out the window at the thick snow, and the plane skids.

"If this plane crashes," I yell to myself, "they'll never know I was on it! Nobody will ever know what happened to me! Not only that, I had to pull some super-secret ticket maneuver to even get on this damn plane!" The plane rises a little, then slams back down to the icy runway. "I am such a fucking douchebag!" I clutch the seat, white-knuckled as the rattling plane lifts off again. The plane drops steeply and I gasp, but then the plane recovers and climbs steadily through the falling snow. I collapse across my row of seats and pass out.

"So...they say God loves an optimist, huh?" Phil laughs as I tell him this story in his office on January 2nd.

"I don't know. Don't they?"

"Beats me," Phil says, "But let's hope so." Phil erupts with a deep hacking cough because he's coming down with the flu. He's sweating and getting worse by the minute, and we cut our meeting short so he can go home to bed. This year's holiday flu is particularly devastating, affecting everyone. Our friends and neighbors are all sick as dogs. Even Tam got nailed with the flu, and she never gets sick. It seems that I'm the only person who's managed to ward off the flu, and I attribute it entirely to my massive unwavering stress while trying to dodge the slammer. Getting sick is a luxury I don't have right now.

In our apartment, things are tense. On those rare occasions when Tamara comes down with something, her most reliable symptom is a manic refusal to admit that she's sick. While Tam is vomiting and feverish, you cannot make any verbal reference to her being ill. Because if you do, Tamara transforms from a sexy young woman who happens to have the flu into a raised-to-kill pitbull with late-stage rabies. Battling this ferocious dementia is always a fun little game, as I try to get Tam to stay in bed and take Vitamin C while inventing reasons for her to do this that have nothing to do with her being sick.

Date: 1.5
Subject: SM trial prep
Steve,
I've dragged my miserable carcass from its deathbed. I need to see you and discuss your trial.
Phil

"You sure you're okay?" I cautiously ask, staring across the desk.

"I'm fine," Phil says, but he looks like he's dying from some Biblical plague, "Your court date is tomorrow."

"And you're up to this?"

Phil nods, then wheezes, "It's your new zero-to-ten day."

"How many zero-to-ten days do people usually get?" Phil just moans so I move on, "So ten days from tomorrow, we rock and roll?"

"Thereabouts, yes," Phil says, wiping his nose.

"And you're still confident?" I ask.

"Absolutely," he replies, "I think this will all be fine."

"Good. Except we've been wrong at every turn," I point out.

"True, but still. Now it's for real," Phil tells me, "We have the truth on our side, and they have a ridiculous case which they have to prove."

"What time should I be there tomorrow?" I ask.

"You don't have to be there," Phil informs me.

"Why not?"

"Well, if you want to..." Phil reluctantly says.

"Not if you don't want me there," I say, "But what's up with that?"

"Nothing," Phil says assuredly, "It should be pretty quick and simple. We'll finally get our requested discovery on Toomey and then get on the calendar."

"Wait...I know Noreen didn't have our discovery back in November. But shouldn't she have had it on that court date on the 19th when I was flying to Philly?"

"Don't ask," Phil moans.

So the next morning, Phil goes off to court for my newest zero-to-ten day. At home, any hope of getting editing done is smashed against the rocks of Tam's steep violent flu-denial. I get her back into bed, but not without a fight, and then sit down at the editing system to worry about my upcoming trial. And I find myself getting caught up in all the old questions all over again. Why has any of this happened? And how will it end?

I pull out my thick file of court crap, and I remember that day in Phil's office when he said he had some idea why this was happening. What does Phil know that he's not telling me? There was definitely something. He was looking at that first letter from Noreen, the one informing me of my false charges. Maybe there's some clue there.

I dig out Noreen's letter. I see the date, from last June, and feel violated. Has this really been going on so long? I read the letter, but there's nothing I can see which would give Phil cause for concern. It's standard bullshit, "You are hereby directed to appear..."

I see my name misspelled at the top of the page, and chuckle about how incompetent these pricks are. My last name's always been a tough one for everyone who's ever encountered it. But Noreen and her friends have butchered my name in an unusual way. They've spelled it "Bevilaque". I shake my head in disgust and give up looking for clues on this page. Then I pause, thinking...and look back at my misspelled name. "That's funny," I think, "The way they've spelled it here, it looks more Latino than Italian—"

I stop mid-thought. My brain gasps. Oh my god, that's it! I can't believe it, but I feel deep down that it's true. Those assholes in the Santa Monica City Attorney's Office assume that convicting me will be a slam-dunk...because they think I'm Hispanic! It hits me like a giant mallet. That might also explain the inexplicable gang statute tacked on my false charges. But that can't be! Maybe that's how things work in L.A., but in Santa Monica with all their self-righteous, high-minded social ideals, do they still go for easy convictions assuming no one will believe some poor Hispanic guy against the word of a white lady?

It suddenly makes sense that nobody has questioned Toomey's ridiculous claims, even knowing that she ran down a pedestrian. They think a conviction for me is a sure thing because she's white and I'm not. But wait, somewhere in the police report is a small "W", indicating that I'm white.

It's right next to the "25", indicating that I'm many years younger than I actually am. But wait, Noreen's never read the police report, at least not while sober. And there at the top of her letter is "Stephen Bevilaque". It's true! She thinks I'm Latino.

I'm sure Phil will dismiss this as me being paranoid, but I know I'm right. I also think he's known about this all along. Suddenly, the mystery of why they'd pursue dubious accusations in such an unshakably rigorous manner is crystal clear. Santa Monica does have it in for me, but only because they think I'm Latino. All they really care about is their conviction record, so they go after easy marks.

And just as suddenly, this explanation is deeply sickening. I'm queasy and, barring the possibility that I too am coming down with the flu, I'm experiencing first-hand what it's like to be a minority in Santa Monica. I now realize that, if I weren't white, I'd definitely be going to prison for this for a long time, no questions asked. Not only for something I didn't do, for something that never happened. It wouldn't matter. They'd all believe Toomey because, as preposterous as her story is, it'd still be good enough to put a Latino guy behind bars. Here in sunny, enlightened Santa Monica. Well, so much for progress.

I have to tell Tam. If anything can snap her out of her fever, it'll be this. I jump on the bed, brandishing my letter from Noreen. "Look at this!" I yell.

"What?" she groggily asks, "Don't get all worked up again. Let Phil handle it."

"Look at my name!" I say, showing her. Tam groans, waving me away, "Your name's never been spelled right on anything."

"But look how it's misspelled!   Does that look Italian to you?"

Tamara wearily looks at my name on the letter, "No, it looks...OH MY GOD!!!" She leaps up and I'm sent tumbling off the bed. The phone starts to ring. A few seconds later, the front door slams behind me as Phil's voice sounds through the answering machine, asking me to come to his office.

vato me...

I storm past the receptionist and charge like a bull down the hall to Phil's office. Wildly waving my letter, I burst in the door and shout, "They think I'm Latino!"

"Mmm," Phil replies, "Sit."

I slam the letter onto Phil's desk, pounding my finger on my misspelled name, "That lush saw my name spelled like this! And that's why she's not talking, and that's why she charged me with the gang statute. And that's why she's been treating this like it's a quick kill!"

I expect Phil to hedge and squirm. He'll never admit to this. That would be conceding something unmentionable, a cancerous flaw in his beloved legal system. But Phil doesn't squirm. He looks me in the eye and calmly states, "I think that is entirely accurate and very astute on your part."

I angrily point at his head, "You've known this from the start!"

"Well..." Phil admits.

"And that's why you haven't wanted me in court! You want to save it for when it will be most effective!"

"Aw Jesus, I just gave you that. I'm not going to comment on this any further," Phil says.

"The hell you're not!" I yell, "This is wrong! How can you not do something about it?!"

"Because, in general, I can't. I handle each case individually, so I'm limited. And in your case, what's the alternative?"

"What do you mean?" I ask.

"If that is what's happening, what choice do I have?"

"What's that supposed to mean?! Yell about it!" I tell him.

"And how will that help? They'll never admit doing it, even if it's true," Phil says.

"If I were Latino, I'd be going to prison for this, whether it happened or not!"

"Yes, probably," Phil says.

An outraged roar comes from my mouth. Phil calmly asserts, "We can't acknowledge it."

"Oh no, because *that* would be wrong!" I yell sarcastically, "This bullshit has been barrel-assing unchecked for seven months, all because they think I'm Hispanic!"

"No, because they assume you're Hispanic," Phil says, "What do you want me to do?! Drag you into court, show you to Noreen McDonough and say, 'Don't do this! He's white!'? Do you really think that will help your case? They'll just prosecute you more vehemently to save face. You've been on the wrong end of a lot of mistakes here."

"They do this all the time, don't they?!"

"Yes, but I'm thinking about you, this time, because that's my job."

"It's just so wrong!"

Phil raises his voice, "Wrong that they do it to minorities, or wrong that they're doing it to you?"

"I don't know!" I angrily think for a second, "Both!"

"Pick one," Phil flatly insists.

"That first one's worse! But the second one sucks! How can you be a part of this?!"

"A part of what? I'm trying to help you," Phil's getting pissed.

"A part of this whole foul system that sends up minorities because it makes the City Attorney's record look good, regardless of the truth!" I blast at him.

"Are you accusing me of being racist?" Phil asks sternly.

"No! I'm accusing you of going along with it," I yell.

"Really? Because it sounds like you're accusing me of being racist," Phil says, with anger building in his eyes.

I stop and exhale loudly. "I don't think you're racist," I say.

"You sure?" Phil asks, still insulted.

"I don't, okay? I think you're a good guy. And I think you're trying to help. I just find this all repugnant. I also just stumbled upon this little insight twenty minutes ago and I'm still trying to sort it out."

"Alright," Phil says.

"Why the hell didn't you tell me?" I demand to know.

Phil laughs, "Are you kidding? Remember what you were like a few months ago? Imagine what would have happened if I'd told you, 'Oh Steve, it's all just because Noreen assumes you're a minority.'"

"Aah!" I yell.

"Can we move on?" Phil asks.

"No! Those pigfuckers! They slam minorities to make it look like they're doing their job, to hell with justice or the truth."

Phil looks at his papers, "Change the world later. It's time for you to focus on your trial."

"Oh, what should I do?" I ask, "Try to seem extra white?"

"Get that superior tone out of your voice," Phil quietly growls, "And trust me, you're plenty white."

"Alright, I'm sorry," I grumble.

"Good," Phil says, "Because you had another interesting day in court."

"Fuck, what now?!"

"This case just never goes smoothly," he says.

"What happened?" I nervously ask, "Was she drunk again?"

"Today, we're attributing it to cold medicine. And we're going to keep moving forward so watch what you accuse me of," Phil warns me.

"I said I'm sorry," I gripe, "What the hell happened?"

"For starters, we finally received our requested discovery on Lauren Toomey."

"And?"

"No hits, criminal or traffic," he says.

"Oh," I reply, disappointed, "Well, how thorough was it? I mean, how shitfaced was Noreen when she finally got around to doing it?"

"No hits, and that's what we have to work with," Phil firmly tells me.

"Can we double check it or something?" I ask.

"I don't think we'll need to," Phil says, "I'm feeling confident about this trial."

"Oh, please." I sigh resignedly, "Hell, who knows? Maybe God does love an optimist."

"There you go," Phil says, "Keep telling yourself that."

"Yeah, all the way to the gas chamber."

Phil moves on, "Here's the real news. Noreen threw a bit of a yelling fit in court this morning. She petitioned the judge to postpone your case for eight months, until August."

"What?!" I scream, "No! How long is this shit supposed to drag on?"

"I sensed that would be your reaction, so I went ahead and countered accordingly," Phil gently says.

"Stop talking like a hotel concierge and tell me what happened."

Phil explains, "Noreen claimed that they're backed up with cases of far greater importance than yours."

"Yeah, once again, my charges are either really serious or really not, depending on how it suits them."

"Well, yes. So then I petitioned the judge," Phil informs me.

"Good for you. What does that mean?"

"After Noreen was done complaining that handling your case now presented an unfair strain on the City Attorney's Office, I pointed out to the judge that your case has been repeatedly delayed. And since we feel that these charges are entirely unjustified, the idea of postponing again, let alone for that long a period, is not particularly agreeable to us."

"Right on, bud!" I yell, "Give 'em hell, in your softspoken way. So they're backed up? I say screw 'em!"

"I did, only in language that would hopefully produce the desired results," Phil evenly states.

"What happened then?"

Phil grins, "The judge agreed with me."

"Ha!" I exclaim, "I love you and take back everything I said. What does this mean?"

"It means they have ten days to start your trial," he announces.

Gearing up for battle, I say, "You told me that they don't let Noreen take cases to trial. Does this mean that we're one step closer to getting past her?"

"Yes," Phil says.

"Excellent! So, who is going to take this dog to trial?"

"We don't know yet," Phil informs me, "Barring any more cheap delay tactics, we find out all that on the 14th. So now we really need to get ready."

"In the fight between you and the world, back the world." – Kafka

Tomorrow's the big day. My first appearance in the Grand Hall of Justice. In honor of this, I have decided to unceremoniously abandon the practice of checking the eWin horoscopes. And just when I could use the sagacious guidance of the online soothsayer. But face it, I've been clicking my heart out on that damn website for months and haven't "won" one cent. So I chuck it, in hopes of giving this absurd situation the gravity it seems to expect.

Another reason for ending the eWin horoscopes is that there simply isn't time. Preparations for my trial have ballooned into a Fellini-style circus in our cramped apartment. Tamara enlisted the art department of her company to make our giant photos and big maps. This afternoon, Tam has brought Jorge the Art Director and his two assistants to our place to show me what they've created, and it's incredible. They've made a map of the entire neighborhood, with landmarks placed on the spots where I was hit by Toomey's car, and then tracing the entire path of stalking and screaming. Jorge has created stick-on representations of me, Toomey, and Tamara, that can be used with the giant map. Phil will be able to colorfully re-enact the whole prolonged incident with these fantastic visual aids.

Liz has arrived and she's brought her boyfriend Gary. Gary reads star charts for a living, but he does it in a bizarrely academic fashion like a medieval alchemist, with huge leather-bound volumes of tables and symbols, which he's piled all over the editing system as he zealously compiles the predictive charts of everyone involved with the case.

Allie's come to help command the chaos, and she's arguing with Liz about some Asian-New-Age-hippie thing. "You may know China," Allie yells, "but don't tell me about Vietnam! I've been to Vietnam!" Allie points an angry finger at Gary, "And he's fucking Japanese! Don't think I don't know that."

Amy Nextdoor, ever thoughtful, brings over some soda and beer. Dave the actor from the opposing balcony pops in as I'm yelling, "Damn it, Gary, I don't know the judge's date of birth! I don't even know his name!" Now that Gary's set up shop, I suppose the eWin horoscopes are especially unnecessary. And since I don't believe in astrology at all, it's terrific to have my own personal magus right here in the living room.

Dave excitedly tells me that one of his old movies is on TV, which I always love, so we turn it on and see Dave reading a newspaper on a toilet while ignoring a blaring alarm, which causes a dam to burst that sends millions of gallons of water crashing down on poor Christian Slater. I look at Dave, "Boy, you've had to play a lot of numbskulls."

Blodg swings by to wish me luck. He only stays for a minute, nodding and not listening to me while he checks out all the women in the room. He clearly finds Allie intriguing, and rightly so because Allie is never sexier than when she's enraged. As Blodg leaves, he slips me a two pink prescription pills and a fifty dollar bill.

"I'm not taking these," I tell him.

Blodg says, "They're not heavy, man. They just take the edge off."

"What's the fifty for?"

"Because you never know," Blodg slaps me on the back, "Buck up, kid. Remember, it's all a show." I have no idea what Blodg means by this, but I thank him all the same.

Jorge is showing me the Toyota Corolla that Phil can slide across the map to demonstrate Toomey running me down, when Liz runs to me shouting that Gary needs to know what time my mother went into labor with me. I sigh, "I've already told you the date, the day of the week, and the exact time I was born. That's all I know."

"To take it to the eleventh house, Gary really needs to know what time your mother went into labor," Liz says.

"I don't know that," I tell her.

"Call her and ask!" Liz urgently insists.

"I'm not calling my mother the night before my trial to ask her what time she went into labor with me."

"Why not?" she asks.

"Because she'll think I've gone completely fucking insane, that's why! Now stop it!" I yell.

"God, Steve, we're just trying to help," Liz bitches. Jorge pulls out huge photos of the 25-mile-per-hour signs along Rose Avenue, and Liz asks him, "Jorge, when were you born?"

"Liz," I say, "Have a beer and take these pills. Blodg gave them to me but I really want you to have them."

Thankfully, I have to go see Phil. So I grab my legal files, along with some oversized trial aids, and flee the apartment.

Phil is intensely focused, because he's got two cases coming to a head at the same time. There's my case, and a murder trial in Ventura. He's getting that trial postponed because it's going to be more involved than mine, or so he thinks. Phil wants to spend a couple hours on some intensive trial preparation. Phil says he's not really concerned with my testimony, as my story hasn't changed since we started this process months ago, but there are a lot of details to go over. "And no yelling," he sternly instructs.

"Yeah, okay."

We talk about Lauren Toomey. "She has a certain amount of credibility because she's a doctor," Phil says, "She's not much of a doctor, but in theory, she's still a doctor."

"Trust me, in May, she really didn't seem like a doctor. Maybe it was the middle finger, or her love affair with the word 'asshole'."

"Yes, which is where we begin the process of eroding her credibility," Phil says.

"You erode away, sir. By the time you're done, I want to see a new Grand Canyon where that bitch used to be."

"That is my hope," Phil smiles at me. Phil is ecstatic about our giant trial aids. "They're not over-the-top?" I ask.

"They're excellent," he grins. I've never seen Phil this animated, and that's keeping me calm. But after another hour of discussion, I sigh tiredly. Phil asks, "Are you sick of this yet?"

"Completely," I say.

"Good. Then you're ready," Phil announces, "Don't think about it anymore. Just answer the questions you're asked as simply as possible. Leave the rest to me. Get some sleep."

As Phil walks me out, I say, "Given what we've recently learned, I guess I'll try to dress extra non-threatening."

"As your attorney, I can't advise you to do that," Phil replies, "However, I would have no problem with you doing something along those lines."

"Got it. Thanks, bud. See you in the morning."

"Just for the record, I wouldn't go too far. On any given day, you're really not all that threatening."

"Right," I say as the elevator doors shut.

That night, I can't sleep at all. Twisting in the sheets, I can't stop imagining all of the treacherous possibilities of the next day. Are they going to get away with this? Am I going to end up in prison? Every new revelation in this case has been repellent. It has demolished most of what I used to believe.

Just before dawn, I finally drift into a harrowing sleep.

morning wood...

The towering tubercular writer looms over the beach. Marionette strings dangle from his oily palms as he bounces the spastic humans on the sand. The strings suddenly snap, and the humans scramble for freedom. With a sharp crack, the rubber strings fly in all directions, dragging the sad mortals back to their lunatic dance. The monstrous German grins, "HE'S COMING..."

I jump awake, drenched in sweat, two minutes before the alarm is set to go off. It's a bright winter day in California. I grit my teeth and force myself to move. I put on coffee, jump in the shower, gulp down some coffee and run out the door.

Last night, Tam had emptied out the closet, or at least my allotted one-eighth of it, trying to assemble the perfect outfit for my first day in court. She then launched into a debate with herself about each individual garment and the endless implications of them in consort.

"You know, I'm nervous enough," I say.

She tilts her head, considering a shirt, "Still, I'm not sure..."

Fed up, I grab a light blue Oxford shirt and some putty-colored khakis. "I think these are appropriately dickless," I announce, putting an end to the discussion.

Now I'm walking up the long lonely path to the flat wide horrible building that houses the Santa Monica Municipal Court. I nervously look for Phil, and feel like throwing up. Once I set foot inside this building, an unholy union of cops, City Attorneys, and a wacked ophthalmologist will conjoin to warp the truth and try to prevent me from ever leaving it again. I pause and sigh, staring at the long line of people at the door.

This long line exists because every person must walk through a metal detector, a simple process which is hampered by every third person needing the device explained to them. In this day and age, can there be this many people completely bewildered by the notion of a machine that detects metal on them? The journey through this mysterious portal is conducted by a man who looks like Sammy Davis Jr. if Sammy had lived to be a hundred-and-forty years old. Watching this old gent, it's hard to believe that this is something he does every day, because he doesn't seem to understand how the metal detector works either. Maybe it's his first day on the job. I wait my turn with the dehumanized drones, as a woman holds up the line by arguing that the keys in her jacket shouldn't be considered "metal". Shit, am I going to be late because of this?

I make it into the lobby, clutching my letter with the command to "appear" in Room S. This building is rather disgusting, like a high school that's been rotting from syphilis since the 1950's. It's got the type of tile floor that's often wet with sophomore vomit and goo from a half-dissected fetal pig, with dingy gold flecks in marble that's the dark green of the ocean when you're down too deep and certain to drown.

I find Room S and step inside. The cavernous chamber is mobbed with the same crowd of idiots from the line out front. A fat uniformed woman with dreadlocks is yelling that everyone must check in at the desk, a simple enough instruction that triggers a hysteria of mass flailing.

I step forward to check in. The disgruntled dreadlocked woman is having such trouble with my name that I lean over the desk to help her look for it. My name is spelled in a whole new incorrect way on her sheet but I find it and she checks me off. She yells to see my driver's license, which I show her, and she grunts with satisfaction, having successfully prevented someone pretending to be me showing up to get slammed for my false charges.

I turn away and find myself in a crowd of Spanish speakers who are confused about the process. I don't want to sit down yet, so I start to help a confused Hispanic woman check in. I don't speak much Spanish but, for this, you really don't need to. It can mostly be accomplished by pointing. After I get her squared away, I help a few more, looking at their letters and leading them to the woman at the desk, who now loves me because I'm helping sort the chaos. I ask a Hispanic man, "Tu nombre? Oh..." I turn to the big woman, "Is nombre 'name' or 'number'?" She has no idea and you'd think she would since she, too, presumably does this every day. Soon, everybody's checked in. The big uniformed mama grabs my wrist and whispers "Thank you" to me, which means I finally have to find somewhere to sit.

Do I go for the middle of a row and get caged in by people, or do I go for the end of a row and have to get up constantly to let people pass? I opt for the end of a row. The second I sit down, a woman in a motorized wheelchair pulls up to my side and parks, hopelessly blocking me in. I'm never getting out of this row now. I look around for Phil but I don't see him. I sigh. I have a feeling I'm going to be here for a very long time.

I scan this stuffy corner of hell, trying to figure out who's who. These seats are painful. They're made of torturously pressed plywood and feel like they could snap violently out of shape at any second. The paneling on the walls is a dismal shade of yellow, like it's been urinated on for years. That wooden altar at the front of the room is clearly the judge's bench. The placard reads "Hon. Roberta Tynan" but the big chair is empty. Behind the knee-level barrier of piss-colored paneling, there are people gathered in small clusters. To the right, I'm guessing, are the public defenders. There's a pudgy balding man in a pinched suit clearly bought before he put on all that weight. But next to him is a real eye-catcher. She's the other public defender, and she's really something.

She wears a drab, tattered business suit. Her hair is stringy and she's too thin, but her face is pretty, although she could use a little makeup. This woman is helping nine people at once, explaining various court procedures in concurrent conversations. She switches from English to Spanish from sentence to sentence, as if automatically sensing which language she should speak at every moment. It's true what they say about genuine sex appeal coming from within, because despite her bedraggled appearance, this woman is absolutely amazing. I can't take my eyes off her. She's so on top of her game, so great at what she does, that she's unbelievably hot. She clearly didn't even glance in a mirror before rushing to work, yet I find myself getting a defiant morning erection while watching her in action, and this awkward lap development is making it even harder to sit in the painful cramped plywood seat.

I force my eyes away from the public defender of my dreams, to the sinister bunch on the left. And then I see her! Oh my god, there she is! It has to be! That's Noreen McDonough! The sight of Noreen immediately takes care of my erection problem, and I settle back into the seat. At long last, Noreen! And what a freakin' sight she is. She's bony and haggard, in an oversized sweater that looks home-made. Noreen looks drunk and hungover at the same time, sitting there with a sour grimace, bitching to the dimwit woman at her side. Noreen clutches a huge bag of pretzels and is angrily stuffing them into her lipless mouth. She's talking with her mouth full, spitting tiny bits of pretzel at her young associate.

There are huge lists of "RULES" posted on every wall of this horrible chamber. These rules include "NO SLEEPING" and "NO READING." I've actually brought a book with me in an unwitting act of contraband. Good thing there's no detector for that or I'd be in a cell right now. Another rule yells "NO EATING!" Right there in loud warning-red, is the command to refrain from eating, with threats of fines and punishment. And under it sits dear Noreen, openly scarfing down pretzels and spewing them out as she talks. Of course, if Noreen were ever charged with illegal snacking in court, she could always use her old defense, "Sorry your Honor, but I was so shitfaced, I forgot about the no-pretzel thing." Hovering around Noreen is an assorted bunch of self-righteous assholes. I guess that's her "team". I look around, but still no Phil.

Looking at the gallery of defendants, I wonder about the different stories that brought them here...all the tragic circumstances by which they were falsely accused of a crime. Maybe a few are guilty but committed their crimes for good reason. Maybe some are horribly guilty, cold hardened criminals lacking any conscious. That's kind of cool. I pick a few and imagine their dramatic lives of crime. Suddenly, this becomes a room full of engrossing stories, full of twists, irony, danger and even touches of humor.

The judge enters. The big uniformed mama gives a half-hearted "All rise." I jump to my feet, and most of the room gradually follows. The sign on the bench reads "Hon. Roberta Tynan" but as the judge sits, I notice that Roberta Tynan is either a man or the best crossdresser I've ever seen. Is this guy a substitute judge? Did I get a temp on my big day in court? While on my feet, it suddenly dawns on me how insanely out of place I look in my button-down clothes. The other defendants wear ripped t-shirts, sweatpants, even a couple see-through mesh shirts. I get self-conscious and quickly sit back down.

Phil arrives, marching through the double doors. He sees me and waves, then walks past me to somebody else. I stare confused as Phil sits next to a man with his teenaged son, chatting with them. Then he gets up and returns to my row. Pausing at the wheelchair lady, Phil looks at me like I'm an idiot and says, "Come out from there." I climb over the wheelchair lady, apologizing. Phil leads me to another row and we sit.

"Who were they?" I ask, nodding at the man and his son.

"Other clients," Phil tells me, "The kid has a DUI."

"Are you going to get him off?" I ask.

"Not this time," Phil says, "He's lucky he didn't kill anyone. It's easier with drunk drivers when they're not seventeen."

"Hmm, good point."

"But it's containable," Phil says, "He'll be fine. And he's learned a valuable lesson."

"I'm not the judge. Don't waste it on me," I tell him, "And speaking of me, what about me?"

Phil gives a jolly chuckle. I've never seen Phil like this. Court brings out a different side of him. He's animated and glowing, totally in his element here. Phil pats my shoulder, "Just sit tight until you're called."

"Where are you going?" I ask.

"I'll be up there," he says, pointing.

"Am I really not allowed to read?"

"Try to seem like you're interested," Phil instructs me.

Phil walks through a small gate to a special holding area for attorneys. It looks like a petting zoo. Phil greets everyone with friendly-but-quiet hellos and they all look happy to see him, which I find reassuring. I settle in and wait for my name.

As the judge starts the day's proceedings, I return to my fun game of looking at each accused person and imagining their lives outside this courtroom. So many fascinating stories! I'm full of high hopes as the judge begins summoning the defendants to stand before him. As each name is called, I eagerly look around to see which one of this ragged bunch will rise. Sometimes nobody rises and they must call the name over and over, until some sleepy-eyed slob staggers to his feet. "This is amazing," I say to myself, "I have to tell Liz about this place!"

A lanky guy with a long mullet steps before the judge. His Honor informs us that this man has been charged with seventeen counts of driving under the influence. I'm confused as to how this works, but as the judge continues, I realize that it's not seventeen separate instances of DUI, it's actually one DUI incident which led to seventeen separate charges, including hitting four different parked cars over the course of his wasted adventure. "Okay, this guy's a meathead. So much for gross social injustice there," I say to myself. I give up on this defendant and search the crowd for more unfairly railroaded souls like myself.

Then it begins, the parade of crushing disappointment. As the defendants all plod forward, I realize many things in succession. One, I'm an idiot for thinking there was anything interesting about these assorted knuckleheads and their crimes. Two, these people have the longest, strangest names I've ever heard in my life. My long-and-strange last name is a piece of cake next to most of them, yet these other tongue-twisting names all dance melodically off the judge's tongue. Why is my name such an insurmountable spelling and pronunciation obstacle for these civil stooges?

The other thing I begrudgingly realize is that every one of these people is as guilty as the day is long. And they're guilty of things which would've been so easy to get away with if they weren't such imbeciles. As I hear the cases, it's as if each one flagged down a cop and yelled, "Excuse me, Officer, I just vandalized some property and I'm holding narcotics!" How did I get lumped in with these bozos?

The judge works his way down the list. I notice that the defendants who need an interpreter all get one, but then they're pretty much just handed over to be sentenced. All the interpreters seem to do is tell them how long they're going to jail. In fact, there isn't much resistance from any of these accused folks. They simply stumble forward to hear their fate. Some are fined, some are set for trial, some are sentenced. But many of them have their charges dismissed for a wide variety of arbitrary reasons. The defendants don't have to argue, or even ask, it just happens because the judge says so. I'm nervous as hell. I feel like I have no control over the outcome of this, and no idea what affects the outcome. And why the hell doesn't Lauren Toomey have to go through this? She admitted to worse crimes than most of these people are accused of, yet she wasn't charged with anything.

I'm thinking about how long and hard we've worked to try to resolve my case before it reached this point. These people don't seem to have made any effort to work out their problems with the piss-colored court. Most of them haven't even remembered to bring their letter that clearly states at the top "YOU MUST BRING THIS LETTER." Yet as often as not, the judge is dismissing their charges.

My frustration builds until one chubby dope lumbers forward to stand before the judge. The judge calmly explains that this man was charged with driving without a license, and the man nods dully. The judge explains further that the court is aware that this man currently holds a valid driver's license. The man nods again, but says nothing. The judge continues to explain that the man was ordered to bring his driver's license with him today, and all charges against him will be dropped. The defendant just stands there, silent. All this guy has to do is show his driver's license and it's over, he's free to go. The judge asks, "So, did you bring your driver's license?" The man doesn't respond, so the judge repeats the question, "Do you have your driver's license with you?" Then the man shrugs and says, "Um...no." I almost explode.

In my head, I'm screaming, "Sweet Jesus! Do you know how many hours I've put in trying to end this bullshit?! And all you have to do is show your goddamn driver's license!" I grab the arms of my chair to keep my thoughts from being shrieked aloud. All that escapes from my mouth is a muttered "Good god..." which still attracts the attention of everyone up front. I glance around, pretending it was someone else who uttered the disgusted comment, and Phil gives me a stern look.

After the entire room has been summoned before the judge, they finally get to me. I can tell because, after pronouncing the most unpronounceable of names, the judge starts stumbling with "Beh...Beh..va...Beliva...Belva..." Noreen McDonough grins smugly and puts down her bag of pretzels. The judge continues wrestling with my name. Everyone up front turns to look at the crowd of scraggly refugees in the gallery. Phil nods at me. This is my big moment! I jump to my feet. Here comes a tidal wave of friendly, crashing through the little gate.

"Hi! That's me!" I give everyone a friendly wave, then say to the judge, "It's Bevilacqua, sir! I know it's a bit of a mouthful. Please, just call me Steve!" I look at Noreen and her gang, flashing my brightest happy-to-know-ya smile.

They're stunned. Noreen's associates look back at the crowd, hoping to find a different me. Noreen McDonough glares at me with such immediate hatred, it almost makes me laugh. She just gave up her whole game with that craggy awful face. The pale young woman next to Noreen stands with her mouth hanging open. Next to her is a middle-aged black man with a gigantic gut who holds a thick file and seems paralyzed with shock. The file slips out of his hand and spills to the floor. The entire room is silent. The judge squints and leans closer, "You're...?"

"Yes, sir!" I smile at him. Phil steps forward, "This is Steve Bevilacqua, your Honor." Phil stands next to me with his hand out, exhibiting me like I'm a refrigerator on a game show. And nobody says anything. They're just staring at me. The silence becomes awkward. I'm starting to feel like the Elephant Man. The uneasy vacuum continues until I finally crack it by muttering to Phil, "Okay, what happens now?" The fat black man sweeps up his papers from the floor, then turns and angrily kicks through the gate. He stomps down the aisle and out of the room. Phil turns to me and says, "I think you can sit back down." Confused, I return to my seat as Phil rushes out of the courtroom.

electric dildo land...

*The Layman's Handbook for Those Falsely Accused of Felonies, page 38...To your **prosecutor**, you are not a real person. You are not even a two-dimensional representation of a person. You are one-dimensional, a mere point, that the prosecutor considers his or her god-given mission to denounce and destroy...*

The fat black man holding the file that's probably about me is a Santa Monica prosecutor named Ned Price. If you ask around about him, you get a mildly negative general consensus with comments like "the laziest man I've ever dealt with" and "if you want to win, just arrange things so that he has do some work." I'm hoping that Phil knows this, and he probably should because it turns out Phil and Ned Price went to the same junior high and have known each other since the sixth grade.

Apparently, Ned Price's pride and joy is his extensive collection of Jimi Hendrix memorabilia, that he keeps enshrined in his home. I can see Price now, with his enormous gut stuffed into the tiny fringed jacket that Jimi wore on *Lulu's BBC Happening* in 1969. The poor little jacket is threatening to burst, but our rockin' City Attorney doesn't care. Foxy Lady is blasting and he's air-jamming on his prized psychedelic Fender Strat. His mortified children beg him to stop, but Price ignores them, down on his knees pretending to set fire to his guitar in a brown-acid-inspired pantomime.

But last night's stone gas seems worlds away in the hallway where it's back to stifling reality for The Ned Price Experience. "God damn it, Noreen told me this was an easy one," he bitches to himself, while Phil tries to wax nostalgic about their days in the junior high band.

I'm planted in a seat near the courtroom doors, craning my neck to hear what's going on in the hall. As people enter and exit, I catch quick snatches of conversation. I hear Phil saying, "He was there but..." And the door swings shut on my impending fate. Then the lady in the motorized wheelchair tries to leave but gets stuck in the doors, and I hear Phil say, "...the right person, but what he's accused of..." The wheelchair makes it through the door, and I can't hear anymore.

I suddenly notice Noreen McDonough glaring at me, burning with hatred, and squinting. But maybe Noreen only appears to be squinting with animosity when she's actually drunk and struggling to see anything at all. I'm starting to get nervous. Phil appears at my side. He touches my shoulder, "Can you come out here, please?" I jump up and follow him out the door.

In the hall, Phil, Ned Price, and I form a small circle, blocking the way for the bustling masses. Phil introduces us, "Steve, this is Ned Price. He's a good man. I've known him for many years." I smile and say hi, then hold out my hand for him to shake. Price ignores my hand. Thinking he just hasn't seen my hand yet, I continue to hold it out. Price makes an annoyed face, shifting his massive body weight to make the point that he's ignoring me. "Ooh, snubbed!" I think to myself. So I drop my hand and give Phil a smile that says, "Your friend's a dick."

We're impeding foot traffic in an obnoxious way, so I try to subtly step aside, but no one follows my lead. The next room houses the juvenile court, and the hallway around us is crammed with surly teenagers and their put-upon parents. Phil's trying to be conciliatory but he seems put off by Ned Price's attitude, which is as sullen and difficult as the zit-faced teens clogging the hall by Room T. I stay silent as Phil discusses my case with Price, who continues to act like he doesn't want to be there, or has to go to the bathroom, or both. Price is not budging. He insists that "the people" have a strong case and are confident that they can put me away for a while.

Phil mentions that the complaining witness hit me with her car. Price grumbles, "So what if she did?" Phil points out that Toomey's story contains many obvious lies and contradictions. Price simply frowns. Phil asks Price if he's spoken to Lauren Toomey. Price makes a face indicating that Phil must be insane. I find all of this confusing. I'm wondering what the Santa Monica City Attorneys base their arguments on, since the obvious choices like statements and evidence don't seem to concern them too much. Phil's being too civil and we're getting nowhere, so I jump in.

I ask Price what exactly these specific charges refer to. I tell him that there's Toomey's story and there's a charge of assault but I don't know which part of her story is considered the assault. Price mumbles something about me punching Toomey in the street, and then again at the store. I tell him that I didn't hit her at all, and he rolls his eyes. Then I point out that the two alleged incidents are separated by a quarter mile and thirty minutes of Toomey stalking, yelling, and grabbing me. "And this was after she hit me with her car," I amiably point out. Price starts to make his standard dismissive face but, as what I'm saying sinks in, he stops. Price looks a little uncertain, and glances down at his file.

Then Price strikes back, clearly resenting the effort it involves, "You said in your statement to the police that you admit doing what she claims."

"That's impossible," I announce, "I never gave a statement to the police. I even went into the police station and asked them if I should make a statement, and they told me that there was no need to."

"I don't believe that," Price announces.

"Well, it should be easy enough to find out, don't you think?" I reply.

"How?" Price asks.

I stare at him for a second, confused, and then explain, "Because if I gave a statement to the police, there should be some record of it, right? You people don't just make this stuff up, do you?"
Price shrugs, dismissing this as well. But we seem to be making some progress, not so much in proving that I'm innocent, which he clearly doesn't care about, but in making my case seem like it's going to require some effort, which irritates him to the bone. Price says, "But you did commit the robbery. You stole something from this woman...Something valuable."

"It was a piece of paper," I say.

"No, it was..." he pauses, painfully uninformed and not sure where to go.

"If it had any value, I wasn't aware of it. I ripped it up right in front of her."

"But you did take it," he loudly asserts.

"Yes, I took it, but I don't know that I actually stole it," I say, "And I only took it because this woman was threatening my girlfriend. She was using that paper to write down my girlfriend's license plate number and make good on her threats to stalk her. I also dug the paper out of the trash and brought it to the police when they asked me to."

I seem to be giving Ned Price diarrhea. Phil jumps back in, "Perhaps you'd like to speak with the witness?"

"Witness?" Price asks, finally achieving idiot status.

"Yes, the witness," Phil says, "The young woman who was also accosted by Lauren Toomey that day, as mentioned in the reports. You can speak with her if you'd like."

Price abruptly shuts down, groaning and walking away. Price looks at me with scorn, and then beckons Phil closer. Phil and Price move deeper into the throng of troubled teens, and I step against the wall to watch their urgently hushed discussion. Then Phil leads Price back to me and says, "Call Tam."

I call Tam at work, where she's climbing the walls waiting to hear from me. "Hi!" I say.

"Oh my god, how did it go?" she asks.

"It's still going," I tell her, "This guy wants to talk to you."

Tam asks, "Who?"

"The prosecutor," I say.

"What does he want to know?" Tam asks, tensing up.

Phil takes the phone from my hand, "Tam hi, I'm going to put a man named Ned Price on the phone. He just wants to ask you some questions. Nothing to worry about, just tell him what you know." Phil hands the phone to Price, who ventures back into the teen crowd.

I stand watching Price talk to Tamara on Phil's phone. Are they going to try something tricky with Tam? How low will these fuckers go? Phil sees the look in my eyes and says, "He's just asking her about what she saw. You have nothing to worry about."

"Yeah, I've heard that before," I say, inching closer to Price's back to eavesdrop. "How enraged?" Price asks into the phone, "She said what?!" Phil grabs my arm and pulls me back, then plants himself firmly between me and Price. Two minutes later, Price hands Phil my phone.

Price looks exhausted from the phone call. In an attempt to diplomatically suggest that the prosecutor get some grip on what the hell he's doing, Phil says, "Perhaps you should speak with the complaining witness." Price releases a cranky sigh, but then his face lights up. "I don't think that will be necessary," he excitedly announces, "because we have evidence that he's guilty."

Phil calmly asks, "What would that be?"

Price digs into his file and pulls out a large brown envelope, "We have photographs of this woman's injuries from when he attacked her."

My heart stops. Shit! I forgot about the photographs! Phil and I look at each other, suddenly forced to confront the question of what Lauren Toomey did to herself to impress the police and succeed with her false charges. Seeing our reaction, Price proudly waves the envelope in our faces. Phil humbly asks, "May we see the photographs?"

Puffed up like the Hindenburg, Price grandly bellows, "Of course!" Price opens the envelope and whips out the photos. I'm afraid to breathe but Phil remains steady. We watch as Price's smirk evaporates. He rifles through all the photos, suddenly very confused. Phil asks again to see the photos, and Price weakly holds them out.

This is it! At last, we see the long-dreaded photographs. Phil and I look at the photos. Then we look at each other, astounded. Because there's nothing there! Nothing at all! We flip through nine photos of Lauren Toomey and don't see a thing wrong with her. Just Toomey's frowning, blotchy, injury-free face.

Phil's more shocked by this than I am. He was clearly expecting much worse. The threat of these damn photographs is the reason that this case got as far as it did, and all this time, nobody ever bothered to look at them! Phil and Price are silent, so I speak up, "If you can find one scratch on this woman, please show me, because I don't see it."

Deflated, Price doesn't speak. He and Phil examine the photos again, and then something astonishing happens. Presumably in an effort to distract from his embarrassment, Price actually makes a joke...about how ugly Lauren Toomey is. Phil follows Price's cue and counters with a joke of his own. I stand there in disbelief as these two officers of the court laugh about the photos like a couple of junior-high kids.

Giggling at Toomey's scowling mug, they toss out lame standards like "her face was on fire and somebody put it out with a hatchet" and "a good face for radio." Phil comes to me, still chuckling, and tells me to wait in the courtroom.

Now at a complete loss as to how our legal system works, I wander back into the courtroom and find a seat. I look around, afraid of something I can't quite put my finger on. Only part of my fear stems from what might happen to me in this urinous room. I've always thought that America had the best justice system in the world. Isn't this one of the reasons the rest of the world aspires to be us and resents us at the same time? From the very beginning of this long legal trail of cat puke, not one person has even wondered, let alone cared about, what actually occurred. Each step has been propelled by a series of execrable petty factors from the players involved. Self-serving malice, stubborn laziness, willful ignorance and sheer incompetence, that's what drives this world. At this moment, a major factor in deciding my fate is how well Phil can maneuver the fact that the prosecutor would rather laugh at pictures of a homely girl than resolve justice, and I use the term loosely. Phil finds me in my chair. "Don't overreact," he says.

"To what?" I ask.

"They'd like to postpone it again," he tells me.

"What?!" I yell.

Trying to calm me with gestures, Phil says, "Price would like you to agree to continue it for one more week."

"Why?" I ask.

"Come with me." Phil leads me out to block the hallway with Price again. Price makes his mean-little-girl face at me as Phil attempts to moderate our discussion. "Now Steve, Ned has asked if you would be amenable to continuing this matter until one week from today."

I look at Phil uncertainly as he says, "I think this is with an eye toward dismissal. Ned would like some time to learn more about your case." Phil seems excited about this. Price looks like he'd rather be somewhere eating. I decide to go along with Phil. I reply, "Alright. And then what?" I address the "And then what?" to Price to give him a chance to contribute to the conversation. But he doesn't. He simply infuses more spite into his bratty expression. I'm not sure Phil's right about this. I think this guy's an asshole, and it doesn't seem like he wants to dismiss my case. It seems more like Price wants another week to find a way to screw me.

Price remains sullen and mute, so Phil continues, "This means that one week from today, we meet back here and decide how to proceed."

I say, "So...is that it?" Phil gives me the nod to leave and Price remains an awkward silent obstacle in the hall. As I walk away, I look back. Price stands perfectly still, staring at me with extreme loathing.

Driving home from Santa Monica's Hall of Justice, these familiar streets take on a surreal quality. I don't understand anything anymore, and it seems to be affecting my sense of color. When I get home, I feel like I'm floating up the stairs.

I call Tam, who's dying of curiosity. I explain to her that I don't know the rules, or what governs the rules, and they're as likely to rule that I'm the Easter Bunny than a dangerous street felon. We compare notes on her phone call with the fat man, but we're both clueless.

That afternoon, I'm back across the desk from Phil, asking, "What the hell was that?"

"I'll grant you that was a little odd," Phil admits.

I sigh, "I was hoping this would get better once we were past Noreen McDonough, but this Price guy seems like one surly moron."

"Easy there, pal," Phil says, "Remember, I've known Ned Price for a long time."

"And what was with those photos?" I ask, still amazed.

"That was a major surprise. But a great one," Phil admits.

"Toomey didn't have any injuries, even self-inflicted ones. So you finally believe me now, right?"

"I've never doubted you," he insists.

"Bullshit," I say.

Phil shrugs, "I'm just not used to dealing with the innocent. No one involved with this is. It's not really set up that way."

"You're all a bunch of jaded bastards. Why won't they throw this out?"

"I'm hoping that they will," Phil says, "So now we give them time to absorb their complete lack of evidence."

I sink in the chair, discouraged, but Phil bucks up confidently, "Tomorrow, I'll call Ned Price and we'll talk about it some more. I think he'll be more likely to dismiss."

"Why?"

"One problem here is that they didn't realize they had no case until you pointed it out to them, so it might bruise their egos a little. But with you not there, it will be easier for them."

The following Monday, my steadfast attorney calls me into his office to tell me his latest stratagem in the war against my false charges.

"What's an infraction?" I reply.

"Charge-wise, it's basically the equivalent of playing your radio too loudly. Actually, an infraction is exactly what you get for a neighborhood noise complaint. The good part about an infraction is that it does not result in a criminal record."

"That's cool. Do I still have to go to prison?"

"No," Phil replies, "But I'm sure they'll tack on a fine, just to get their last digs in."

"Did you talk to Price about this?" I ask, not remotely convinced.

"Yes," Phil tells me, "and he seemed receptive."

I wonder aloud, "Do you think that fat buckethead has finally spoken to Toomey?"

Phil gives me his look, "If you mean Mr. Price, I certainly hope so."

I sigh, "I guess the infraction's okay."

"Don't worry. This is all coming to a head, very soon," Phil assures me, trying to end on a positive note.

My new court date arrives and I shuffle through the long line to the courthouse door. Room S is the same tumultuous mess as before. The bailiffs look happy to see me, as well they should, because I'm quickly directing traffic again, "No, this is Room S. You need to find..." What happens when I'm not here? This mob must take hours to organize.

My fellow defendants are a bunch of colorful oddballs like last time. That drab-yet-sexy public defender isn't here today, and the part of the "Hon. Roberta Tynan" is still being played by a mysterious gaunt man with glasses. I see Phil enter briskly with a crisp happy smile. He comes over and shakes my hand, proclaiming, "I'm feeling very optimistic this morning!"

"Well you know what they say..." I reply.

"Exactly. See you up there." With that, he heads through the gate to the petting zoo for lawyers. Noreen McDonough looks extra shriveled this morning, while Ned Price holds a battered cardboard file box, standing irritably like his back hurts.

The judge begins summoning the malfeasant fringe. Again, he has no problem pronouncing any of the long, difficult names on his list. Names like DeAngelistica and Lafianatis roll off his tongue like water. Later that day, the judge gets to my name. I can tell because this is the point when his Honor starts yammering like a barnyard animal that's been granted limited powers of speech. Phil jumps to his feet, "It's Bevilacqua, your Honor. I think, anyway." He looks back at me.

I leap to my feet and bound through the little gates, wearing my most affable smile. Noreen looks away in disgust. I say "Hi!" to all, daring them to try and prove that I'm a threat to society. Suppressing a grin, Phil re-directs me back to my seat.

Phil and Ned Price confer with the judge, then head out to the hall. I sit there, waiting. For some insane reason, I think things might go well today.

to the mat...

I am soon summoned for my date with destiny, to our favorite spot by the jailbait court. Price holds his sloppy file and Phil looks sickened. The color has drained from Phil's face, and I'm wondering if he's having a relapse of the flu. I say hello to Price and he ignores me, so I play along, pretending he's not there either. "We've been discussing your case," Phil tells me, distraught.

I look at Price, who's giving me the mean-little-girl look, which is losing what little effect it ever had. "The City Attorney has rejected the idea of you pleading guilty to an infraction," Phil informs me.

"Oh...Then what are you guys talking about?" I ask. Phil shakes his head forlornly. I turn to Price and force the question in a matter-of-fact tone, "What would you like me to do?"

Price glowers at me, still trying to seem intimidating, but I'm not buying it. I plow ahead, "I asked you to tell me what you'd like me to do."

"You can plead guilty," Price snarls.

I don't flinch, "Nope, I didn't do it, so that's out. I thought we were here to discuss compromises and solutions. That's neither."

Price barks, "I'm telling you that you should plead guilty!"

"Why?" I ask Phil, who shrugs and rubs his eyes. "Did you read the police reports?" I ask Price, who responds with a twisted frown. I try again, "Did you talk to Lauren Toomey?"

"Yes, I did," he says.

Maintaining a matter-of-fact tone, I continue, "I didn't do anything. Toomey's lying."

"It's in your best interest to plead guilty," Price announces.

"I didn't attack or rob Lauren Toomey. She's lying about the assault and she's lying about the sunglasses!"

Price irascibly blurts out, "We know she's lying about the sungla-" He stops himself, and looks like he just wet his pants a little.

My jaw hits the floor. Stunned, I feebly ask, "What?"

"What?" Phil also asks, looking shocked. I look to Phil, but then turn back to Price and ask, "Did you really just say that you know she's lying?"

Price doesn't respond. Phil's overcome with revulsion, and nobody's saying anything, so I keep at it, "And you know she hit me with her car?"

Price sneers defiantly, "So?"

This all just sunk to a new level. I can't believe this guy just admitted that he knows Toomey is lying. I face Price again, "Then you also realize that she attacked me through the streets after fleeing the scene of the accident."

"This isn't about what she did! It's about what you did." the prosecutor replies.

I take a breath, thinking out loud, "You know, I think all along, despite everything, there was a part of me that still believed this was all a big misunderstanding. So you really don't care that I got hit by a car?"

"I told you this isn't about that," the fat man growls.

"And you know she's lying?" I ask.

Price gives me a look of contempt, "Yes."

I sharply announce, "Then I have no respect for you or your court. Let's go to trial."

Price chortles with disdain, "Oh please, you're really going to go through a whole trial for something as small as this?"

"It's not that small to me," I tell him, "This could result in prison time, and probably will as long as I keep trying to deal with the likes of you. You even know that I'm innocent."

"I know nothing of the sort," Price puffs up his big fat chest, "By your own admission, you've committed a crime!"

"Which is more of a relative concept than I was led to believe," I reply, "Toomey committed crimes too, but you don't seem to care about that."

The prosecutor yells, "This isn't about what she did, and don't make me say it again! You broke the law when you took that piece of paper! And you've admitted it."

This has strayed so far from reason that the hallway begins to warp in my peripheral vision. Price gets in my face, "You broke the law and you're going to pay for it!"

"Well, she broke the law and she's not going to pay for it," I throw back.

"That's not the point!" he yells, "You're going to pay for what you've done!"

"Despite everything else?"

Price roars, "I don't care about anything else!"

Phil jumps in, sensing that I'm about to lunge at the prosecutor's neck, "Gentlemen, please!" Price glares at Phil, who matches his glare and says, "I find this proceeding essentially disgusting at this point. So, after all this woman did, running down a pedestrian, stalking him, and then lying to the police about being assaulted, you're going to tell a jury that's he the one who should go to jail?"

"Yes!" Price yells, "Because when he took that piece of paper from her hand, he technically broke the law!" Price turns to me, his face warped with anger, "I'm going to tell the jury that they are absolutely obligated to convict you!"

Genuinely curious, I ask, "Wow, do you think that will work?"

"Of course it will work!" Price bellows.

"I want a trial," I say.

Price smirks, "Trials can be very costly. I don't think you're aware of that."

I respond, "Listen, I've already had to cough up for the trial or this nice man wouldn't be here by my side. We're past pre-trial, or so I'm told, which is why I'm enjoying the indescribable pleasure of speaking with you."

Price protests, "You don't know-" but I cut him off, yelling to the entire hallway, "I want a trial! And it's going to be the hardest trial of your fat fucking life."

I turn to Phil, "I am asserting my right to a trial."

With a nod, Phil tells me, "I'll handle the details. You should go." Price says, "But..." as I stomp away and leave them there, not looking back.

Later that day, the twitch in my left eye seems to be returning as Phil grins at me from behind his desk, "Believe it or not, I was proud of you in there."

"I thought you wanted me to be nice," I say in a very subdued tone.

"I've changed my mind," Phil says, "I guess sometimes 'nice' can be a problem. You know, if you had talked to the police back in May the way you talked to Price today, they probably wouldn't have done this to you. You always try to make people like you, and it's a slippery slope. Some people will never like you. Just accept it."

"I've always thought that because I'm friendly, people assume I'm stupid."

"That too, probably," Phil concedes, "But they definitely think they can walk all over you."

I take an unsteady breath, "So we're going to trial."

Phil sees my growing anxiety, "Listen, there are a few times in everyone's life when you just have to go to the mat. For you, this is one of those times. God knows why, but these people really have it in for you. But after today, I have never been more confident in your ability to go in there, be yourself, and walk out a free man."

"You think?" I ask, still squeamish.

Phil smiles, "This is going to be the most painstaking review of an entirely insipid incident that court has ever seen. I'm going to make them beg us to end it."

"Okay!" I reply, gaining confidence from Phil's renewed energy.

Phil adds, "Just stay away from the word 'fuck'."

"Right..." I say, "So when's this go down?"

"Next Tuesday."

Phil and I meet every afternoon for the rest of the week. Phil gets almost giggly when discussing the fact that the Santa Monica City Attorneys are going to put a complaining witness on the stand whom they know is lying. Phil's also eagerly anticipating his plan to repeatedly call her "Ms. Toomey" until she snaps and yells "It's DOCTOR Toomey!"

"God, that's such a cheap trick," I point out, "You think it'll work?"

"I'd put money on it," Phil grins. Phil predicts that the jury will hate Lauren Toomey as much as everyone else who's had any contact with her. "For Christ's sake, even Price hates her," he gleefully says.

"He just hates me more," I reply, and Phil simply shrugs.

I become somewhat bi-polar this week. When I'm with Phil, I feel positive about my impending trial. At home, however, I get very tense. My friends are growing impatient. "God, Steve, when the hell's this trial going to start?" Liz snaps at me, and she seems to speak for all. Even Tam is losing patience at how long this ax is taking to swing down.

I can't sleep at all, still plagued by totalitarian nightmares. While awake, I tell myself that it's no big deal to go down for this, that I did everything I could, and that it's just one of those things. But when I'm asleep, the plain truth bursts from its shallow grave. I can tell myself anything I want to, but in the end this is the most pointless drag, ever.

The clock of doom is pounding deep in my head, making it very difficult to get anything done. I sit at the editing system, staring blankly at the footage, when a wacky, but not entirely bad, idea comes to me. I always make a point to try to make the best of a lousy situation, and transform a disadvantage into an advantage. This way, I can kid myself into thinking that there's a reason for everything. Now I see a perfect opportunity to turn this epic waste of time around.

I'm going to film my trial!

I call Tam and she likes the idea. Who knows, maybe we'll get something out of it and maybe not. But it's worth a shot. We'll keep it simple, a few small video cameras in the gallery. They won't even know we're there. Maybe, once they get used to us, we can get cameras closer to the bench and other interesting angles. Tam and I decide this will be cool as hell, and we're really excited about it. That afternoon in his office, I tell Phil about our swell new plan. And he explodes.

"No! Absolutely not! Dammit, I knew you were going to crack! You cannot film your trial!"

"Why not?! It's my trial and I want to film it!"

"There's no way," he insists.

"Why the hell not? They filmed O.J.'s trial," I say.

"Not in Santa Monica, they didn't! And this isn't O.J.'s trial!"

"So what? I want to film it!"

"Not a chance!" Phil's really furious about this. Trying to lighten things up, I ask, "Aw, you're not camera shy, are you?"

"That has nothing to do with it," he scowls.

"Then why not?" I ask.

"One, it will seriously affect the entire tenor of the trial, as well as its outcome. And two, because they almost never allow cameras in the courtroom in Santa Monica. You have to petition the judge for special permission to do so."

"So will you petition the judge?" I ask.

"No! I won't! I'm trying to get you out of this. These people hate you enough. If you go ahead with this dopey plan, I swear they'll try to hang you! I can't believe you want to turn this proceeding into some kind of circus with cameras!"

"Right, because it's all played out with such dignified purpose so far," I retort.

"Think about your future," he sternly says.

"I am. Maybe I can salvage something usable from this wreck. And maybe these clowns will think twice about trying to nail an innocent guy on some pigshit technicality if it's going to be recorded for posterity"

"Forget it," Phil announces, "I will not be a part of this!"

"Come on!" I plead.

"No! You do that, you do it without me," Phil states firmly.

"Shit..." I say, "Alright, fine! So much for that big idea."

Phil stares at me weirdly. "I hope you're not going to go nuts with the pressure of the trial."

"You're no fun," I tell him.

"I'm trying to keep you out of prison," he says angrily.

"Well, this way if I do go to prison, at least there'll be an upside to it," I say, "A sequel."

"Get out of my office! Forget that you ever had this stupid idea," Phil yells, "And come back tomorrow."

While I feel that Phil is overreacting, I decide it's probably best to abandon the filming idea. As I said, I always try to make the best of a bad situation. Sadly, it usually doesn't work.

On Monday afternoon, Phil and I have one last meeting before the first day of my big trial. Phil tells me that Day One won't be too bad. We wait until we're summoned before the bench, then we're assigned a courtroom, and then we find out who our judge is. Next, Phil and the prosecution will do their pre-trial motions, which will take up most of the day. And then, if there's time, we could possibly begin jury selection.

That night, I'm tossing wildly in bed, imagining all the various stages of my trial. As Phil explained, jury selection should last a couple days, and then the trial really begins. I'll get to haul in our elaborate visual aids that are piled up in the corner. Then comes the part when Atticus Finch wows us with an inspiring speech that reaffirms all that's best about America. Maybe we don't get that part.

MY TRIAL – DAY ONE:

Back in Room S, the drums of war beat an ominous march as I head up the aisle. "You're back!" the bailiff happily exclaims. I nod and start sorting out the confused masses. People now seem to think I work there, as they wander up and show me their papers. I help some check in, send others to the right room, and explain to one clueless woman that she's come on the wrong day. Then I find a seat near the back.

The routine plods along. The judge enters and starts summoning the accused. Phil keeps looking back, giving me encouraging looks. Noreen and her crew are perched like vultures around their table. I don't see Ned Price. Maybe he's going to call in sick and drag this mess out even longer. Then again, maybe a colossal earthquake will send Santa Monica to the bottom of the sea where the fucking place belongs. The judge begins his usual stumbling over my name. Phil leaps up and cheerfully announces, "Your Honor, I'm hoping this is your last chance to get that name right. It's Bevilacqua." The judge doesn't even look up. He shifts one tired eyebrow and grunts, "You know what I mean." Phil waves for me to come forward.

As I approach the bench, the big doors fly open and we all look back to see Ned Price march up the aisle carrying his sloppy cardboard box. The judge looks at Phil. "Are you ready?" he asks.

"Yes, your Honor, we are!" Phil announces like a cheery soldier.

At long last, this is it! THIS IS MY TRIAL! After months of preparation, anticipation, strategies, oversized maps, and instruction in the ways of the court, it all comes down to this. The judge looks at Price, "Is the prosecution ready?" And then it happens...

"Um," Price says. With his trademark surly expression, Price walks to Phil and mumbles in his ear. Phil turns to me, "We're going to have a quick conference. Wait here."

Phil and Price scamper to the hallway while Noreen McDonough tries to kill me with her stare. The judge shuffles papers, looking bored. This painfully awkward moment lasts for five minutes until Phil and Ned Price return.

"What's going on?" I ask Phil.

Phil smiles, "They're declining your case."

"Huh?" I ask.

Ned Price sullenly mumbles to the judge, "The people decline to take this case to trial."

I'm flabbergasted. All amped up for my trial, I completely deflate and before I can stop myself, I mumble "Oh, you suck" to Price.

"Excuse me?!" Price yells.

Phil grabs my elbow and whispers urgently, "What are you doing?!"

"Sorry, it slipped," I whisper back.

The judge looks up from his papers. This has caught his attention. "I'm sorry, your Honor," Phil says, "but we have worked for months in attempts to not waste the court's time by taking this to trial."

"But they wouldn't listen," I add. My contribution makes the judge bored again, and he looks back down at his papers. Phil notices my effect on the judge and gives me a look like we've defused the bomb. Noreen McDonough suddenly slams down her coffee mug. She and Price whisper furiously at each other.

The judge beckons Phil and Price to the bench. They mutter officiously while shuffling papers back and forth. The judge squints at a form and then scrawls on it, then Phil and Price resume their positions. Back at my side, Phil is almost levitating.

I'm confused, and the judge starts to speak, "Mr. Beh..." With an exhausted sigh, he tries again, "Mr. Bev..."

For everyone's sake, I say, "Just call me Steve, Your Honor, please."

The judge rubs his eyes sleepily, as my amazing soporific effect on this bulwark of justice continues. Then he says, "These charges against you will be continued for one year then dismissed, provided that you do the following..."

I'm standing eager and attentive, but very puzzled. The judge reads from the sheet, "You stay away from the victim."

"Toomey?" I ask Phil, who nods. I look up at the judge and smile, "Done!"

The judge nods, "And you obey all laws."

Confused, I confer with Phil, "I don't get it. Doesn't that go without saying? What laws am I allowed to break now?"

Phil replies, "You can't get arrested."

I look to the judge, "Okay!"

The august judge proclaims further, "And this court orders you to undergo three hours of sanctioned anger therapy."

"What?" I turn to Phil, "What for?"

"Just do it," Phil whispers.

I grin at the judge, "Terrific!"

The judge asks if all the parties are content with this arrangement. Phil happily announces "Yes, your Honor!" Noreen and Price grunt and nod. The judge looks at me and says, "Mr...um...You are free to go."

"Thank you, sir!" I tell the judge. Phil and I turn and hurry down the aisle. I ask Phil, "What-"

"In the hall," Phil says, cutting me off.

Outside the doors, I turn to Phil, "What the hell just happened?"

Phil shakes my hand, "You're a free man!"

"Really? Did they just wuss out after talking such a big game all these months?"

"That wouldn't be entirely inaccurate," Phil smiles.

"What happens if I do get arrested?" I ask.

"Have you ever been arrested?" he asks back.

"No," I tell him.

"Then what are you worried about?" Phil asks, "Besides, it will be the same dog of a case then. They still have a complaining witness who's lying."

"So that was the big factor?" I ask.

"Just one of many. I've never seen a mess like this," Phil says, "We should talk about your terms, but I can't now. I've got a murder client facing a lethal injection in Ventura. Let's meet tomorrow afternoon. Bring Tamara, it'll be good to see her." Phil hurries off to save a murderer's life, and I stand there, dazed. What a bunch of pointless assholes. Suddenly exhausted, I head down the hall.

Tamara is ecstatic when I call her. That night, she's still excited, but I'm not. I feel violated and drained. "We should go out and celebrate!" Tam exclaims.

"I don't feel like celebrating," I say, "I wish none of this had happened."

"Well, at least it's over," Tamara happily announces.

"It doesn't feel over," I reply. And it's not. But my wretched legal odyssey is about to take a radical new turn.

pangea...

The translucent galleon hovers just offshore. The ghost captain laughs while his suicide bride sobs by his side. Human heads hang like party lanterns around the deck, and butchered hands still clutch the riches in the chests. The young fisherman on the sand yells, "It didn't work! I'm free of you!" "For now," the pirate roars, "But the gold is mine..."

My eyes snap open in the pre-dawn blue, "That ghost pirate is right! I've been fucked out of twelve-thousand-five-hundred dollars."

Never mind the stress and wasted time, with my current situation, I will never pay off these debts. I guess Toomey did win after all. So did Noreen McDonough, Ned Price, the dickhead cops, even that satanic beast Detective Bender. Maybe I managed to stay out of prison, but they succeeded in completely ravaging my life with their demonic games.

The Layman's Handbook for Those Falsely Accused of Felonies, page 91...Life after being falsely accused will never be the same.

Fight doggedly to regain the worldview you had before the system left its scars. It is difficult, and in some cases impossible, but you must try or the sinister forces will succeed in forever indenturing a piece of you...

Tam and I go to see Phil, who's still bouncy from yesterday's escapades in court. In the spirit of celebration, Phil has us sit in his firm's stately conference room with its leatherbound volumes and gigantic antique globe. With an unshakable smile, Phil reviews the terms by which the demigods of justice have agreed to dismiss my charges.

Tam is confused, as am I, by the court's second condition that I'm not allowed to get arrested. "What happens if he gets arrested?" she asks, "What will they do, arrest him for getting arrested?" Phil explains that it's just something they tacked on. I'm still unclear about this, "But if I do get arrested, does this case automatically go to trial?"

"Not necessarily," Phil says, "You've never been arrested in your life. Are you going to go get arrested now, just to test this?"

"No, that would be stupid," I point out.

"Exactly," Phil responds, "There are some things in life we never find out. Let this be one of them."

"But I'm worried about how this could come back and attack again. Yesterday Noreen McDonough looked like she wanted to murder me."

"I think you're safely out of her clutches," Phil assures me, "Remember, there's the double-jeopardy clause of our constitution that precludes you from being tried for the same charge twice."

I reply, "There is no doubt in my mind that there are ways around that when it suits them."

"I suppose," Phil says, "But if they do try something like that, I'll still be here." Phil looks back at the form, "The next condition you must perform, or we will end up back in court. You need to complete three hours of anger management therapy by March 11th. That's four weeks, shouldn't be too hard to pull off." He hands me a yellow Xeroxed list, "I picked this up for you at the courthouse. It's all of the court-sanctioned therapy programs." Phil circles one name on the list, "A colleague of mine has had decent experiences with this guy, so you might want to try him."

Distracted, I take the list from Phil and he pointedly asks, "Why aren't you happier?"

"Well, aside from the obvious," I say, to which Phil replies with a conceding shrug, "Despite what the monkey court claims, Toomey is not the victim here. And neither am I. The real victims here are a guy in Boston, one in D.C. and some nice folks in Pennsylvania who are out a lot of money that I won't be able to pay back for decades. And that's what really pisses me off."

"I think you should sue," Tam sharply announces.

"I agree," Phil says, "I think you have a very strong case. Both of you."

"Me?" Tam looks confused.

"Absolutely," Phil continues, "In some ways your case is even stronger than his. You were nothing but a witness to this incident, yet Toomey falsely accused you of a major crime. And you were the one the police brutalized because of Toomey's deliberate misstatements."

Tam and I look at each other. A righteous fire seems to be growing inside of Phil. He suddenly announces, "You know what? I'm looking into this! And if you decide to go ahead with a lawsuit, I'll help you."

I ask Phil, "You want a cut or something? You can have one. I just can't afford to pay you any more."

Phil shakes his head, "I've been paid. But I'll stick around for this. I want to help you set things right." Phil smiles with newfound drive, "I love this idea! I'll talk to my colleagues and see what they think."

The Layman's Handbook for Those Falsely Accused of Felonies, page 82...If your false charges are **continued,** *they are not dead. They are simply dormant, hovering in an ethereal state above your everyday existence. These charges may become active again at any time prior to the continuance's expiration date...*

The spectral lingering of my charges prohibits any sense of closure. This is probably why my disturbing dreams persist, but these latest dreams tend toward the baroque, and are threatening in more oblique, even stranger, ways.

I jump to the task of enrolling for my court-ordered therapy, pulling out the list that Phil gave me. Piles of these yellow lists are placed near stairways in the courthouse, and they're printed with bold letters stating **"Los Angeles County Probation Department APPROVED BATTERERS' PROGRAMS."** Excellent! I get to hang with a bunch of batterers in an approved program, or I get to hang with a bunch of 'approved batterers' in a nondescript program. I'm not sure which because their phrasing is vague. The name that Phil circled is Dr. Jacob H-, PhD. The listing says to call for an appointment, and that there are "Women's programs available for those batterers who are female".

I call Dr. H- and, despite my hopes, I soon sense that this may not be the program for me. I tell Dr. H- that I need some court–ordered anger management therapy (or A.M. as it's called by insiders), and Dr. H- immediately launches into prescribing an extensive course of psychotherapy. He doesn't ask what I've done to create this need for anger management, and when I try to tell him what happened, the doctor interrupts me and says that we won't get to that until my fourth or fifth session. Dr. H- then starts rattling off the costs of all this therapy, and it's steep. He lists the dollar figures in chunks, possibly hoping that I won't think to add them up in my head. He's approaching the six thousand dollar mark when I interrupt, "Um sir, I only need three hours."

"Pardon me?" he says.

"Three hours of anger management. That's what they said."

"That can't be," he scoffs.

"No, really," I reply, "That's all I need."

"Well then, you're going to require extremely intensive therapy. I'm going to insist on at least six sessions before we even approach your rage counseling."

"Why is that?" I ask.

"Because three hours isn't nearly enough time to address all of your anger," the doctor diagnoses.

"How do you know?"

"Because I'm a professional," he responds, "Three hours will not be adequate."

"Maybe I don't have that much anger to manage, and that's why they only ordered three hours."

"That can't be," Dr. H- insists.

"It's not like they spun a wheel and it landed on three. Maybe I don't need that much therapy."

"Impossible," the doctor snorts.

Okay, I'm already thinking that, for a therapist, this guy doesn't listen very well. I can see where this is going and, frankly, I'm not a good candidate for therapy in the first place. I am up-front to a fault, and I suspect that therapy with Dr. H- will be a lot like when I was forced to go to confession as a kid in Catholic school. Kneeling in the confessional, I would make up sins to confess because, being a normal ten-year-old kid, I hadn't committed anything close to a genuine sin. But if I stepped out of the confessional too soon, the nuns would slap me and send me back in, so I'd keep talking long enough to keep the fascist brides-of-Jesus happy.

Dr. H- continues plotting his convoluted web of therapy, but then he makes his fatal pronouncement, that three hours probably won't be enough to cure me and there's no guarantee that he'll sign off when they're done. I thank Dr. H- for his time and hang up.

And it's back to the list. I examine the different programs, fascinated by the wide variety of approved batterer counseling. Anger therapy comes in Spanish, in a "lesbian-sensitive" format, for the deaf, and for the visually impaired. There are programs marked "For Parolees Only" and "For Veterans Only". There are A.M. programs in Armenian, Thai, Farsi, Vietnamese, Pacific Rim, and "Mildly Retarded". It's a wide world of anger management and I feel inadequate for my run-of-the-mill anger. I'd love to talk my way into the A.M. class for deaf lesbian vets, yet I suspect that's not going to happen. I guess I'll simply pick the one that's closest to home.

Venice has more halfway houses and rehab centers than any neighborhood in the city, but Venice doesn't seem to have any anger management programs. The closest one is a place called Fresh Start in Santa Monica. I like the name, it smacks of the low-rent generic institution I desire.

I call Fresh Start and a cheerful young woman answers the phone. I tell her that I need to sign up for anger management. "Super!" she chirps, then she asks if I can come in at 4:30 to fill out forms and meet someone named Jerry.

At 4:30, I'm in front of a brick two-story office building on Santa Monica Boulevard that houses a travel agency, two telemarketing firms, and Fresh Start. I find Suite 202, and recoil immediately. The reception area is disgusting. It's musty and smells like old vomit. The battered chairs are those distinctive pressed-wood-with-gray-cushions type you used to see on public access TV shows. These chairs are stained in the most suspicious ways, and I smile because this is exactly what I'd hoped to find, your basic no-frills social-services program. No fancy expensive psychoanalysis going on here.

Sitting behind the uneven counter is a hyper-sunny Latina named Becky. "Oh my god, are you Steve?!" Becky jumps up and throws out her hand like it's the best day of her life. I shake her hand and she squeals, "Okay! Well, let's get you started!"

Becky hands me pile of forms stuck to a clipboard. "First, you need to fill these out. You can have a seat right there," she ecstatically points to the stinking, revolting chairs, "Then Jerry will see you! Do you have a pen?"

"Yes! I have a pen," I smile, trying to keep up with her super-terrific attitude.

"Good for you!" Becky beams, "Because we're a little low on pens. We're a little low on everything, as you can see." The office behind Becky looks like a garage sale. There's an ancient typewriter, thick with dust, sitting on a counter that's propped up with boxes. On the desk is an ancient computer, straight out of a 70's movie depicting "the future", that doesn't seem to be working. The shelves on the wall are crooked, with a dead plant sitting perilously close to the edge. The file cabinet doors hang at weird angles, and there are two faded posters on the wall. One poster has a list of rules that must be obeyed to remain in Fresh Start therapy, written in big rainbow letters. The other poster has an inspirational quote written in a flowery script, but there's a stain over some of the words so it's hard to make out what the inspiring message says.

In her happiest tone of voice (at least I hope, if this girl gets any happier, she'll be floating off the floor), Becky starts outlining the rules of Fresh Start. First and foremost, it's cash only. They don't accept checks or credit cards. As I'm currently living on credit, I want to complain about this but I look around the tattered office and respond, "Oh alright."

Becky begins telling me the different meeting times, then she stops, "Oh wait, are you Narcotics Anonymous?"

"No. Anger Management," I tell her.

"Oops, sorry," she giggles.

"Do I look like I need Narcotics Anonymous?" I ask.

"No! I think you look cute," Becky laughs.

"Thank you, Becky," I smile.

"And you don't look like you need A.M., either," Becky adds, "But we have a space in the Wednesday evening class. Now, are you twenty-six or fifty-two?"

"Twenty-six or fifty-two what?" I ask.

"Weeks."

"Oh no, I need three hours," I inform her.

"That's only two weeks," Becky says, confused.

"Cool," I say.

"The sessions are an hour and a half each week," she explains.

"Well, put me down for two, then."

"But...that's impossible."

"Why?" I ask.

Becky hesitates, "Um, because nobody needs just two weeks."

A gaunt, hollow man in worn-out clothes steps out from the back and stares curiously at me. Becky seems uncomfortable and acts like she doesn't know what to do with her hands. With quick frantic gestures, Becky gets the man to follow her into the back office.

Standing there alone, I notice the disgusting carpet. Unlike the walls and furniture with their individual stains, the carpet contains one massive central stain that covers the entire floor. This stain is shaped like the prehistoric colossal landmass before the continents shifted to their current positions. You can find each individual continent as part of the greater stain, then imagine it leaving the pangea and shifting across the carpet to its destined location. I like Fresh Start. It's a smelly disgusting new beginning for every individual who passes through that cracked doorway.

Becky returns, "I don't think you can come here." She then explains that court-ordered anger management is doled out in two forms, twenty-six weeks and fifty-two weeks. Becky and Jerry have never heard of anyone doing just two weeks.

"Oh," I reply, "So what should I do?"

"Are you sure it's not a mistake?" Becky asks.

"Becky, this whole thing is a friggin' mistake. But no, I really just need three hours."

"Jerry says you're going to have to get something from the judge, Sorry." She flashes a sympathetic smile.

I sigh, "That's okay."

"You're so nice! I like you!" she exclaims, bouncing in place, "You really don't seem the type for anger management."

"Well, I'd go for a different class but that's the one they're making me take." Becky laughs like it's the funniest thing she's ever heard.

Date: 02.10
Subject: Smack my bitch up
Phil,
I can't enroll in anger management. They don't believe that I only need 3 hours. I think I may need something from the judge. Help!
Steve

Shortly thereafter, the phone rings. "Steve, it's Phil."

"Hey! How are you?" I ask.

"Murder trial in Ventura," Phil says with a sigh, "So what's the problem?"

I explain, "The nice lady said that anger management only comes in doses of twenty-six or fifty-two weeks."

"Really?" he asks.

"Yeah, I almost jumped over the counter and ripped her fucking head off."

"Cute," Phil replies, "Alright, let me look into this."

The next morning, I get a call from Phil who's stuck on the freeway in his SUV. He's discovered more about my anger management dilemma, and he's got news about my proposed lawsuit against Lauren Toomey, so we set a meeting for that afternoon.

"And we're back!" I announce from my old spot in front of Phil's desk, "Again, thanks for everything. I'll be recommending you to all my criminal friends."

"Swell," Phil says, "I've looked into the issue regarding your enrollment into an anger management program. Your case continues to defy all standards of criminal prosecution."

"Excellent! So what do I do?" I ask.

"I thought a letter from me to the anger management administrators would suffice, but I've since learned that that's not the case. So I've written this for you." Phil hands me a letter on his firm's thick elegant stationery, "You need to go back to the courthouse. Present this letter at Room K and they'll give you a form with the judge's instructions. Then take that form back to the anger management people and it should all work out."

I look at the letter. It's written half in English, and half in some strange code. Phil continues, "You need this completed soon, so don't waste time."

"First thing, Chief," I say.

"Good. Once you've completed your required hours, the anger management people will give you an additional form which you'll need to take back to Room K."

"Okay, simple enough."

"Yes. Magic is easy once you know the secret," Phil grins at me.

"And this is magic, isn't it, Phil?" I say.

"Alright, let's talk about your civil suit."

"What's the news?"

"Well," Phil shrugs, "I've spoken to my colleagues and they all feel that you have an extremely strong suit. Tam also has a very solid case against Toomey."

"That's good," I say.

"Yes. However, they've all turned down your case."

"Damn, why?"

Phil slips into his undertaker tone again, "While you have a case that, according to them, you're certain to win, there's not much money there."

"I'm not trying to make a lot of money. I just need to pay off my legal debts."

"There's also the issue of collection. Toomey is such a loon, that even after a judgment in your favor, you may never collect any money. That could take a lot of work."

"If she blows off a court settlement, won't that screw up her credit rating and stuff?"

"Yes, but Toomey's an idiot who probably won't realize that until it's too late," Phil somberly informs me.

"She can declare bankruptcy and evade the whole thing, can't she?"

"Bankruptcy is a nightmare for anyone, let alone a doctor who's trying establish a practice. But again, Toomey is such a dunce, she may not figure that out until it's too late. My colleagues were more intrigued by the idea of suing the City of Santa Monica. Much deeper pockets there, but it's harder to prove anything deliberate. They'll try to lie their way out of it, and it could go on for years."

I shake my head, "And they'll cite a million technicalities to cover their worthless asses. I'm not going there. Toomey's the one who's really liable for all of this."

Phil thinks, "Have you asked your friends for referrals?"

"Working on it," I say.

Phil tells me, "You're going to have to find a lawyer who wants to do this, as opposed to one doing it for the money. These are civil attorneys we're talking about. Ninety percent of them only go after insurance companies, and they don't care too much about setting things right. They only care about dollar figures." Phil leans back, thinking, "You know, one of my colleagues did have an interesting idea, based on the dollar amounts in play."

"What?"

"Small claims court," Phil says.

"Huh?" I ask.

"The limit for small claims in Santa Monica is five thousand dollars. If you and Tam both file, that's ten. You're still short the last few grand, but it's better than nothing."

"As a last resort, I'll consider it," I reply.

Phil says, "There's one more place you can look."

"Where?"

"The Yellow Pages," he tells me.

"You think?" I ask.

"Why not? Some of them are as good as anybody. You only need to find the one right attorney for your case. And if you find one that way, I'll look into them for you."

"Cool, thanks," I say.

"Keep me posted. And good luck," Phil says with a hopeful smile.

wonderland...

Bright and early the next morning, I'm in the glacial procession outside the Santa Monica Courthouse. After shuffling through the portal of wonder, I begin searching for Room K. Room K is on a floor below my old haunt Room S, and down here it's like the 70's *INVASION OF THE BODYSNATCHERS* with blank-faced people in bad clothes trudging along the grim hallway making no eye contact with each other. In the queasy light I manage to locate Room K, but it's not open yet. A long line of empty souls waits along the drab tiled wall. I get in line. And wait.

The clock that hangs from the ceiling is broken, furthering the impression that time is standing still, but eventually the door to Room K swings open and people start stepping inside, one at a time. As the line inches forward, I clutch the letter from Phil like some protective fetish. I finally reach the front of the line and start to step inside, when an elbow comes from behind and pushes me aside as a scratchy voice burps, "Move!" I turn to see my old friend Noreen McDonough forcing her way past me. Noreen doesn't appear to recognize me. Of course, Noreen doesn't appear to recognize anything, lumbering forward in a cantankerous funk. Obediently remaining in my Noreen-appointed place, I peer beyond the doorframe to see what she's doing in there but I can only see her hunched bony back, draped in another seemingly homemade sweater with a crooked pattern.

Noreen grunts at the person behind the glass and turns away. I smile at her as she shoves me again for no reason. I watch Noreen hobble down the shadowy hall. "Why, she's making such a difference!" I think to myself as voice inside Room K roars, "Next!"

Inside Room K, I'm confronted with a wall three feet from the door. A sullen obese woman glares at me from behind a thick plexiglass window. I say hi and slide my letter from Phil through the slot. The woman takes the letter and, without a word, disappears into the maze of cubicles behind her.

Lists of regulations are posted on every inch of the walls in this cramped municipal burrow. Newer lists are taped over the older lists, obscuring the previous rules. Their directives are written in an odd style with certain conditional verbs in big bold capital letters. **"You HAVE to present..."** and **"You CANNOT request Form B without first presenting..."** I stand there for a few minutes, reading the rules on the walls, then the fat woman returns, holding a new form which she slides to me through the slot. I look down at the form and the woman bellows, "Next!"

The clock still says 1:18 as I walk down the dark hallway trying to make sense of the form in my hands. This document is a foot-and-a-half long with columns of empty boxes that could be checked but aren't. Next to each box is a series of complicated codes. Below the fifty unchecked boxes, someone has scribbled "3 hours of anger management" at the bottom of the page.

"I speak differently from how I think, I think differently from how I'm supposed to think, and so it proceeds into deepest darkness..."
– Kafka

That afternoon, I'm at Fresh Start, showing Becky the scribble at the bottom of my form. She's happy as a bouncy little clam, and soon I'm filling out lengthy questionnaires about my likes and dislikes, like at a dating service. Only this dating service asks about drug convictions and the impulses that trigger me to punch someone. I sit on a stained chair for a while until Becky gleefully chirps that Jerry will see me. I think Becky is super. She can manage my anger any day.

Becky leads me along a crooked corridor of shabby offices. Everything in this place is held together with tape. The doorways along this hall are of different sizes and it's disorienting. I guess I've always taken uniform doorways for granted, because it's hard not to stare at them. Becky ushers me into a stuffy windowless room and giggles that Jerry will be right with me.

I sit at a wobbly round table, waiting. To pass the time, I test the table, seeing how much pressure from my finger it takes to send the whole thing rocking. A few social-service pamphlets slide back and forth on the table, like we're at sea. I decide to help by taking the pamphlets and shoving them under the short leg of the table. Bent over, I hear "Why are you putting our pamphlets on the floor?" I look up to see the skeletal hollow man. He checks his clipboard, "Mr. Beh..."

"Hi! Just call me Steve. Please."

"Good," he gives me a weak but grateful smile. "I'm Jerry," he says as I shake his fragile hand. Jerry gently lowers his sweatered bones into a chair. Jerry looks like the mummified remains of a 60's folk singer and exudes the air of someone who's been through every multi-step improvement program ever devised. I have no idea what Jerry's been addicted to, or how he's been traumatized in his past, but it's left him a frail husk of a man who could crumble to dust at any moment. Jerry pores over my answers to the pages of questions. He stops reading and looks at me uncomfortably. "Three hours?" he asks.

I nod and he keeps reading. Jerry is now confused, and asks me to tell him the story of what happened. My tale only makes him more uncomfortable. I can't gauge Jerry. He seems shocked, but I can't tell by what. He maintains a steady weak nod as he asks me about my life in general. Then Jerry starts asking me how I'd react in certain situations. As I answer, I try to inject a little non-threatening humor into the scenarios. But Jerry doesn't laugh. I think Jerry's laughing days were over about thirty years ago and now he's grateful just to get through the day. Jerry puts down the paperwork, "You don't need anger management."

"I do if I want these people off my back," I say.

"This is a place for people with problems," Jerry clucks.

I'm thinking fast because I need to make this happen. "Jerry, I do have a problem. My problem is that I'm going to go on trial for something I didn't do, unless you let me into this program. Please!"

He shakes his head, "You don't belong here. For god's sake, you just said 'please'."

I see two options for myself at this moment. I can get really pissed off and start yelling, hopefully demonstrating to Jerry my uncontrollable rage. Or I can beg. "Jerry, I will get on my knees for you to let me into this program. I have to do three hours here or I go back to facing a mandatory prison sentence for an incident that never occurred. It's the only way to appease the court and get my life back."

"You won't fit in here," Jerry tells me.

"I don't care. I'll do my best to fit in, if that will make you happy. I need this."

Jerry exhales a long, tired sigh. He thinks for a minute. "Okay."

"Thanks, Jerry. I really appreciate it."

"I still don't think this is right." Jerry flips open a book, "I'll put you in Frank's group. Wednesday nights are okay?"

"Excellent!" I reply. Jerry stares at me like I'm some agreeable freak, wondering whether to change his mind. That was way too friendly, I'll have to watch myself around here. If I seem too un-angry, I might get thrown out.

Back in the reception area, Becky is bursting with glee as she explains that it costs sixty bucks to enroll, then twenty-five dollars for each session, so this whole program will cost me a hundred-and-ten bucks. I smile, "Becky, that is totally cool."

"You are SO super-nice!" Becky says, "Wait til the guys in A.M. get a load of you!" I pause uncomfortably, wondering what the hell that means.

The grand search for a civil attorney begins. Tam and I cast a wide hopeful net, asking for referrals from everyone we know. Ian, my tech-whiz buddy, tells me to call his pal Oswald, who just graduated from law school and can't find a job, so I call Oswald but he doesn't seem to know much about our options. Last time I dealt with a lawyer who didn't know what he was doing, that idiot insisted I call Detective Bender again, which was simply courting disaster.

Tam calls Blodg to see if he has a civil lawyer guy, but Blodg can't help us because he's never sued anyone in his life. "He only knows criminal lawyers and divorce lawyers," Tam informs me. "Well, that's our Blodg," I reply.

I call Ken in D.C. and ask him for ideas. Ken's still ranting about the entire Toomey ordeal but I tell him to focus his slobber into helping me find a civil attorney. I remind Ken that his firm has an L.A. office, and he says that he'll see if he can find anyone there to help me.

My Dad calls to inform me that a lawyer pal of his in Philadelphia knows a big-deal civil attorney here in Los Angeles. Dad adds that the guy may be retired since he's over eighty years old, and he gives me the phone number. The old lawyer's name, weirdly enough, is Red Browne.

Then I open the Yellow Pages, where there are forty-eight pages listing thousands of attorneys. Starting with the A's, I begin to compile a list of anyone who looks remotely promising. This instantly grows tedious so I take a break and look into this Red Browne character online. It turns out Ol' Red is quite a legend in legal circles. During his career, Red broke new ground in raising the dollar figures awarded in lawsuits to astronomical heights. In fact, Red's one of the pioneers of this twisted era of the preposterously gargantuan monetary settlement.

I'm already having doubts. My case is not a big deal. And Red Browne helped to create this current, seemingly irreversible, legal trend that has landed our country into a ridiculous state of imbalance. There's a big difference between believing that human life is priceless and deciding that some poor slob deserves half a billion dollars because a doctor made a mistake. Attorneys like Red Browne have thrust this country's legal system into impotent absurdity, rendering dollar figures meaningless and forging a fantasy kingdom of court-rewarded-opulence in which valid claims go unaddressed in hopes of winning the new lawsuit lottery.

Okay, clearly I have some unresolved issues about lawyers like Red Browne. Nonetheless, I call his office and speak with the nice Southern lady who answers the phone. She tells me that due to Red's advanced age, he doesn't come to the office much anymore, but she'll give him the message. In the interest of time, I offer to explain all in a fax. "Why, aren't you clever!" comes the soothing Southern belle's reply, "That would be marvelous!"

I write a letter to Red, politely explaining my predicament, and fax it off. Then I remember Gavin Dodd, that first criminal attorney we met. I bang out a letter to Dodd, in which I re-introduce myself, flatter the hell out of the shiny pitbull, and ask if he knows a civil lawyer who might be interested in taking my case.

Editing the movie gets shoved aside once again as the hunt for a civil attorney balloons into a full-time job. The ads in the phone book ejaculate come-ons like "HAVE YOU BEEN INJURED?!" and "OVER 120 MILLION COLLECTED!" Most of these lawyers deal exclusively in worker's comp and malpractice, but I start to call the names on my list. With each call, I keep imagining the same cluttered fake-wood-paneled office, with a little oscillating fan by an overflowing inbox and some mustached guy with his feet on the desk. If I'm going low-rent, I want the whole works, a genuine old-school L.A. shyster. It's not entirely my fault, the names of these guys really lend themselves to my pulpy scenarios. They've got names like Shanks, Ameche, Smoker, and Gleg. Gleg's ad has a photo of him, and he's even got the right mustache. If he were wearing arm garters, he'd be right out of a Warner Brothers Depression-era flick.

My list is very long, so Tam offers to call some of these lawyers. We argue over who gets to call Gleg, and I let her win. Two hours later, Tam calls back. She's spent a good long time on the phone with Mr. Gleg, telling him the whole story. "Gleg was riveted," Tam tells me, "He loved the story, said he's never heard anything like it."

"Cool! Does he want to meet?" I excitedly ask.

"Well, no," Tam says, "Gleg said we've got an excellent case and we'll probably win, but there isn't enough money in it and we'll never collect."

"Oh," I say, deflated. I had high hopes for Gleg. Maybe it was the mustache. Tam goes on, "But he wished us luck. And here's the best part. Gleg has a brother, who's also a lawyer. They're both partners in the firm."

"You mean?"

"Yes, the firm is actually called Gleg & Gleg."

I'm on the phone all day, calling lawyer after lawyer but each time, it's the same. At first, they claim to be too busy to listen, but then I start telling the story and they're hooked. I spend a long time on the phone with each one, and they're hanging on every detail. They react loudly, often without meaning to, and usually at the same points in the story. Then, when I'm done my tale of woe, they all say exactly the same thing. They declare that in their X years of practicing law, they've never heard anything like what happened to me. They tell me that I've got an excellent case and will most definitely win. Then each one turns down the case, and for the same reason...the money. There's not enough dough in it for them, and I'll never collect a dime from a wackjob like Toomey. They thank me for telling them the story and wish me luck. Repeat this thirty times, and you have my day.

Four days later, I've told the story so many times that I can't stand it anymore. I've been turned down flat by the slimiest ambulance chasers in this city. Yet they all love listening to my disastrous tale.

Ken calls from D.C.. He's told the other lawyers in his firm about my case. "They all say they've never heard of anything like this in-"

"Yeah, I know," I say, cutting him off, "But will any of them help me?"

"Well, no," he says.

"Shit. Why not?"

"They all say you've got a great case, but there's not enough money in it, and you'll never collect."

"How about doing it pro bono? At this point, I'll take charity."

"I already thought of that," Ken tells me, "And they all said no. You're not dramatic enough. For pro bono, they like gross social injustice so they can milk it and look good. Evicted grandmas, amputees, that kind of thing. You don't make the grade for that. Sorry."

The next day, I'm still on the phone, telling my story to lawyer after lawyer and it's grown stupefying in its aggravation. Then a lawyer I left a message for a couple days ago calls me back, a fast-talking fella named Milligan. Like the rest, Milligan tells me that he only has a second to talk, yet is soon sucked into the story. When it's over, he says the same thing as everyone else, begging off and wishing me luck. But then he stops and says, "You know, I think there's somebody who'd take your case."

"Really?!" I jump because, after two hundred calls, this is the first potential bite. Now we're getting somewhere! Milligan says, "He loves cases like this. Tell him I referred you."

Milligan's buddy is a lawyer named Stigman, of Stigman & Stigman. I guess, like Gleg, he's got a brother. I call Mr. Stigman, hoping for the best. As I talk to Stigman, he continually spouts a rapid-fire manic stream of "Uh-huh, uh-huh, uh-huh." I can't tell if the uh-huh's mean that he's agreeing with me, or simply comprehending what I say. However, at the end of the story, Stigman does not beg off from getting involved. Instead, Stigman asks a lot of questions about the case, but all of these questions are about the police. He continues saying "uh-huh" as I provide answers and, before I know it, Stigman is orchestrating an elaborate landmark lawsuit against the police departments of both Santa Monica and Los Angeles.

"Whoa! Sir..." I interrupt him, "I don't want to spend years suing the police for seven-figure sums. I just want to recover my damages. The cops will concoct all their usual sob story excuses and drag this out forever. I want to go after the driver who caused all of this."

"Then why are you calling me?" Stigman says, "I only handle lawsuits against the police."

"Really?" I ask.

"Yes. Didn't Milligan tell you that?"

"No, he didn't. You only sue the police? Exclusively?"

"Yeah," Stigman tells me, "And I think you've got a really strong case. You should pursue it."

I sigh, not liking this idea at all. While I appreciate Stigman's fiery commitment to a thankless specialty, I don't think he's the lawyer for us. Face it, what happened to me with the cops was probably them on a good day. But I need my life back from the incidents of May 7th of last year and Stigman's definitely not the person to do that.

The search for a civil attorney is growing futile. I follow up on my letters and faxes, calling Gavin Dodd and Red Browne. Dodd blows me off completely, but the nice Southern lady in Red Browne's office takes a message and, an hour later, the phone rings.

"Steve, I'm not even going to attempt to pronounce your last name," a creaky old Southern voice asks through the phone.

"Good for you, sir. That's fine. Please just call me Steve." Ol' Red and I get to talking. He thinks my story is interesting and that I have a strong case. I find myself liking Red Browne, despite myself, probably just like all those juries who awarded hugely exaggerated sums to his past clients. As I attempt to keep up with Red's impeccably genteel Southern manners, Red finds himself liking me too. So he decides to help.

Red wonders aloud whom to go after to get the most money. He's already anticipated that the police will lie for each other and cover their tracks. "But that doesn't mean we can't nail 'em," Red laughs. Red considers going after the City of Santa Monica, because it's "a much deeper well to dunk in." Then Red switches tracks drastically, "The problem I see with your situation, is that it's a woman who accused you. You say she hit you with her car?"

"Yes, sir."

"But she won't be in that car when she's up on the witness stand."

"That is true," I say, not following this at all.

"You see, what's happening here is that you got this hot lil' tamale coming in and accusing you of stuff. It won't matter so much that she was in a car and you were on foot when they see her fine tush walking to the bench."

"I'm sorry, what?"

"What's she like?" Red asks.

"She's horrible," I tell him.

"But is she big?" Red inquires, "You know, in the bosom?"

"Huh?"

"How ample is her chest?"

"I didn't really notice."

"And what's her rear like?"

"I...don't know."

"Son, what's the little lady look like? Describe her to me."

"She looks like something you'd pull out of a drain."

"Well, that's something, but when she's all dolled up for court, it'll be a different matter. Remember, this is a guy-on-girl situation and I don't know if the jury's going to swallow it. You say your girlfriend got in on this action?"

"Yes."

"What's she look like? How's her figure?"

I start to describe Tamara, which gets Red very excited. He asks for more details, inquiring about her eyes and what she looks like from behind. "Now that's much more promising! See, a girl-on-girl scene is far more enticing for a jury to get into. Tell me, during the altercation, were the two women close?"

"Yes."

"Mmm, sounds good. How close were they?"

I'm sitting with my hand over my mouth as this octogenarian continues to discuss my civil suit in graphic terms normally used to describe porno flicks. Red's getting breathless and aroused from all the hot girl-on-girl action, and I'm politely trying to get off the phone. Then Red shoots his load, exhaling deeply and informing me, "Well, I'm mostly retired now. I don't know if they told you that."

"Yes, sir."

"But I like your case. It's juicy. I think I know someone who can help you."

Excellent! The old perv is going to hand me down to one of his junior sharks. Red Browne gives me the name of another attorney, but one at a different firm. His name is Alex Gatman and he's in Beverly Hills. I thank Red Browne, hang up, and squirm from having just had phone sex with an eighty-year-old man.

I call Mr. Gatman of Beverly Hills and a shrill woman answers the phone, "Alex Gatman's office!" I give her my friendliest hello and tell her that Red Browne sent me. "We'll get back!" she screams and slams down the phone.

A few minutes later, the phone rings. I answer it and "Who referred you to Mr. Gatman?!" slices through my eardrums.

"Mr. Red Browne referred me."

"Hold!" Their hold button makes a sharp piercing ring. No lame music for this office, just the most annoying sound I've ever heard through a telephone. Soon enough, she's back.

"You said Red Browne?!" she screeches.

"Yes, that's right."

"Please hold!" The skull-shattering tone returns. And then she's back. "How do you know Red Browne?" she shrieks.

"I was referred to Mr. Browne through a family friend," I say, and she yells, "Hold!" As the deafening sound comes back, I pull the receiver away from my ear.

"Mr. Gatman will see you Thursday at five!" She hangs up on me before the word "okay" is out of my mouth. I call Tam and tell her about my hot 'n horny chat with Red Browne and his subsequent referral of this Gatman guy.

"I'm coming!" Tam announces, "I want to see this."

"I think that's smart. If this guy is anything like Red Browne, I'll keep his attention longer if I bring a hot lil' tamale with me."

Another long day on the phone has left me sucked dry, but tonight's the big night! My first, of two, anger management classes! I decide to lie down for a quick power nap before venturing into the jungle of court-ordered social services.

The little girl looks the mutant grinning cat in the eye. "What a strange land this is!" she exclaims, "Everything here is topsy-turvy!" "You mean topsitty-turvitty!" replies the giggling hat, while brain-damaged twins ogle her like a pair of matching pedophiles. "No, I don't mean that," the girl protests, "This place sucks dog dick! I'm sick of the whole fucking lot of you." The freakish creatures all gasp...

and whiskers on kittens...

Fresh Start is in a terrifying state of chaos. I stop dead in the doorway, confronted with a deafening prison riot in the reception area. My hesitation is cut short as I'm pushed forward by more people forcing their way into the raging mob. Explosions of shouting and frenzied laughter erupt around me as I cautiously fight my way to the counter. There's a desperate vibe to this pack, like civilization has collapsed but they refuse to acknowledge it, choosing instead to fill the void with manic small talk and forced mirth.

I'm pressed against the counter that's bending and threatening to crack, where a besieged woman holds out her hand without looking up. Overwhelmed, I don't respond quickly enough. The woman's weary eyes rise to meet mine and she asks with dread, "Are you new?"

"Yes," I inform her, and the woman's shoulders collapse.

"Omigod! Hi!" rings a familiar cheery voice. It's Becky, thank god, who squeaks, "I'll take care of him!" Getting flattened from behind, I yell to Becky over the thunderous crowd, "Thanks!"

"Wait here!" Becky says as she leaves to retrieve my file. When Becky returns, I hand her my enrollment fee of sixty dollars. Becky struggles to stuff the bills into a tiny envelope, that she seals and writes on with a little pencil from a miniature golf course. I give Becky the twenty-five bucks for tonight's session and she forces that into another tiny envelope. All money here goes into these ridiculously small yellow envelopes. I haven't seen anything this low-tech since the milk money was collected in kindergarten.

Becky smiles, "Okay, you're all set!" She hands me a xeroxed set of rules and I make my way into the screaming jungle. I need a place to stand, and notice an empty spot along one wall. Wrangling my way through the pandemonium, I press against the wall, trying not to look nervous. I look at my list of regulations, pretending to have something to do. These rules involve confidentiality, and no physical or verbal threats. There's a rule against "negative/secret contracts with peers." Another rule announces in big capital letters "NO GLAMORIZING ALCOHOL OR DRUGS WHEN SHARING." I look back at this rule, and cringe at the idea of being forced to participate in "SHARING." This is going to be horrible.

Suddenly, on some cue I've missed, half of the crowd starts quickly herding out through a doorway. Confused, I start to follow them. Becky dives onto the counter and grabs my arm. "No, you don't go there! That's Cocaine Anonymous."

"Oh. I thought they seemed a little jumpy."

With a giggle, Becky puts a finger to her mouth to shush me. "You go that way," she says, pointing to another doorway. The reception area is draining fast.

I timidly step into the anger management room, where the air is downright stifling. Fresh Start's trademark stains are everywhere, even on the ceiling. An assortment of damaged, mismatched chairs form a large oval, and on these chairs sits the toughest, meanest sharing circle on the planet. I walk to one empty chair and start to sit down. "THAT'S FRANK'S CHAIR!" comes a roar of eighteen pissed-off voices before my butt has even made contact with the stained cushion. I jump up and say, "Sorry." I quickly look for another place to sit. There's one other empty chair, next to the biggest guy in the room. He's a terrifying shitkicker, with cut-off shorts, giant workboots, and an angry, confused scowl. To the ogre's right is the break in the chairs for the door, and to his left is the only remaining seat. It's clear that nobody wants to sit next to this guy, but I have no choice, so remembering the rule on the list about no threats, I brace myself and walk to the empty chair. I make a casual gesture to inquire if the seat is taken. The frowning giant grunts, and I quickly sit.

We sit in awkward silence. The tough guys' eyes keep darting to empty chair as we wait for Frank. This goes on for about ten minutes. The pained silence is shattered as Becky bursts into the room. Becky's brightening effect on the group is immediate. "Hi guys! Frank is going to be a little late. He had an emergency intervention." The men grumble but stay on their best behavior because it's Becky, the Sweetheart of Murderers' Row. "Don't worry. You're all on the clock starting now and you won't have to stay late." Becky gives us a little wave and hops off, plummeting the room back into excruciating, stuffy silence.

Sitting next to Frank's empty chair is a tall handsome cowboy with long wavy hair, straight off the cover of a western-themed romance novel. This cowboy seems to be the de facto leader of the group in Frank's absence. He also seems to be grinning at me. As I start praying quietly, "Dear god, please let this guy not be looking at me," the cowboy says, "Hey, new guy..."

"Fuck! No!" I scream to myself as I force a smile and say "Hey."

"What's your name?" the handsome cowboy asks.

"Um, Steve," I say, desperately flailing to act casual.

"Hi Steve, I'm Patrick," he says. The entire sharing circle is now staring at me. A shaved-head-and-tattooed demon asks, "How long you got? Year? Year-and-a-half?"

"No. Just...three hours." And the room detonates in a chorus of loud reactions. "Shit, dawg, you must be innocent!" yells a menacing gangbanger.

"Yeah, pretty much." I say uncomfortably.

Patrick gives me a wide smile, "Well, while we're waiting, why don't you tell us what brought you here?" *Where the fuck is the instructor of this class?!* I reply, "Aw, you guys don't want to hear that."

"Yeah we do!" comes the angry group response.

I skittishly grin, "Uh...alright." The shitkickers all lean forward attentively like it's story time. I take a breath. "One Sunday last May, I was crossing the street..." Twenty minutes later, the entire room is glued to my tale. These guys are an eager and involved audience, interjecting loud cries of "No!", "Shit!" and "Dang!" I reach the end of the story with "...and that brings me here."

Patrick stands up. He walks to me, and holds out his hand. "Welcome to our group," he smiles.

"Thanks," I say, shaking his hand. As Patrick returns to his seat, I realize that the frightening colossus at my side is staring down at me, very intensely. I look up at him. "Sounds like some crystal meth bitch to me," he says.

"That's funny," I reply, "That's exactly what I thought."

"You want me to go kick the shit out of her for you?"

"Huh?...No!"

The giant scowls, "Somebody should smack some sense into that whore."

"Um, listen...I appreciate the offer. And you're right, somebody probably should smack some sense into her. But I don't think it should be you. I mean, it looks like you've had one scrape with the law already, but...thanks."

"Yeah, you're probably right." The monster holds out his Godzilla-sized hand, "I'm Erik."

"Steve," I say, shaking his hand. The whole room is gawking at me, looking mildly impressed. I get the feeling this is the first time Erik has shaken anyone's hand there.

Almost an hour into the session, a paunchy black man hurries through the doorway wearing a frayed tweed jacket. I figure this is Frank, because nobody yells when he sits in

Frank's chair. With Frank is a pale, trembling man who lingers in the doorway. "Everyone, this is Howard," Frank says, "We just had a bit of an impromptu session. Howard was wondering if he could sit in on tonight's group."

Patrick speaks for all, "Absolutely, no problem. Hi Howard." Howard just stands there with a hollow, jittery stare. Frank says, "Howard, why don't you have a seat?" Only there isn't a chair for poor Howard, so somebody goes and gets one from the reception area. Disorganized and cranky, Frank starts fumbling in his briefcase. "Are you Steve?" he asks.

"Yeah, hi," I smile and wave.

Frank looks over my paperwork, confused, "Why are you here?"

I shrug, and Frank sighs tiredly, "Let's start with Howard."

Howard begins telling his tale, pausing frequently to exhale anxiously. It seems Howard has a wife and a baby, and a job in an office somewhere. And from what I can tell, earlier today Howard came very close to embarking on a massive ultra-violent killing spree. A few of the guys in the circle ask what Howard did and how long he has to be there. Frank replies that Howard hasn't done anything. "Not yet, anyway," I think to myself. Frank explains that Howard's not there by order of the court. Howard stares blankly ahead, twitching. "But he's trying to get help," I tell myself. Forget it, this guy's a fucking time bomb.

Frank asks Howard if there's anything he'd like to share. With a jerk of his head, Howard says that he'd really just like to listen, if that's okay. So Frank moves on to the regular gang, starting with Patrick, in the chair to his left. Patrick says that he's fine, he's had a good week, and doesn't have a whole lot to report. Frank nods and says, "Good." Frank moves on to the guy on Patrick's left, a pudgy slacker in a concert t-shirt who's name is Evan. Evan's a slob, but he seems harmless. Quite soft, actually.

With his whiny, nasal voice, Evan begins his tale. It seems Evan's troubles center around his ex-girlfriend, whom he beat up badly enough to get arrested and sent here. They have a baby together. Evan kicks off his week by calling his ex-girlfriend and leaving a message on her answering machine, despite the fact that he is legally barred from contacting her.

"Do you think that was a good idea?" Frank asks.

"I dunno," Evan says. Later that day, the ex-girlfriend calls Evan back and leaves a message on his answering machine. When Evan returns her call, she's not home so he leaves her a message. Evan's tale continues as his girlfriend calls again and leaves another message on his answering machine, then he calls her back and leaves her a message. After five more minutes of message-leaving, Evan and his ex-girlfriend manage to actually speak on the phone. They chat about nothing in particular, mostly the ex-girlfriend's job. "I think she was happy to talk to me, I don't know." Evan then launches into a lengthy examination of the perceived tone of the ex-girlfriend's voice.

But Evan's not finished yet. His thrilling yarn continues, when he calls his ex-girlfriend the following night and leaves a message on her answering machine. Then, in an exciting twist, the ex-girlfriend calls back and leaves him a message. By the time Evan is finished with his voicemail saga, we're out of time.

Frank stands, "Okay, we'll pick this up next week. Sorry I was so late." I look at poor Howard, who's staring blankly at the floor. I don't think listening to Evan's adventures with the answering machine helped Howard very much. The stampede for the door begins and Frank notices me, "Oh, right. Steve, we'll get to you next time, if that's okay."

"Sure, that's great," I smile at him.

"Three hours," Frank says in a tone between a question and a statement.

"Yep," I reply. Frank shakes his head, irritated. I shuffle out the door with the rest of the group, leaving Frank to pick up the pieces of Howard, who isn't moving.

With my much-needed first session of anger management therapy behind me, I get back to finding a civil attorney to handle our lawsuit. Tam and I go to meet Alex Gatman, the attorney Red Browne referred us to, on Rodeo Drive in the ghastly, ostentatious heart of Beverly Hills.

I rarely go to Beverly Hills because I find the place unbearable. The horrific denizens of this place have sucked all the fun out of having money. Despite their tasteless bling and six-figure cars, the idol-worshippers of Beverly Hills never seem to be having a good time, which makes me want to yell to these garish, chronically irritated clowns, "If you're so rich, why the hell aren't you happier?!" Nonetheless, I'm here now, sitting with Tam in the tacky reception area of Alex Gatman's office.

An hour and ten minutes later, we're still sitting there, listening to explosive outbursts of shouting from the back and watching harried people rush past. Then Tam and I are led into a conference room with a glass table, glass walls, clear plexiglass chairs and wide windows looking onto the mecca of Beverly Hills. "Why, it's all so transparent," I say to Tam as we sit down. We wait another fifteen minutes for Alex Gatman to appear but he finally does, with his spindly frame in a suit that's obviously expensive but downright ugly. Gatman's in his 50's with curly gray hair and piercing beady ferret eyes. True to Beverly Hills form, he never smiles, opting instead to keep a nauseated sneer plastered on his face. Gatman doesn't acknowledge that he's an hour-and-a-half late so I let it go and say "Thanks for seeing us" with my friendliest smile. Gatman snorts "yeah" and slams his spidery ass into the chair at the head of the glass table.

Tam senses that this guy is an epic asshole, and suspects that my gregarious Hi-I'm-Steve approach will accomplish nothing, so she handles the small talk. Gatman cuts Tam off in the middle of a sentence and shifts his caustic expression to me, "Red Browne sent you?"

"Yes, sir," I say.

"Hmm," Gatman cocks an eyebrow. This guy oozes scorn from every hole, but he seems to have a modicum of respect for Red Browne. Gatman demands to know how I know Ol' Red. I begin to answer when Gatman interrupts me, hissing "Tell me about your case."

While I tell Gatman the story, he looks like he's suffering from a major bout of acid reflux disease. When I reach the end of the story, Gatman clucks, "Give me that," and snatches my file with his knuckly talons. Gatman pores through my legal paper trail, sighing and grunting. Then he starts commenting, saying the word "idiot" over and over. He stops reading and squints at me.

Gatman proclaims that I was an idiot for doing what I did, and he's probably right. But then he tells Tam that she was an idiot for doing what she did. Apparently, in Gatman's world of light and laughter, everyone's an "idiot", as he coughs out a nasty tirade condemning the cops, Detective Bender, the Santa Monica City Attorneys, Phil, and the judge. Then, amazingly, Gatman holds up the sheet from the court which details my initial charges and snorts, "I have no idea what this even is."

I don't how to respond. This guy just accused everyone involved of being an idiot, now he's clenching a court document which is as self-explanatory as anything you're ever going to find in Santa Monica, and announces that he doesn't know what it is. I begin to explain what it is, but Gatman groans with disgust and tosses the paper aside. "You got fucked," Gatman scornfully announces, "I've never seen anything like this. And I think you have a case."

Thinking this may go well after all, I brighten up. "So, do you think you can help us?"

Gatman shakes his head. "There's no money here. We'd have to sue the City of Santa Monica to justify a lawsuit of this size. This idiot doctor doesn't have shit."

"Does the lawsuit have to be that big?" I ask.

Gatman glares at me, "Do you know how much it will cost to depose everyone involved? Do you know how many hours a case like this will take?"

"Not really," I say.

"No, you don't! Idiot," Gatman replies.

Tam jumps in, trying to keep things on track, "It may not take as long, or cost as much, if we keep it on the smaller side. We're not looking for a multi-million dollar settlement."

"You don't know what you're talking about either!" Gatman yells at Tam. And the smile leaves my face for the first time since meeting this prick. It's one thing to talk to me that way, but don't do it to Tam. Gatman notices the look on my face and backs off. He looks down at the papers, pretending to read. Always the trooper, Tam asks Gatman in her most conciliatory tone of voice, "What would you suggest?"

Gatman sighs, "Like I said, I think you were completely screwed and I think you have a strong case. In terms of damages, we'd have to be creative to find money to go after. Now," he points at Tam, "You're okay. You know what the problem with this case is?"

Tam and I both shrug slightly. "What?" I quietly ask.

Gatman thrusts a bony finger at me. "You. How am I supposed to get a jury to give a shit about you? You sit there smiling like some happy stupid asshole after all this happened? And it's your word against a doctor's. Juries like doctors."

"You haven't seen this doctor," I say.

"It doesn't matter. Next to a sickening moron like you, they'll still find for her!"

"I can act like more of a victim if you want." I say, trying to be helpful.

"I doubt that," he spits at me with disgust.

Tam looks at me. We have identical 'How do we get out of this room now?' expressions on our faces. As Gatman keeps ranting, "No sane person is going to believe-" I leap to my feet and interrupt him with a commanding, "Okay! Thank you!"

Gatman looks confused, "I wasn't finished." Walking toward the door, I say to him, "I appreciate your insight and I'll be sure to tell Red Browne how worthwhile this was."

"Wait!" Gatman shouts. I pause as Tam hurries out the door. Gatman comes after me, hands me his business card, and says, "I think your case has potential. Let me know what you decide." I look at him like he's got rabies. "Yeah, keep in touch," I say as I run after Tam. As we flee, Tam pauses to ask the receptionist if they validate for parking, and woman responds with a cynical chuckle. Downstairs in the parking garage, Tam and I learn that we have to fork over twenty-eight bucks apiece to get our cars back.

Driving out of Beverly Hills, I shudder. I feel tainted from my meeting with Gatman. Dealing with these civil attorneys has been a demoralizing experience. They're all dirtbags, only some have more expensive offices. I miss Phil. Maybe he's a part of this same putrid system, but he does it with a certain sincerity which I'm beginning to suspect is extremely rare.

That night with Tam, I try to laugh it off. "Could you believe that guy? He totally hated me."

"Yeah, he did," Tam replies with an ambivalent tone.

"Should I have done something differently?"

"He may have a point. You could seem a little more damaged by the ordeal."

"He called me sickening and said the jury will hate me."

"Well, maybe if you stopped being so goddamned friendly." Tam's definitely pissed off about this.

"Sorry, I just wanted to seem easy to deal with so he'd want to help us. Do you want me to be more of a dick? Would that help?"

"It's just..." Tam mutters, but she doesn't finish the thought.

The next day, I visit Phil. "Then the asshole actually hands me his card and tells me to call him. Stop laughing! I'm completely tubed here."

Phil covers his mouth but continues giggling. "Sorry," he mutters, "That's what a lot of lawyers are like."

"It's been twenty-four hours and I still feel a thick, lingering stain. These days, it seems like people would like me better if I were more of a prick."

"No, they just think they would," Phil says, "If you became more of a prick, they'd say 'God, what happened to you? You used to be such a nice guy.' You can't win there, I'm afraid."

"My civil suit is in the toilet. We've called legions of lawyers and that vulture yesterday is the only one who would even meet with me. It's extra frustrating because every single one of them says I'll win, but I'll never collect a cent. I'm about to concede defeat." Phil looks disappointed, but I continue, "Except for one possibility."

"What's that?" he asks.

"You mentioned something about small claims court."

Phil's eyes light up, "I did!"

"Tell me about it."

"Well, you're limited to five thousand, but Tamara can bring a separate suit for another five."

"But Tam didn't have any monetary damages," I say.

"True. But that might not matter, considering."

"What about this weird-ass 'continuance' of my criminal charges? Will that be a problem?"

"The status of your criminal case should not preclude you from suing Toomey," Phil says with confidence.

"Yeah, well a lot of 'should not' stuff has happened along the way here. I'm sure I'll get screwed somehow. But that's not going to stop me from trying." Phil smiles because the game's back on, which means a minor victory for his hopeful view of the system despite my continual evidence to the contrary. "There's still the collection issue," I say.

"That will be an uphill battle," Phil admits, "But if you get a judgment against Toomey, there are processes to help force her to pay. They can be somewhat devastating, especially for a doctor who deals with malpractice insurance and things like that. And I will gladly help you."

"Cool, thanks."

"My pleasure," Phil grins, "Now, you can't have lawyers in small claims court. I'll guide you through it as much as I can, but when it's time to throw down, you're on your own." Phil chuckles, "Small claims court, huh? I like you, bud. Nothing squashes you for good."

Back home, I inform Tam that both of us are suing Lauren Toomey in small claims court, and she smiles. Like Phil, she seems bolstered by my never-say-die approach. "Screw those scumbag lawyers," Tam says. "I like this idea."

But Tam will stop liking this idea very soon, once she discovers where it's going to lead her.

nice finger...

Just as Tam, Phil and I begin our new, small-claims, plan of attack, I'm slammed with the devastating flu that's been ravaging the nation. Tam and Phil have already been laid flat with this tenacious strain, but my mountain range of stress seems to have shielded me from it. That is, until now, when the virus crashes into my head like a failed Soviet satellite.

I need to shake this flu immediately, so I resort to my emergency-remedy plan. It's time to go on the 'Quil. It's a simple plan, really. Suck down half a bottle of Nyquil, sleep like a corpse for twenty-four hours, and then wake up all better. It's worked in the past, so five shots of Nyquil later, my fingertips are tingling and I'm sinking into a semi-hallucinatory state. I hit the sack and have some of the most disturbing dreams in my long, deranged history.

I wake up, not knowing who I am or where I am, as the sun's going down. I throw myself into the shower to shake my hazy Nyquil cocoon. The flu symptoms seem to be gone. I step out of the shower and see Tam. "I think I'm better," I tell her.

"You had a rough time of it last night," she says, "You were babbling, and drenched in sweat. I got soup for you." Tam tells me about her day while I have some soup, but something she says makes me stop short, "Wait a minute...What day is this?"

"It's Wednesday," she tells me.

"I thought it was Tuesday."

"No, you've been out for two days. That flu really is nasty."

"Shit!" I jump up from the table, "I have anger management tonight."

"Can't you skip it? You're sick."

"I'm better," I tell her.

"Just do it next week," Tam says.

"No, there are penalties for missing class. There are rules about it, but I didn't read them. Damn it, I'm late!" I run out the door, then rush back in to borrow some cash from Tam to pay for the class. Seconds later, I'm in the car, racing to Fresh Start. I'm still woozy from the bottle of Nyquil, and my throat feels scratchy, but I plow forward. The fever is rushing back into my head as I'm parking the car.

I run into the building and up the stairs, then stop dead in the doorway, again confronted with the crazed mob. My symptoms are back with a vengeance, but I am going to get through this. I take a breath and stumble into the crowd. At the counter, Becky gives me a big smile as I pull out my twenty-five dollars and then drop the money to the floor. I suspect that I took way too much Nyquil because I'm seeing double and my hands keep missing the bills. Wobbling, I finally succeed in handing Becky the money and ask, "Is it like a million degrees in here?"

"Yeah, the heater's broken again. We can't turn it down, or off, and we don't have the money to fix it. It's kind of neat, though. It's like summer!"

"Yeah, on Venus maybe," I say as I wipe the gushing sweat from my forehead. I push through the crowd, drowning in my tropical fever. I find a spot on the wall and shove myself against it, trying not to fall over.

We're herded into the anger management room where the empty chair next to Erik the giant is waiting for me. This room is even hotter than the reception area. The anger boys are all complaining about it, and taking off their shirts. If these guys realize that I'm sick, they might kill me for bringing in the flu. Hopefully, they won't notice. Erik nudges me and "Dude, you sick?" So much for faking it. "I'm okay," I say, trying to sound tough. But the crowded room is starting to blur.

Frank rushes in, bitching to himself and looking miserable. "Let's get started," he irritably announces and the circle of sharing begins. Patrick the cowboy tells us he's learned that you have to be careful at all times. "Because your whole life can change in one split second," he observes with a laidback drawl. I like Patrick. He seems to be the second-most-well-adjusted person here, right after me and just before Frank, who's such a surly malcontent he should really talk to someone.

I feel my stomach starting to churn. "Splendid," I think, trying not to swallow as I concentrate on not puking. The healing spotlight moves on to our old pal Evan, the slacker whose waltz with his ex's answering machine continues into its second week. "Well, I left a message for Ren on Thursday. No, wait. Yeah, it was Thursday. Then she left a message-" Frank interrupts, asking Evan point blank if he's seen or spoken to his ex-girlfriend since last Wednesday. Evan says no, then begins to elaborate but Frank cuts him off again, saying that we can continue this next week.

Next up is a heavy-metal mullethead who mumbles so badly that it's hard to understand him, but he's saying something about learning to control himself when he sees a police car. Apparently, this guy vandalized multiple police cars in plain view of the police. I mop the sweat from my face onto my sleeve. The room is starting to melt before my eyes. Frank notices me and asks if I'm okay, which makes me bolt upright with a shot of self-conscious alarm. I tell Frank that I'm fine and he shifts his attention to the next secret-sharer, a sharply dressed pimped-out player who manages hip-hop artists. I can't tell what this guy did to get sent here because his diatribe is so completely bizarre.

The player explains that he keeps himself from acting on his rage because the next time he's arrested, he'll be sent to prison. But it's not the criminal record or loss of freedom that prevents Mr. Slick from exploding in anger. It's this...

"I hate men," he says with a glazed expression, "Groups of men, I hate them. I hate the way they look. I hate the way they smell. I hate lots of men together. The thought of being cooped up with a group of men makes me insane. The way they smell..." The whole room is put off by this guy, even Frank, which is understandable because this player is a major psychopath with problems that run far deeper than his

300

anger. Frank clears his throat, "Okay, well that's good, that's...for now, you're staying on track." The shitkickers seem relieved that the player with "man issues" is finished for the night.

The room seems to be getting even hotter, or my fever's getting worse. My shirt is soaked. I put my hand to my mouth each time I feel like I'm about to vomit, knowing damn well that my hand won't prevent anything if it's really time. The best I can hope for is to direct the spew away from anyone who'll murder me if I throw up on them.

The next person to share is a mild-mannered fellow named Chad who seems oddly gentle for this crowd. I don't know what Chad's in for. I only know that it sounds severe, he doesn't deny doing it, and this was his second strike. At his court date next week, Chad expects to be sentenced to sixty days in jail and he has two big problems. One, he doesn't have enough vacation time to cover his jail sentence and he's going to be fired from his job as the shipping manager at a warehouse. Two, Chad takes care of his brother who has Down's Syndrome and can't get by on his own. Chad has no relatives who can help his brother while he's in prison. I'm disintegrating badly. My eyes stare blankly down at the stained carpet while Chad's story wafts through my Nyquil-and-fever-induced haze. I am profoundly moved by Chad's situation. My mouth is hanging open and I think I'm about to cry. The last thing I hear is Chad describing how much he regrets what he's done, not so much for his sake, but because it affects his handicapped brother who relies on him for everything. That's when I completely zone out.

Some undetermined time later, I realize that a new voice is speaking. I'm annoyed that I don't know what's going to happen to Chad's poor brother while he's in jail. But the path of sharing has jumped the break in the circle allowing for the door, and the voice drifting through my delirium is that of Erik, the scary mountain by my side. Erik is describing something that happened to him last Saturday. People look surprised that Erik is sharing at all. Despite my best efforts to hang on, I find myself relapsing into my sickly coma while Erik's story dimly seeps through.

Erik's tale involves a typical L.A. road rage incident. Somebody switched lanes, the other driver looked at Erik funny, and so on. I can barely hear Erik over the rumbling furnace in my skull. I'm gripping the bottom of my chair, about to topple.

"I can't believe the way that fucking asshole looked at me. I wanted to kill him! I chased him for a while, but I lost him. So I drove around looking for him, and I found the stupid piece of shit in the Ralph's parking lot. I floored it, right up to his car. That pussy was scared shitless. I guess I should've been thinking about the stuff you talk about in here, but I was too pissed off. I threw that asshole against the car, and I was about to kick the shit out of him, when a cop pulled into the lot. So I ran back to my car and took off before the fucking cops could arrest me again."

There is a profound silence. Finally, Frank speaks up. "Okay, um...Does anyone have anything to share, any comments?" The tense silence continues as the whole room gawks wide-eyed at Erik. Without meaning to, words suddenly spill from my woozy head, "Jesus, what the fuck is wrong with you? Why don't you evolve a little?"

The room gasps. Frank blurts out, alarmed, "Okay Steve, we try not to judge people here."

Delirious and half-dead, I keep going, "I'm serious. Think about it. You don't know this guy. Why would you want to know this guy? He's an asshole. Let him go live his asshole life and move on. Think about yourself, man. Think about what's important for you-" At this point Frank leaps from his chair and dives at me, yelling "Stop!"

Frank's shouting in my face snaps me from my sweaty daze. I glance around the room. Everybody's frozen, and Frank looks petrified. I slowly look up at giant in the next chair.

Erik is about to kill me. His eyes bulge with fury as he glares down at me. Frank's about to run from the room to get help. I stammer, "Um...I'm sorry."

Erik clenches his gargantuan fist. But he pauses, thinking. Then he looks ready to kill again. Frank yells for Becky. Then Erik opens his mouth. "You know what?!" he roars. The whole group hangs in the air, waiting for me to respond. I can't breathe but finally yelp, "What?"

"You're absolutely fucking right, dude! Fuck that guy! Who gives a shit about him? I'm gonna remember that! Thanks!"

Frank groans a huge sigh of relief and rubs his face. Erik lifts his giant hand and gives me a friendly slap on the back that sends me tumbling off the chair.

Drained, Frank trudges back to his seat as Erik picks me up with one hand and places me back in my seat. I give him a weak smile and start praying to get the hell out there. Frank apparently feels the same way because he sharply announces, "I think that's enough for tonight. I'm going to let you guys out of here a little early." The whole group excitedly jumps to their feet, including me.

"Hey! Wait!" booms through the room, and we all turn to see Erik still seated.

"Yes, Erik?" Frank asks.

"You haven't gotten to Steve!" he says.

Shaking with irritation, Frank growls "Okay." Everyone sits back down and stares at me. Frank shoots me a look of death and growls, "Steve, how you doin'?"

I shrug, "Um, okay."

"Great! That's all for tonight," Frank stands up and asks, "Steve, can I see you for a minute?"

Wiping more sweat on my sleeve, I stand there as the group shuffles past me. Each one glances over with weird fascination as if seeing someone who's cheated death. Erik pounds my back, "See you around, man!"

Frank's fumbling with my paperwork. "Sorry about that," I say, "I'm kind of fighting something off and I didn't-"

"Just shut up!" Frank shouts, "There's no reason for you to even be here! Except to cause trouble." Frank angrily fills out my forms, ripping through the paper with his pen. I'm dying to know what he's writing because I have to present this at court. I casually take a peek as Frank writes, "Mr. Bevi- has completed 3 hours of anger management. Progress cannot be determined due to the minimal hours." I hope that will do.

Frank shoves that form into my hand and begins the second one. "Thanks," I say and Frank just scowls. I feel terrible, having made this put-upon guy's life even harder. "You know," I say, "I think you're doing an awesome job here."

Frank frowns, "I'm filling out your forms. You don't..." He aborts the thought and keeps writing.

"I'm serious. You're really helping these guys. They listen to you." Frank keeps writing, ignoring me, but I continue, "I know it might not seem like it in the daily grind of this place, but you're making a difference with these people. And I think that's great."

Frank shoves the second form into my hand and says, "You're cured. Get the fuck out of here and don't ever come back."

"Okay," I say, "Thanks."

"And if you've given me the flu, I'm gonna find you! And all the anger management in the world won't help you then! Get out!"

Leaving Fresh Start, I double over and throw up all over the sidewalk. Once home, I stagger into our apartment, leaving a trail of clothes to the bedroom.

"How did it go?" Tam asks.

"Still sick," I blurt out as I drop to the bed and pass out dead.

The goblin armies march over the sand. "When do we eat?" one goblin inquires. "Silence!" his deformed captain yells, "The Troll Queen approaches!" The hideous Queen hisses down at them, showing her crooked scabby middle finger. "Nice finger," the goblin says, unimpressed, and the captain grabs his whip, ready to restore some purpose to the little creatures...

the great curve...

With the flu and Nyquil flushed through my system, I sit with Tam in our favorite hangout, Phil's office. "So what happens in small claims court?" I ask.

"You tell your story," Phil tells me, "Keep it short and simple. That's important in small claims court. They hold it against you if you waste their time."

"Okay, then what?" I ask.

"Then Toomey tells her story and the judge will decide."

"I don't know about this," I sigh.

"What's wrong?" Phil asks.

I reply, "In Santa Monica, people bend the facts to make excuses for Toomey while twisting them to screw me. Why won't it go that way this time?"

Phil gives me his usual patronizing nod, "For one, because this is a different case, to be judged on entirely different criteria. We're no longer debating whether you did something criminal. Now we're questioning whether Toomey's deliberate misstatements to the police cost you a lot of money, and it's very obvious that they did."

"That's assuming they believe Toomey's statements to the police were false."

Phil assures me, "At this point, I don't think that will be much of a problem."

"You know, I've heard shit like that from you before."

Phil says, "This is no time to turn chicken."

"Yeah!" Tam adds, "Especially if you're dragging me with you."

"Face it, I'm going to end up in jail somehow because of this," I say.

"Just don't talk too much," Phil says, "Go file the suit, get your court date, and have her served. Do not serve the papers to Toomey yourself, because that's a violation of the terms of your criminal case."

"So I need to find someone to do that for me?" I ask.

"The Sheriff can do it for you," Phil informs us.

"That sounds good," Tam says with a grin, "Let's do that."

The next morning Tam and I drive to the Santa Monica Courthouse. "Oh, it's been so long since I last saw the place!" I say.

"Let's just get this done," Tam replies.

There's the customary logjam at the courthouse door, where a woman is arguing with Old Sammy the security guard, and refusing to walk through the metal detector. Tam, true to her no-nonsense manner, sees no reason why rest of us can't pass through instead of standing there like cattle, so she casually tosses her bag on the conveyor belt and walks through the metal detector. The metal detector doesn't make a sound, but Sammy has what appears to be a mild stroke. He runs after Tam and pulls her back, "You...you...can't do that! Go back!"

Tam's confused, "Why? I didn't set it off."

"But...she hasn't gone through yet!" He points at the woman who's refusing to go through the metal detector. Annoyed, Tam walks back to where I'm standing in the herd. "I can't believe this," she grumbles.

"Welcome to court," I reply.

I've brought my coveted anger management completion form to bring to Room K. "I'll just drop it off," I tell Tam as I lead her down the shadowy corridor, but the line to Room K stretches so far down the dim hall that it's hard to see where it ends. Tam stares unhappily at the seemingly infinite line outside Room K and asks, "What's in that room?"

I decide to come back and do this later. Now we need to file our small claims suits. I think aloud, "The directory says the

Small Claims Office is in Room 224. Would 224 be before or after K?"

"I'm just following you," Tam says glumly.

"I'm guessing Room 224 is on the second floor." And I'm wrong, it's on the first floor, but we eventually succeed in finding it.

Room 224 is set up like Room K with a three-foot space that leads to a bullet-proof window. There's no line at all, which is a relief. There's also nobody on the other side of the plexiglass, which could be a problem.

"Hello?" I call out. There's no response, so I try again. Then we hear "Berightwithyou!" in a sing-song falsetto with an incredibly thick accent. A young Latino guy pops up in the window like a hand puppet. He's slight and exceedingly friendly, which is rare in this godforsaken place.

"HelloImHernancanIhelpyou?" he says and I don't catch a word of it. "I'm sorry, what?" I ask.

"WhatcanIdoforyou?" he chimes with a big smile but I don't understand one syllable due to his musical tone and extreme accent. However, I decide to proceed simply assuming he said what I expected him to say.

"I need to file a small claims lawsuit. And so does she."

"Ello!" Hernan beams at Tam. Hernan gushes a fountain of words that I'm hoping don't matter, and waves some forms at us. We take the forms and fill them out. I write '$5000 for attorney costs due to false statements to the police.' We hand over our completed forms. Hernan says something incomprehensible but rather pretty, then rushes away. Five minutes go by and Hernan returns with some papers that he starts sliding through the slot. He's speaking the whole time but I have no idea what he's saying. I assume he's explaining these forms to us, but they're reasonably straightforward, basically repeating what we wrote on the first forms. At the bottom, I see our court date.

"Now we have to have Toomey served," Tam says.

"Right." I look to Hernan, "We need to have this woman served with the papers." Hernan responds with a cheerily unintelligible outburst.

"We need the sheriff," Tam tells him.

"Ah!" Hernan exclaims and he continues his rapid-fire speech without missing a beat. The amazing thing about Hernan is that, while I can't make heads or tails of what he's saying, he seems to have absolutely no problem understanding us.

Some minutes later, I'm still asking Hernan where to find the Sheriff. I ask him to draw a map, which he does, with written directions.

Out in the hall, I look at the sketched map with directions. "His writing is infinitely better than his speaking, but I feel kind of bad."

"Why?" Tam asks.

"Because I just made that guy draw us a map showing how to get to the room next door," I say, looking at the door by our side, "I think this is it."

We walk through the door and find ourselves in the County Sheriff's outpost in the Santa Monica Courthouse. An immense mountain of uniformed flesh with a name tag that reads "Tashia" asks if she can help us. I explain that we need to have Toomey served with her court papers and Deputy Tashia informs us that it will cost thirty bucks apiece. Then we jump to the task of filling out a new pile of forms.

Tam stops writing, "Wait, this is Toomey's home address."

"Yeah?"

"I want her served at work," Tam says.

"You do?"

"Hell yeah. Those cops threatened to come to my office. Let's see how she likes it. I want as many people as possible to see this." Deputy Tashia gives Tam a sly smile and says, "That's fine. You know where she works?"

"No," Tam says, deflated.

"I do!" I say, opening my file.

As we write the eye clinic's address on the forms, Deputy Tashia explains the serving process. What the deputies like to do is show up at peoples' homes at five in the morning. They do this on their way to or from work, and they get paid extra for it. Tam hands over a check and Deputy Tashia says it's as good as done. "But how will I know when it's actually done?" I ask.

Deputy Tashia replies that they'll make three attempts, and if they don't find Toomey in person and serve her, we'll have to come back and pay for three more tries. "How many times can I do this?" I ask.

"As many times as you want, honey," she says with a mischievous wink.

Back in the car, Tam is bouncing with glee because, after months of forced passivity, she's finally able to fight back. "That may be the best thirty bucks I've ever spent!" Tam drops me off at home and heads to work. I get in my car and drive right back to the Santa Monica Courthouse, where I take my place in the long line to Room K.

One thing I actually like about interminable lines is that they give you a chance to think. I should be thinking about the latest scenes from the movie that I'm piecing together, but my mind quickly drifts and I see a seedy eye clinic in Hacienda Heights. In thunderous slow motion, the door opens and a burly Sheriff's deputy stomps in. The big guy marches toward the reception area with an attitude announcing he's not taking shit from anybody. But our macho deputy stops dead...when twenty patients with jarring lazy-eyes all turn to look at him. Unnerved by the off-kilter gaze of so many crossed-eyes, Deputy Badass tries to remember why he's there.

The deputy feels those wall-eyes drilling into his back as he approaches the receptionist. "Two good eyes, thank god," he thinks as he puffs up his intimidating posture again. The dyed-blonde ninny frantically hits a button, "I need Dr. Toomey up front ASAP!" The deputy grunts and starts to turn, when he remembers the crossed-eyes behind him, so he fixes his bullying gaze on the door to the examination rooms. The handle starts to turn, the door creaks open and-

"Next!" comes the shattering cry from inside Room K. I hurry into the cramped chamber with walls smothered by lists of rules, and say "Hi" to the obese lady behind the glass. Everyone who works in this building is either too fat or too thin, I think as I slide my anger management completion forms through the slot. The woman glances at them and bellows "Next!"

I leave Room K with a spring in my step. Three days later, Tam and I both receive notification from the Sheriff's office that Lauren Toomey has been served with her court documents. Things are starting to move. I call Phil to tell him that we're in business. "Excellent! When's your court date?" he eagerly asks.

"April 9th," I tell him.

Phil tells me the exciting news about his newest client. A bigshot TV producer got arrested boarding a plane at the Burbank Airport with a carry-on bag crammed with illegal drugs. "Congratulations!" I say, "You think you can get him off?"

"This one's mostly about containing the damage," Phil replies.

Things soon cease to move forward, hitting a snag on March 28th, when Tam and I both receive identical suspicious letters in the mail. They're wrinkled envelopes with our names written in unsteady scribble and no return address, like notes from a terrorist. Fearing anthrax, I tell Tam to put hers down while I cautiously open mine. Inside the envelope is a smudged Xerox of a court form. "It's from Toomey," I tell Tam.

"What's it say?" Tam asks as she rips open her envelope. The blurry documents inform us that our court date has been postponed at the request of Ms. Toomey, for the reason that she will be "in Florida that date."

"She's trying to get out of it," Tam says with scorn.

"Well, I think she just did. But hopefully it's only temporary."

"When's the new date?"

"Doesn't say," I reply, searching the murky form, "But apparently Toomey will be in Florida on the 9th."

The next morning, I call the Small Claims office and get my pal Hernan on the phone. Ten minutes later, I'm still trying to figure out when our new court date is. Finally, I make out something that sounds like 'website' from the melodic stream of nonsense coming through the phone. "Website?" I ask, "You guys have a website where I can find this?"

"Sionlyputinyourcasenumber," Hernan sings, or something close to it, so I go online and find the Santa Monica Court website. I type in my Small Claims Case Number, and up pops a readout in reverse chronological order detailing all the exciting highlights of my case so far. I see the latest entry: **Request for continuance/postponement of defendant Lauren Louise Toomey is granted. Matter continued for Small Claims hearing on the 30th.**

So she did get out of it, but only for another three weeks. I call Phil and tell him about this. "Let her run to the 30th. We'll be there," Phil says. But I'm uneasy. Lauren Toomey is plotting some new sinister stunt. I sit at the editing system, unable to get anything done as dire suspicions chew inside my skull. On the monitor, I see Toomey wheeled into the courtroom in full traction, or pretending to be blind and stumbling to the judge's bench. The authorities have never questioned her malicious lies. They've even assisted her in compounding those lies. This is driving me crazy.

Liz bounds through the door, "Gary's giving a massage and I can't go home until four. Let's hit the Rose." I tell Liz about my nagging fears, "I can't figure out what her new evil scheme is. She might be lying about being in Florida on our court date."

"God, you're such a dope," Liz groans, "Toomey's not going to Florida." Liz grabs the phone, "Where's her office number?" Liz snaps her fingers impatiently as I find the number, and then she calls the Hacienda Heights eye clinic.

"Well, I'd really like to be examined by Dr. Toomey," Liz says into the phone, "I've heard such good things about her. And I need to come in on April 9th." Liz rolls her eyes while the receptionist consults the appointment book. "Do you have anything earlier?" Liz asks, "And this is the 9th, right?" Liz hangs up and gives me a superior look, "There. She's lying. You happy now?"

"No! I am not happy now! What does this mean?"

"It means she's a liar! Which, by the way, is something you've known since the day she attacked you. You can't come to the Rose if you're gonna be that spastic little bunny you become when you're worried about something stupid."

I start pacing around the room, but Liz pulls me toward the door. "Come on," she says, "Let's get coffee and talk about people we hate."

At the Rose, I can't stop trying to figure out Toomey's new plan. Then Liz yells at me, which I deserve, if for no other reason than I forget to tell her that Phil's new client is the TV producer who got busted with illegal drugs at the airport. Finally losing patience, Liz ejects me from the Rose for being a drag.

That evening, I'm pushing a cart down a supermarket aisle as Tam compares soy sauces, and I tell her how Liz proved that Toomey's lying about being in Florida for our court date. "Of course she's lying," Tam says, "Toomey's a liar. That's what liars do."

"But what new lies will she tell this time?" I wonder.

As we carry the groceries into the apartment, I'm still stressing about Toomey's upcoming attack. "If I had some experience with small claims court, I could fight whatever new bullshit she's going to pull. I need that money to pay back everybody."

I put the groceries down and see the red light flashing on the answering machine. I hit the button and whine, "I wish it were like on TV. At least then, I'd have some clue what to expect."

The machine beeps and a voice says, "Hi, my name is Cassandra and I'm a producer on the Judge J- television show. We'd like to talk to you about your upcoming court case..." I stare at the answering machine, speechless. Tam stops putting away groceries. She looks over at the answering machine. "What was that?" she asks.

Suddenly, I realize what's going on. I grab the phone and dial. "Liz, it's me! Very funny, ha-ha. Pick up the goddamn phone!"

Liz stops screening, "Hi!"

"That was cute. I liked that," I say.

"What?"

"Whoever you had call and say they were from the Judge J-Show."

Liz laughs, "Oh, what a great idea! That would've totally fucked with you."

I pause, thinking. "I'll call you back."

"Wait, did somebody really-" I hang up on Liz and play back the message. Tam slowly steps closer as I write down the phone number. "It was Liz, right?" Tam asks, her unblinking eyes growing wide.

I dial the number. Tam hovers nervously by my shoulder, "What did Liz say?" I'm connected to the Judge J-production office. I punch in the extension and get the voicemail for Cassandra the producer. I put down the phone, "Well, that explains it."

"It's a joke, right?" Tam anxiously asks.

"No, it's real."

oracle of the airwaves...

"He kept expecting the street to finally turn toward the Castle. It was only this expectation that kept him going." – Kafka

Tam backs away from the answering machine and drops to the sofa. Looking white as a ghost, she mutters, "I don't want this story to be on TV." Then she recovers, laughing to herself, "That's insane. Why would anyone go on one of those shows?"

I'm frozen, weirded out by the very idea, "I'll call this woman tomorrow and tell her no."

Tam responds with a very loud silence and that's the end of the discussion. The next morning I call Cassandra at the Judge J- Show. She's extremely friendly, but that's only because she doesn't yet realize she's going to get nowhere with me.

"I really think you should come on the show," Cassandra says.

"Not a chance," I tell her, "How did you find us, anyway?"

"It's public information," she tells me, "You're listed on the court docket. And your story sounds interesting. I'd really like to hear about it."

"Listen," I say, "this has been a total nightmare for everyone involved, and I don't want it broadcast on TV. I want it over."

"Fine, forget the show. But I'm intrigued by your case," Cassandra says, trying to draw me in, "Tell me the story."

I chuckle, "Cassandra, I see where you're going with this, and it's not going to work. There's nothing you can say that's going to get me on that show."

"Okay, I got it," she says, "You're not doing the show. But now I'm curious. Just tell me. What happened?"

I sigh, "Oh, alright. One Sunday last May, I was crossing the street..." Fifteen minutes later, Cassandra is hanging on every word, and like everyone, gasping involuntarily at certain points.

"You have to come on the show!" Cassandra shouts.

"No!" I laugh, "I know, this isn't your typical you-didn't-pay-your-share-of-the-phone-bill kind of story, but there's no way. Besides, that's assuming a lot."

"How so?" she asks.

"Even if I did agree to go on your show, which I'm not, how the hell are you going to get Dr. Nutso to go on TV and admit that the first thing she did after taking her medical board exams was run over a pedestrian with her car?"

"That's my problem. You have to do the show! Please!"

"Aw shit. Cassandra, if I'd known it would just make you more insistent, I wouldn't have told you the story."

Cassandra exhales, thinking fast, "Steve, you really should do the show. We can help you."

"Alright, I'm hanging up now."

"Wait! Listen to me. You have an excellent case, and you're probably going to win. But if you do win, there's no way you're ever going to collect. This woman's crazy, and she's never going to pay you!"

"I know," I grumble, "I've been told that by several hundred people already, thanks."

"But that's why you have to come on the show," Cassandra eagerly tells me.

"Why?" I ask, irritated.

"Because if you win here, the show pays you!" Cassandra says, and the planet stops turning. I suddenly can't breathe, and it's not because my hand is over my mouth. I can't believe I just found a way around the settlement-collection issue that seemed insurmountable to every lawyer in Los Angeles County.

"Say that again?"

"If you win on the show, we pay the settlement," Cassandra says, "You won't have to worry about collecting from this woman."

This bit of information is an overwhelming combination of good and bad. I didn't see this coming at all. Shit! What now? Oh hell, it's out of my hands.

"I'm in," I tell her.

"Great! I'm going to call this defendant, and get her to come on the show."

"Wait!" I yell, "It'll never work. There's a problem."

"I'm sure we can figure it out," Cassandra says with a false air of assurance.

"There's no way Tam is ever going to agree to this."

"Who's Tam?" Cassandra asks.

"My girlfriend, the one from the story. She's suing Toomey too, for falsely accusing her of driving the getaway vehicle in the robbery."

"Oh my god, that's amazing!" Cassandra exclaims.

"Shut up! It is not! Tam's never going to do this. Not in a billion years."

"You have to convince her!" Cassandra orders me, "It's the only way you're going to pay back your legal fees. Do you want me to talk to her?"

"No! Let me try."

"Work it out, Steve," Cassandra says, "I think we can help you."

My intestines tangle further as I hang up the phone. "Fuck!" I yell, when Liz barges in. Within seconds, Liz is cackling, "Oh my god, Tam's gonna kill you! She's perfected the art of dodging out of snapshots like no one I've ever seen. She acts like an aborigine who thinks the camera steals your soul. You really think she's gonna go get yelled at on some shithead TV show?"

I decide to make dinner for Tam and ease her into the idea. That night, Tam comes home from work and sees the table set. "This is nice," she remarks as we sit down to eat. "Did you talk to the Judge J- people?" Tam casually asks, and I bring up my conversation with Cassandra. "NO!" Tam yells as she storms away from the table. I run after her, explaining that it's the only way to get around the collection issue.

"I don't care!" Tam yells, "I am not going on TV!"

"I need to pay everyone back, and this looks like the only way I can do it," I frantically plead.

"How do you even know you're going to win?"

"Cassandra said so," I tell her.

"Of course she did! They tell everybody that! They're trying to get you on their show so they can make a jackass of you."

"Maybe..." I say, pausing to ponder that idea, "But we have no choice."

"Yes, we do!" Tam declares, "We can choose not to go on the stupid TV show!"

"Come on, it won't be that bad," I reply uncertainly.

"Yes it will!" she screams, "Oh god, this whole thing has been such a fucking nightmare!"

"Well, it hasn't been fun for me, either." Tam graces me with a fiery look of loathing, and snarls, "Up until now, this has only been horrible. Now you want to make it humiliating, and there's a big difference!"

"I need that money."

"Figure out something else!" Tam yells, "I can't believe you want me to go on TV, so the whole world will know that my sadsack fucking boyfriend got hit by a car and somehow managed to almost get sent to prison for it! No!"

"Please?" I ask.

She doesn't budge, "Why do you think this will work?! For Christ's sake, the real court fucked this up beyond comprehension for months. Do you really think some dumb TV show's going to get it right?! They're not even gonna try! They're just going to make us look like a couple of trailer park bozos arguing on afternoon TV!" Tam's so upset, she's about to cry, "You want me to look like a fool."

"No, I don't. I just...I have to do this."

"Fine, then you do it."

"But you have to come with me," I reluctantly point out.

"Why?!"

"Because you're my witness."

Tam lets loose an animal cry of frustration, then angrily marches out of the apartment with a slam of the door that shakes the walls. I feel terrible. I plunk down on the sofa, wondering if this is the straw that really ruins my life. Tam's been through a lot with this. It never crossed my mind that I could lose her because of the Toomey ordeal, but it suddenly seems very possible. Granted, this hasn't been a very good year for us, and Tam could probably do a lot better than me, especially these days. I don't know how to make this right. I'm never given any decent fucking options.

For me to proceed with my plan, Tam needs to confront one of her deepest irrational fears...being on camera. Even worse, this is being on TV. And this isn't the *'Woo-hoo, look at me! I'm at an awards show!'* kind of being-on-TV. This is the kind of being-on-TV that's just one notch up from having your corpse airlifted from a canyon on the local news. I sit on the sofa for an hour and twenty minutes, wondering where Tam is. I don't move. I'm watching her cell phone in the spot where she left it, next to the regular phone.

Finally, the door opens and Tam quietly returns. "Liz says I should man up and do it."

"That's where you went?"

"Yeah, we had a glass of wine and I calmed down."

"And how's Liz?"

"She was laughing when I got there and laughing when I left."

"You don't have to do this. I don't want you to. It was a stupid idea. But I feel obligated to tell Stu F- about it. After all, it's his money that's not getting paid back. But he won't want us to do it, not when he hears how upset you are."

Thirty minutes later, my jaw is hanging open as Stu F- howls through the phone, "Oh my god, I can't believe you're going on Judge J-!"

"I'm not going on Judge J-," I inform him.

"The hell you're not!"

"Tam seriously doesn't want to do it," I tell him.

"Tough shit!" he laughs.

"I'll find another way to pay you back."

Stu cackles with wicked glee, "I don't care if you ever pay me back, you have to go on Judge J-!"

"Oh shit. To be honest, Stu, this isn't what I thought you'd say."

Stu laughs, "She's gonna scream at you guys on TV, and it'll be the funniest thing ever! You probably won't even win, she'll hate you. And it's totally worth the money."

"Listen, Tam's never going to forgive me if she really has to do this."

"I don't care!" Stu replies, "You owe me five thousand dollars and I say you have to go on Judge J-!"

"Fuck," I hang up the phone.

That night in bed, I'm still trying to convince Tam. "Come on, it won't be that bad," I repeat for the hundredth time. Tam rolls over, refusing to speak.

Tam's stony silence continues in the morning. She goes to work, where she mentions the call from the Judge J- Show to her co-workers, describing it in her most severe, eye-rolling, can-you-believe-my-asshole-boyfriend tone of voice. However, the people in Tam's office think it's the most exciting idea they've heard in a long time, especially Tam's boss. The general opinion by the coffee machine is that Tam should stop being such a spoilsport and help me pay back my legal bills by going on the show. This sentiment snowballs through the company, and soon Judge J- is all anybody can talk about. That afternoon, I get a call from Tam. She simply says, "Fine, I'll do it," and hangs up on me.

While Tam has agreed to go on television, that doesn't mean the problem is solved. Unlike her colleagues, I know firsthand how Tam freezes in front of a camera, with a wide wolfish grin and glazed eyes. It's the only time she ever loses her grip, which is why she overreacted so much to the idea. I'll have to keep an eye on her to see if, at some key moment, she's going to implode.

I call Cassandra to tell her that Tam and I will do the show. Cassandra is elated, but I'm not close to convinced that this is actually going to happen. "Why not?" she asks.

"Because you have to get that lying loon to agree to this."

"I'm working on that," Cassandra assures me.

"You think she'll do it?"

"I'm not sure yet. She says she has to talk to her husband."

"Husband? What husband?" I ask.

"I think she's lying about the husband," Cassandra admits.

"Maybe he's in Florida," I suggest.

"Why's that?" she asks.

"Never mind," I reply, and Cassandra moves forward, "We want you on the show next month. It's turning out to be a little tricky with your criminal charges continued in that vague way." So I offer to call Phil to see if he can help.

"No way!" Phil screams with uncharacteristic abandon, "Judge J-! I love that show!"

"You watch Judge J-?" I ask incredulously.

"Hell, yeah! Get in here!"

Phil is giggling at me across the desk. He is ecstatic, and I am astounded. It turns out the Judge J- Show is a huge hit among Phil's high-powered attorney pals, and his excited colleagues keep sticking their heads in the door to ask, "Is this the guy?"

"Un-fucking-believable," I gripe to Phil, "You know, lots of your clients are big-time celebrities."

"Yeah, but none of them go on Judge J-," Phil replies like a pre-teen girl, "This is the coolest thing ever!"

"You think we'll win?" I ask.

"Who cares about that anymore? You're going on Judge J-!"

"I care! This matters a lot! I need to..." But Phil's not listening. In fact, he's turning red in the face from laughing, so I give up. "I'm sorry, what were you saying?" he asks.

"Nothing," I sigh, "But you'll talk to them?"

"Absolutely! I'll be happy to explain your continuance to them to get you on the show," Phil says, "You really aren't like my other clients." I leave with Phil still giggling. I don't know if I like the way this is turning out. My grueling nightmare is becoming a huge joke for everyone but me. So I go home and call Ken in D.C..

"You're what?!" Ken gasps into the phone, "You can't do that!"

"Why not?" I ask.

"I don't know, you just can't!" he gurgles.

"I'm worried that it will all be decided on what makes the loudest TV episode. That might not go my way. What if they decide to take Toomey's side? All the real authorities bought her insane story for no good reason."

"What do you think's going to happen?!" Ken yells, "They're not running a court, they're running a TV show!"

"But in a real court, I'll never collect," I remind him.

"But here you won't even win! You'll just be exploited for cheesy shock value," he whines.

"I know! But Stu F- says I have to, and I owe him more than I owe you. And now everybody's laughing at me, even my lawyer."

Ken groans, "I can't believe you said yes to this."

For once in my life, I agree with Ken. This is going to be a disaster. My ordeal and my legal debts are going to be reduced to a half-hour of cheap entertainment for shut-ins and the unemployed. All of America will temporarily feel better about their miserable lives while I get screamed at on some dumbass TV show. And Tam's going to hate me for it.

When Tam gets home from work, she's tense but won't acknowledge it. I tell her about my conversation with Cassandra, especially that strange part about Toomey's 'husband'. "What husband?" Tam shoots back.

"That's what I asked."

"She's lying about the husband," Tam says.

"That's what Cassandra thinks too."

"She's right."

"But that's so weird," I say.

Tam glowers at me with contempt, "Why do you have that look on your face? How can you be surprised by this?! Toomey lied about hitting you with her car. She lied about you committing a felony strongarm robbery. She lied about being in Florida for the trial. Everything that's ever come out of her mouth has been a lie, yet you still get bent out of shape every time like it's never happened before! She's lying! She doesn't have a husband." Tam walks into the kitchen, shaking her head with disgust.

The situation takes another toxic twist the next day, when I run into Amy Nextdoor and Dave the Actor outside our building. Amy excitedly tells me that there were deputies knocking on our door at five in the morning. Dave adds that they were there the day before as well. "That's strange," I say, "I didn't hear anything. Did they wake you?"

"No, I was up," Amy replies, "I've started taking yoga at five-thirty."

"But that's insane. Why?" I reply.

"It's the good class," Amy assures me.

"How can it be the good class? It's at five-thirty in the morning," I turn to Dave, "Did they wake you?"

"No, I had a six a.m. call time yesterday. I did a guest spot on *THE PRECINCT* playing a cop who dies of Ebola fever."

"How was it?" I ask.

"Awesome," Dave tells me, "By the end, my face is melting off."

"Did the deputies say what they wanted?" I ask, imagining some new fascist nightmare courtesy of the Santa Monica PD.

"No, they just said hi," Amy tells me. The big loud gears start grinding furiously in my skull. I walk inside and see the red light flashing on the answering machine. I can sense a horrible new piano about to land on my head as I press the button and hear Cassandra urgently instructing me to call.

I get Cassandra on the phone, and she is seriously amped, "Can you come in a week from Thursday?!"

"I thought you said next month. Why the sudden rush?"

"Because your case is so much better now," she says.

"How so?" I ask with dread.

"Oh my god, don't you know?"

"Know what?"

"About the countersuit," Cassandra breathlessly yelps.

"What countersuit?"

"Lauren Toomey is suing you!" she gleefully exclaims.

"What? For what?!"

"Oh, a whole long list of things," Cassandra says.

"Cassandra, I'll call you back." I slam down the phone and rush to the computer. I guess that explains the deputies. I go online to the Santa Monica Court website and call up my case, then stare shocked as I read the latest entry. Lauren Toomey has filed a lawsuit against me, for five thousand dollars, **"Because monetary damages due to assault and**

battery, strongarm robbery, property damage, intentional infliction of emotional."

That last item makes even less sense than the rest of this nonsense. Apparently, Toomey is claiming that I've intentionally inflicted 'emotional' on her. I'm assuming that she forgot the word 'distress' or 'damage', but who knows what Toomey actually intended to say. Either way, that lunatic's emotional damage and distress were both firmly in place long before the day she hit me with her car.

Panicking, I call Phil but he's in court. I ask his assistant to have him call me and, within seconds, my phone rings. "Steve, it's Phil."

"Geez, that was fast."

"You caught me at a break. What's going on with Judge J-?" he eagerly asks. I tell him about Toomey's countersuit. "I'm not at all surprised," Phil replies.

"Why not?!" I ask him.

"Didn't you expect this? Toomey's a lying, vindictive piece of trash. Don't worry about this at all. I think you're good."

"They've pushed us up for the show because of it," I tell him.

"See? There's your silver lining already. I've got to go back in. We'll talk about this later." Phil hangs up.

I call Tam to tell her that I'm being sued. "I can't believe it!" Tam says, "Is she suing me, too?"

"How could she sue you?" I ask.

"I don't know," Tam replies, "I wouldn't put anything past that hemorrhoid."

"Point taken. But no, it didn't say anything about her suing you."

Tam's fired up, big-time. "You know what?" she says.

"What?"

Tam roars, "I have had enough of Lauren Toomey! Let's go on that fucking show!"

"How's next Thursday?"

"Done!" she yells. I get off the phone before Tam has a chance to think about it, then I call Cassandra and inform her that we're on for next Thursday. By the time Tam gets home from work, she seems to have lost some of her afternoon bravado about going on the show. There's an underlying tension that I'm trying to gauge as I cautiously bring up the subject. "So, you're cool with this, right?" I ask.

"I guess," Tam mumbles, staring off at nothing.

Well, so much for gauging Tam's tension. I think for now it's best left under the surface, because I don't know what to do about it. We enjoy a grim, quiet night, until 11:10 when the phone rings. It's Phil, who's still at his office. "You're working late," I say to him.

"This murder trial isn't going very well. And while I'm trying to keep my client from being sentenced to death, I've also just spent the past two hours trying to get you on the Judge J- Show."

"Christ, what now?"

"The producers are concerned about your criminal charges. I've made it clear to them that the charges are as good as dropped, despite the continuance, and I've drafted a document stating that as well. I think this will be enough to convince them, but if not...I may get to discuss this with Judge J- herself."

"You'd love that, wouldn't you?"

"Do you know how cool that would make me look to the other lawyers here?! However, I've made this document sufficiently thorough that it probably won't be necessary for me to speak with Judge J-, as amazing as that would be."

"Does your bigshot TV producer client know how girly you get at the very notion of Judge J-?"

"Steve, it's late. I have a family at home, and a client headed for Death Row. Let me finish. I'm sending you a copy of this thing I just sent the TV show." A few minutes later, the letter comes through. It's written in more of Phil's code, so I give up trying to read it and go to bed.

The next morning at 5:15, I awake to the sound of rapping on the front door. Groggy, I stumble out in my boxers and open the door. Outside, I see three sheriff's deputies with shotguns aimed at me. Then I see Toomey pointing as she yells the order to fire, and the deputies shoot, blowing me back into the living room in a blood-splattered tangle of limbs.

I snap awake and jump out of bed. I rush to the door and throw it open. No deputies, just Dave the Actor walking to his car. I smile and say hi. The clock says 7:45. I look for Lauren Toomey lurking in the shrubs or near the parked cars, but she's not there.

She's hiding inside the TV.

rub the lamp...

As Tam and I inexorably slide toward our televised fate, time passes both slowly and quickly, depending on which is worse at any given moment. A thick throbbing ball of tension grows in the living room, like a giant mutated white blood cell attacking the infection that is currently our lives. Of all the possible scenarios racing through my head, only one is good. The other nine thousand form a scale between disastrous and suicidal.

Blodg pops in, upset because the Screen Actors Guild is "hassling" him about his pension. "God damn it, Troy Donahue warned me about this, those motherfuckers," Blodg gripes. I have no appropriate response to this, so I simply stare at him.

Blodg needs to unearth tapes of some old TV appearances so he can get his full pension. Among other things, Blodg must track down two episodes of *"DEATH VALLEY DAYS"* and footage of his nine-month stint on a forgotten daytime soap opera called *"NEVER TOO YOUNG."* Blodg asks Tam if she'll help him search for these shows. In an effort to reverse her doom-laden state, Tam tells Blodg about the Judge J-Show, but Blodg, being an ever-surprising combination of now and then, has no idea what the Judge J- Show is. "It's a gas your fella got that guest spot but what's up with the court thing?" Blodg asks. After a few more attempts to explain to Blodg that the TV appearance is the lawsuit, I sense Tam's tension skyrocketing out of control and decide to leave the apartment.

Outside, I run into Amy Nextdoor, who's all a-titter. "My yoga instructor had the best idea!" she squeaks, "I'm coming on the show with you!"

"You're what?"

"I'm going to be the witness, and then I can use the footage for my reel!"

"What reel?"

"I'm trying to get into commercials," Amy informs me, "And Ramesh says this is just what I need." I tell Amy that I'll ask Cassandra about it. Word seems to be spreading, because we now start getting phone calls from struggling actors, all eager to lie their way onto the Judge J-Show. "I'll pretend to be a witness or something!" each one says. After the seventh call from a friend-of-a-friend, I start to yell at them to leave me alone. I ask Cassandra about this, and she's not surprised. "People try this all the time," she says, "If you bring your neighbor, Judge J- will throw you off her set."

"She'll know?"

"Yeah, she'll know. There's nothing this Amy person saw that Tamara wasn't there for. Judge J- will say you don't need more than one witness to explain that the cops stormed your apartment. She'll toss you off the show, or rule against you for being a dope, and then I'll get yelled at letting it happen. You're not bringing anybody on the show."

Armed with Cassandra's refusal, I shoot down a few more calls from schmo actors. The phone rings again and I groan. I pick up the phone, ready to yell, when I'm cut short by a booming brassy New York accent, "Oh my god, Steeevie!"

Pulling the receiver away from my ear, I say, "Roz?"

The Layman's Handbook for Those Falsely Accused of Felonies, page 67...A **court observer** *is inexplicably fascinated by the mundane details of the judicial process. Court observers may prove a valuable resource, provided that what they describe is accurate...*

"I can't believe you're going on Judge J-!" Rosalyn B- can only yell. Her quietest whisper is louder than most of us will ever get. Born and raised in Manhattan, Roz is extroverted to a degree noticeable from outer space. She's a pal from college, having lived with me and Ken in a ramshackle off-campus house in an extremely dangerous neighborhood.

Roz, while completely crazy, is now a high-end uptown Manhattan shrink. I haven't seen Roz since Ken's wedding when we got hammered and she told me stories about her patients, including the surgeon who has to say a Hail Mary before he can urinate in a public bathroom and the air traffic controller who would sob uncontrollably in the closet after having sex. Tam was meeting Roz for the first time and she asked, "These are your patients. Should you be telling us this?" Roz loudly responded, "Oh, who cares? They're fucking crazy!"

The Judge J- news is making Roz even louder than usual because it's her favorite show. Roz records the Judge J- Show every day and watches it at night with her stockbroker boyfriend, who also loves it. Roz considers Judge J- her hero. "I love her! I just love her!" she yells loudly enough to render the telephone unnecessary.

"Roz, bring it down a little. You're weirding me out."

"Aren't you psyched?!"

"No, that wouldn't be remotely accurate. I never even watch this show." I pause. Cue lightbulb. "And you do...Oh my god, tell me everything about it!"

"Why don't you just watch it?" Roz asks, "It's the best show ever!"

"I've tried watching since we learned we were going on, but each time, I start gagging. I'm really nervous, Roz. I need this money to pay back my legal debts. And now it's all in the hands of some dopey TV show."

"It's the best show ever, Stevie. Don't you mock it."

"Fine. Tell me what to do."

"Okay," Roz begins, "First off, never and I mean NEVER, talk back to Judge J-."

"Easy enough. Why would I?"

"You wouldn't believe the people who go on this show."

"Oh, beautiful," I mutter, "What else?"

"Never look at the other person. Keep your eyes on Judge J-
at all times, or she'll yell at you. And you don't want that.
Never talk to the other person directly and NEVER interrupt
the other person. Keep everything you say very brief. Don't
talk for more than a few seconds or she'll yell at you to shut
up. Let her ask the questions. Remember, it's her court."

"When did you turn into this weird TV groupie?"

"This isn't TV, it's Judge J-. Remember, Judge J- is a real
judge, a tough judge from New York. She's like me..." Roz
trails off, "God, you know, you're way too nice for this
show. She's going to rip you to shreds."

"Don't tell me that!" I yell.

"You know what really matters? You've got to make Chuck
the Bailiff like you."

"Who?"

"Her bailiff, Chuck. If Chuck likes you, you'll win. That's
how it always goes down. If he takes something from you to
give to the judge, be sure to thank him really loudly."

"What happens if he doesn't like me?" I ask.

"Then you're fucked," Roz tells me, "The people Chuck likes
are the ones who win."

"What the hell kind of court is this?"

"It's a real court!" Roz yells, "I've been to court, I know."

"It doesn't sound like a real court."

"Just roll with it, Stevie. If it all blows up in your face, at least you'll have a good story to tell."

"No, you'll have a good story to tell. I'll be screwed, and humiliated."

"I can't wait!" Roz laughs the same laugh that seems to come from everyone these days, only more ear-splitting.

Roz calls five more times that day, bursting with excitement. She tells me that all she's been discussing with her patients is my upcoming doom on the Judge J- Show. I ask Roz if that's fair since they're paying her to listen to their problems. "Aw hell, they're all so miserable," she says, "It's a nice distraction for them."

Tomorrow is the big day and Tam has stopped speaking, to me and everyone. She now exists in another dimension of terror-stricken detachment. The phone is ringing non-stop, and I've stopped answering it. At 4:30 in the afternoon, I hear Cassandra leaving a message on the machine. She sounds upset so I pick up the receiver. "We have a big problem," Cassandra says, "The show's off. Toomey pulled out."

"Why?" I ask.

Cassandra sighs, "She says her husband won't let her."

"Christ, not the 'husband' again. Who is she kidding?"

"I don't know," Cassandra says, "I'm very annoyed. She said that she'd do it."

"Wow. So that's it? We're done?"

"Looks that way," Cassandra glumly replies, "I'll give it another shot later. But for now, the whole thing's off."

So that's that. We're not going on Judge J- after all. I call Tam and tell her the news. After a quick tirade about the 'husband', Tam announces, "Fine! We'll get her in a real court and win there."

I call Phil to let him know. "Oh no!" Phil sounds heartbroken, "It's not that stupid continuance again, is it? Because I'll talk to them."

"It's not that. Toomey bailed," I tell him, "She says her husband won't let her do it."

"What husband?" Phil replies.

"That's what everybody asks."

"She's lying about the husband," Phil says.

"Who the hell would lie about a husband? That takes this to a new level of bizarre, don't you think? I need to get this case back into an actual court, the kind without commercials."

"Right," Phil says, "We'll talk about it later. Hold on to that document I wrote the show. You may need it."

When Tamara gets home, she seems relieved on an almost molecular level. She asks if I'm upset about the show being off, but I'm so confused by this point, I don't know what I think anymore.

At 11:20 that night, Tam and I are in bed, fornicating our little heads off, when the phone rings. The machine picks up and Cassandra's voice echoes through the apartment, "Steve, you're back on! I need both of you here at ten tomorrow! And I need you to call me and let me know that you got this message. I'll be here late. Call me!"

Tam immediately stiffens. I get out of bed and go to the phone where, naked and confused, I call Cassandra's office. "What happened?" I ask.

"Don't worry about that," Cassandra replies, "I'll see you in the morning, right?"

"Sure," I say. I hang up and go back to bed, where Tamara clutches the sheets, staring up like the ceiling's holding a gun on her. "It'll be okay," I tell Tam as I climb into bed, but rigor mortis has already set in.

The sickly writer sits in his beach chair. His portable TV is tuned in to the Execution Channel and a parade of ritual state-sanctioned termination flashes before his eyes. "There really is a cable channel for everything," he thinks, glued with sly wonder at the hanging-gas-electric-guillotine programming. So amused is the writer under his dark umbrella that he doesn't notice the towering tsunami crashing towards shore, about to destroy all...

I wake up sweaty and the phone's ringing. I've writhed through this torturous night, plagued by alarming dreams and then by the phone, which has been clanging off the hook since about five. There are over twenty messages on the machine. The first six are all from Rosalyn B-. After that, the messages are mostly from Rosalyn, with other people squeezing in to wish us luck. I ignore them all and head for the shower. Then I start to wonder if any of those messages are from Cassandra, so I let them play out, half-listening while I make coffee.

With no new updates from the show, Tam and I drive to Hollywood to find the studio from which Judge J-commands all. Tense and pale, Tam is so quiet, it's unnerving. Tam has a wide range of emotional states, but 'quiet' is not one of them. We park in the lot across the street, as instructed, and then check in with the security guard at the gate. A short, sturdy young woman with a headset runs forward to meet us. "Are you Cassandra?" I ask.

"No, I'm Leah. Come with me!" she urgently barks as she hurries away. We struggle to keep up with Leah who, like a little ram with a clipboard, plows through people and then into a building. Leah pauses in the doorway just long enough to bleat, "Hurry up!" Scrambling in her wake, we trot after Leah through a maze of corridors, up some stairs, around a corner and into a sudden dense throng of people. Shouting and shoving her way through the crowd, Leah grabs us and pulls us through.

The next stretch of hallway is completely deserted, then we hit another jammed section. I'm already starting to panic. Leah stops short, throws open a door and shouts, "In here!" Tam and I step inside the room, and Leah slams the door shut behind us. Confused, I turn back and open the door, but Leah is gone. "SHUT THE DOOR!" a deep voice yells from outside.

"They want that door closed, baby. Every time we open it, that man yells at us." Tam and I look at each other, then turn to face the room. The room is deep and wide, with a few scattered people in it. Is this the mythical 'green room'? It is vaguely green, but I think that's just what the white paint faded into. In one corner, there's a rail-thin blonde woman with a big Bubba guy in a Harley-Davidson muscle shirt. Hovering by a long folding table are three boisterous black women, who are laughing and rehearsing insults for some good-for-nothing man. While the white couple is dressed for a tractor pull, these women are done up to hit the town. Tam and I timidly sit down on the edge of a sofa. I'm nervous, but Tam is beginning to seize up dangerously.

I see coffee on the long table and ask Tamara if she wants some. She doesn't respond, which I take as a "yes". I walk to the table, where the three loud black women say hi. I get some coffee for Tam and return to the sofa. Still silent, Tam drinks her coffee like a half-charged robot, which makes me more nervous, so I wander to the door and open it a crack. "GET BACK IN THERE!" a huge man roars. I jump to the ceiling, then quietly explain that I need a bathroom. The guard scowls and points.

I spend my time at the urinal trying to figure out how we can escape from this place. There are no windows, the exits are guarded, and I've lost all bearings on where we are in relation to the car. But I'm having trouble breathing and I need to get the hell away from here. Washing my hands, I notice a strange grin on my reflection's face that I'm pretty certain is not on my face. "This is it," my reflection says.

"What?" I ask the me in the mirror.

"The point where you finally totally fucking lose it." My reflection laughs, and I feel myself leaving my own body. Pulling away, I see both of me, but only one's laughing.

"No!" I shout at my sinister reflected self.

"Looking a little tenuous," my reflection taunts with a sneer.

"Fuck you!" I yell. I'm watching myself from a point above that continues drifting further away. I slam my fist down on the sink, "I've been attacked and bullied and slandered and kicked around, and it all stops now!"

"You think?" my reflection chuckles. There's violent pounding on the door. The doorknob starts shaking, and I hear the guard yelling outside. I look back to the mirror, "Okay, honestly, I don't know. But I sure as fucking hell hope so."

"Unlock this door now!" the voice outside bellows. I'm sucked back into myself. I unlock the door and the big guard shoves it open. He looks around the bathroom, suspicious, and asks, "Who else is in here?" I shake my head like I have no idea what he means.

The guard escorts me back to the holding room. As we reach the door, my insides are tightening up. I step into the room and see Tam with a wolfen grimace on her face, tightly perched on the edge of the sofa. The blonde Southern woman is talking to her, "You look just like that actress, what's her name? You know, the one on that show about the slutty girls in New York City." Tam unwittingly crushes her coffee cup and the remaining coffee dribbles on her knees. Tam makes a gurgling noise, and her breathing grows panicked.

"Oh honey, it's just coffee, I'll help you with it," the Southern woman says.

I lunge forward, "I'll get that!" Grabbing some napkins, I wipe the coffee off Tam's skirt and try to talk her out of her autistic coma, and the blonde woman retreats, looking concerned. Tam snatches the napkins from my hand and shoves me away, still not speaking. The black women are getting even louder with their exaggerated insults for this bastard who three-timed them all. I look at them, thinking, "Weren't you warned not to do that? Didn't Rosalyn B- find out you were going on the show and call you a thousand times?" I urgently grab Tam's shoulders, "Are you going to be alright?!"

"I don't know!" she snaps, and I don't press any further. We sit there for another two hours, periodically looking over at the door, hoping to make something happen. The minutes pass like centuries of infinite discomfort, and I'm worried that Tam is going to be permanently scarred from this. She's not responding when I talk to her, so I stop trying. I'm in a deep lonely hole.

Finally, the door opens and two people charge in, but they're not here for us. They want the Southern people. They go over a pile of paperwork while discussing children and various drug charges. I have no idea what the Southern couple's case is about, but it sounds pretty drastic. The fun black women, on the other hand, seem to have a case that only involves who called whom a bitch, and this dude they all had a turn with before he stepped out with their cash. But the Southern couple seems so fired up to be here, despite the custody battle and drug arrests, that it makes me wonder. Their case sounds horrible, let alone having it decided on TV...but maybe that's it. Maybe the excitement of being on the show makes the crashing reality of their dire situation manageable.

I look at Tam, who may have actually passed away at some point in the last half-hour. She's not blinking, and I'm not entirely sure she's breathing. Perhaps we're approaching this thing all wrong. Maybe the Southern folks are right and the fact that we get to be on TV makes this whole awful experience worthwhile. Whoa! That didn't work. The very thought of rationalizing it that way just made me dry heave. Let's not try that again. Instead, let's just get it over with. We're now shifting into the gear marked 'I' for 'Ignore'.

We wait more. There's no clock in this room, just a lot of half-eaten doughnuts lying on a table. I try to position myself so I can see the time on Tamara's watch without having to ask her, but she senses something every time and shifts uncomfortably, so I stop. I try to gauge the time by comparing the increasing amount of casual litter scattered through the room. I finally decide that it doesn't matter what time it is. There's no universe outside these dingy walls. For all practical purposes, time has stopped. It's like being dead and waiting for something eternal to kick in.

The door bursts open and people run into the room. An attractive black woman yells behind her, "There's no way she's going on camera with those sunglasses!" Walking closer, the woman sees me and smiles, "Are you Steve?" I give her a weak half-smile. "I'm Cassandra," she says. I shake her hand and say hi. A nondescript man in pleated khakis steps forward and laughs, "This is the guy?" Cassandra shrugs, "Yep." Confused, I shake the man's hand and he says, "I'm Jeffrey."

Cassandra and Jeffrey look at each other and chuckle. Cassandra says, "Sorry to keep you waiting so long, but we've been dealing with..." She trails off and Jeffrey changes the subject, "This is Karen, she's from Legal." Karen comes forward and slams a stack of paperwork onto the coffee table. Cassandra leans over to guide me through it, mumbling, "And hopefully this will go a little more smoothly..."

"A little more smoothly than what?!" I yelp, my voice cracking. Cassandra and Jeffrey look at each other, grinning. "Nothing," she replies.

I point at Tam and announce, "She is scared out of her head right now and all this mysterious smiling shit is not helping!" Cassandra looks suddenly embarrassed, "Oh my god, you must be Tamara. I am so sorry. I'm Cassandra."

Tamara just stares at them, so I poke her with my elbow and plead, "Come on, snap out of it. I'm dying here!" Tam takes Cassandra's hand and mumbles, "Hi." I sigh. This is exhausting, and we haven't even started yet.

Cassandra steps back, hoping to start over, "Listen, there is absolutely nothing for you to worry about. You guys are great..." I stare at her as if she's speaking in tongues. "Really," she says, trying to bring me around. Karen from Legal snaps, "Can we do this now?! There isn't much time!"

I look down at the field of paperwork. Cassandra says "Steve, we need you and Tamara to sign all of these." Nodding, I look at Tam. "You okay?" I ask. "Fine!" Tam snarls. I begin to read the forms, but I get to the third line of the first page and stop immediately. "This is wrong," I say.

"What?" they all ask at once.

"You have this wrong," I repeat, "The woman I'm suing is named Toomey. This says Bennett." Karen from Legal groans with disgust. "Bennett is the name she's using," Cassandra reluctantly explains.

"What?" I ask.

"Just sign it!" Karen barks at me.

"She's insisting on using that name," Cassandra informs me.

"Hold it," I say, "Why does she get to use a fake name? Toomey's her name on all these other court documents."

"She can call herself anything she wants to," Cassandra says, "It doesn't matter. It's still her."

"Fuck that!" I yell, "She was Toomey when she hit me with her car. She was Toomey when she lied to the police. She can be Toomey when she's on TV!" All three groan this time.

Cassandra sighs, "It's the only way she'll go on the show. Just let her have her way. It's still legally binding, no matter what name she uses. We just went through this for hours."

"With who?!" I angrily ask, the implications not yet sinking in. But nobody answers that question, so I continue, "I don't like this." Jonathan and Karen moan again, but Cassandra doesn't. "Why not?" she asks.

"Because you're already bending the rules for her, which is exactly how this whole mess happened. She hits me with her car but that's okay because she yells about it. Then I have to go to court charged with crimes that never occurred because she's screaming louder and they're trying to make the hateful bitch happy. This is bullshit, and I don't know if I trust you."

"Sign the papers or you're not going on the show!" Karen shrieks.

Cassandra turns to her with a commanding tone, "Karen, would you let me handle this, please?" Karen angrily stomps away, but stops too near the laughing black women, gets uncomfortable and then moves again to a spot by the wall.

Cassandra plunks down next to me. "I'm sorry," she says tiredly, "It's been a really long morning." And then it hits me. I suddenly realize what's been happening. They've been going through all of this with Toomey! And they're clearly damaged from the experience. But it finally sinks in, that Lauren Toomey is here! Probably just in the next room. My god! She's really here! I'm about to be reunited with that festering monster for the first time since she capriciously decided to make my life a living hell a year ago. "Yeah," I say to Cassandra, "I've had my share of long mornings too."

Cassandra looks grateful that somebody understands what she's been going through, someone who knows the mind-bending agony of dealing with Toomey. Cassandra pats my hand as we tacitly bond over the universal plague named Lauren Toomey. "I'm really not comfortable with this," I tell her.

"Honestly, it won't matter. It makes no difference what name she uses here. Legally, it's all the same."

"Where did Toomey pull this other name from?"

"She says that..." Cassandra stops, stifling a giggle.

"What?" I ask.

"She says it's her married name." Cassandra and I both bust up laughing. I hear something, and turn to see Tamara laughing too. "God, she's crazy," Tam laughs. Excellent, Tam's back!

I ask Cassandra, "Wait, is the 'husband' here? Have you actually seen him?!"

"We shouldn't be talking about this," she replies.

"What does that mean?" I ask.

"Let's get through the paperwork," Cassandra says, "They're almost ready for you."

At the words "ready for you," I hear a slight gasp come from Tam. I turn to Tam and say, "You know, for better or worse, I don't think you have as much to worry about as I do." Tam blesses me with a murderous glare, and Karen from Legal screams at me, "I need those signed now or you can't go on!"

"Please sign them, Steve," Cassandra pleads, "We're really behind. Toomey took a lot longer than we expected."

"I'm not going to let you bend the rules, just so that horrible shrew gets her nasty way again." Cassandra looks at me with eyes of quiet desperation. I find myself wondering how long she's been with this show, and how much today means to her. "It will be fine," Cassandra says, "Trust me."

I take a breath, "Okay. Let's do it." Then it's sign here, sign there, initial this, and that, first me then Tam and then we're done. Cassandra scoops up all the paperwork and hands it off to Karen, who grunts and dashes to the door. Cassandra grins, "We'll be right back for you! You guys ready?!"

"Sure," I tell her, but I don't think anybody's listening anymore as Cassandra and Jeffrey run out of the room. I turn to Tam, "I think Cassandra seems nice." Tam takes my hand and clutches it like steel.

An hour later, we're still sitting in this room, dying a thousand ready-to-be-televised deaths. My mood has swung up and down so many times by now that I'm entirely drained. I no longer care what happens on this stupid show, but I force myself to stay alert because somewhere in this building is Lauren Toomey, the source of all evil in the universe. I can feel her monstrous presence. I'll bet she's bitching at someone right now.

At last, the door flies open and Cassandra yells, "Okay, let's go!" Cassandra and Jeffrey frantically lead us through more empty and crowded hallways. They seem almost panicked. Hurrying to keep up, I want to ask what the big rush is since we've been ready for hours, but I have a feeling that this is the way it always is here, and that there's no actual reason for it. We march through more people until we come to a door. "Wait here!" Cassandra yells, like there might be armed guerillas around the next corner. She ducks inside the door, and we wait. Cassandra pops back out and urgently commands, "Now! Hurry!"

Nervous, Tam and I run into the room where we see two women, two chairs and a big mirror. "Oh, it's just makeup," Tam says, relieved. "I had no idea makeup could be so dangerous," I whisper when the two women yell, "Let's go!"

Tam and I jump into the chairs. One woman starts applying makeup to Tam, while the other one sits by my side, reading a magazine. After five minutes, Tam looks great and the woman tells her that she can go. "Am I okay?" I ask. The woman with the magazine glances at me and shrugs. Cassandra appears in the doorway, "You ready?!"

Tam and I head out the door. Cassandra leads us into the dark, cavernous soundstage, crowded with towers of sinister clutter. "Careful!" Cassandra shouts. What are these people so afraid of? What fiend lurks in this shadowy soundstage? Granted, there's Toomey, but that can't be it, she's never been here before. Cassandra stuffs us into a cramped triangular closet formed of black cloth and tells us to wait. Tam and I are pressed together, face-to-face, in the tiny dark space.

A hunched elderly black man appears with some wireless microphones for us. He's very sweet, with a deep raspy voice and an air of serene wisdom, sort of like Scatman Crothers in *THE SHINING*. "Any advice, bud?" I ask as the old guy works his hands up my shirt. "Don't you worry about a thing. You'll be fine," he smiles. I don't believe him. I don't have time to believe him, because I'm busy being overcome with panic as I hear them coming for us.

Cassandra and Jeffrey cram themselves into the tiny holding pen with us. The kindly sound man excuses himself and squeezes his way out. Cassandra and Jeffrey both ask us rapid-fire questions at the same time. They ask if we've remembered all of our materials. I show them my folder full of court documents, and they ask if they can see it. Both of them reach for the file at the same time and it falls to the floor, spilling my legal papers everywhere. I gasp and drop to my knees, frantically sweeping them back into the folder. "That's great, we have to go now!" Cassandra orders as they lead us into the darkness. I stop, not caring that they're getting away from us, because Tam is starting to hyperventilate. With a fit of desperate determination, I grab Tam and turn her to face me. "Alright, I know you're dying, and I know this is horrible, but we need this! We really need this, so I can pay off my legal debts and we can finally be done with this ratfucking nightmare!"

Tam takes a terrified breath, "You're right. Let's do it."

"Okay," I gasp as I hear Cassandra shout, "COME ON!"

here she comes...

"It is only our concept of time that makes us call the Last Judgment by that name." – Kafka

Cassandra pulls back a black curtain and we rush headlong into the blinding lights. Tam and I stop, adjusting our eyes. It looks like a courtroom, just not a real courtroom. It's more like a courtroom in a high school performing a musical that's set in a courtroom. Cassandra and Jeffrey are gone, but two men appear behind us and escort Tamara up the aisle, instructing me to wait.

A thunderous voice echoes through the studio, "Plaintiff!" I nervously look around for the source of the voice, but I can't find it. "Plaintiff!" the voice booms again.

"Yes?" I ask, still not knowing where to look.

The booming voice instructs me that, when signaled, I must walk up the aisle and through the gates, then move to the table on the right, where I need to stand at the piece of green tape on the edge of the table. I reply with a weak "Okay." Then the voice goes away, and I stand awkwardly.

"Lauren Toomey must be here!" slams through my brain, and I go on full alert, anxiously looking for her. The seats in the audience are full and there's a hunched figure standing against the side wall, but I can't find Toomey. I decide to see if I can locate which person in this crowd might be the 'husband'. I notice one audience member glaring at me, making an effort to look mean and threatening. He's a fat, middle-aged freak with a greasy, gray ponytail and a walrus-style mustache. My god, could that be the 'husband'? That guy looks demented enough to marry Lauren Toomey. So I counter his menacing stare with my best I-see-you-and-I'm-going-to-remember-what-you-look-like-asshole look, which seems to scare the crap out of him. The man jolts in his seat and spins to face front. But I cannot see Toomey anywhere on this stage.

I see spastic production assistants waving me forward, but I hesitate. So this is it. At last, a trial...of sorts. My legal debacle is now officially in the clutches of the hanging judge of syndicated TV. I feel my spleen making a break for it as I start to walk down the aisle.

I head through the tiny gates to my appointed piece of tape. Chuck the Bailiff enters and orders us to raise our right hands. As Chuck leads us in swearing to tell the truth, I realize that Toomey absolutely must be there. I look to the table at my left. That hunched woman from the wall is standing there, but that's not Toomey. It doesn't look anything like her. Oh my god, there's been a horrible mistake. I'm at the wrong trial!

I open my mouth to prevent this from going any further, when I look back at the other table and freeze. Chuck the Bailiff instructs the hunched woman to take off her big black sunglasses and...it's Toomey! She's not just using a false name, she's wearing a cheap disguise! Toomey is wearing huge silly wig and buckets of garish makeup, along with a lumpy sackcloth dress that looks like she stitched together in the car on the way here. Apart from her trademark scowl, this Lauren Toomey bears no resemblance to the frizzy-haired, blotchy-skinned maniac from last May. Now she looks like Patty Hearst about to rob a bank.

Trapped next to this bizarre disguised creature, a convulsive chill rumbles down my spine. The stage lights catch the psychotic glint in Toomey's pupils, and I truly feel the difference between casual crazy, as in an offhanded comment during conversation, and genuine to-the-scariest-fucking-depths insanity. I suddenly realize that I've been underestimating this all along, and that odds do exist that Toomey could leap from the bushes one night with a kitchen knife. She is as profoundly cracked as anyone I've ever seen. And here I am, stuck next to her, going before an irascible judge on a televised faux court. As situations go, this is unimprovable.

"All rise!" orders Chuck the Bailiff. The door to the Judge's 'chambers', or dressing room, swings open. Everybody stands as Judge J- marches onto the set. The first impression you get when you see this pillar of televised justice is that she's really, really tiny. However, all thoughts regarding her size are swept away by the fact that Judge J- is staring at me like she wants to kill me. I tell myself that it's not true. Then I glance around and realize that it is true, her despising eyes are fixed straight at my head. Oh fuck, I don't think this was a good idea. I can't believe I got talked into this. I want to go home.

The Judge climbs to the top of her judicial throne, and introduces the case she's about to adjudicate as an "unfortunate incident". She still won't take her fiery eyes off me, and I feel the contents of my stomach beginning to rise up for their big surprise appearance on the set of The Judge J- Show.

"Mr. Bevilacqua," the Judge snarls. Unlike any judge in any genuine court I've experienced, this judge is actually capable of pronouncing my name with no effort, yet she infuses it with oceans of dripping scorn. I wish she'd stop staring at me like that. She hasn't looked at Toomey at all. I don't want to be here.

The Judge growls that the Santa Monica Court ordered me to attend three hours of anger management, stay away from the victim, and obey all laws known to man. I'm looking extremely guilty and this isn't good. The Judge starts commanding me to produce documents, one after another. I rifle through my folder while she shouts "Hurry up!" I hand over one document after another, until there's one I can't find. It's not in the file! Shit, where is it?! It's back on the floor where all my papers spilled. I glance back, wondering if I can dash back to look for it. The Judge yells, demanding the document again. I cover my mouth and look up at her, terrified.

And then, Judge J- starts screaming. 'Screaming' is a polite word for it, actually. Her screams come from the most constipated bowels of hell, damning me to eat shit for eternity. The Judge screams about everything...my paperwork, the way I'm standing, the way I look, the way I seem, and my general presence. I'm paralyzed with fear, with my mouth hanging open. Out of the corner of my eye, I see Toomey smiling wickedly, and holding a copy of the court document that I've lost. "I have it, Your Honor!" she says, thrusting it forward. The Judge smiles at Toomey and calmly says "Thank you." They seem to share a bonding moment. Then the Judge flashes her sulphurous stare back on me and continues screaming. The Judge seems to take offense at my very existence. I don't know what to do, or how to react. The last thing I remember is the Judge shrieking about the way I'm looking at her as she roars, "You think I'm not a REAL JUDGE?!!!"

The room starts to spin. All I hear now is my own voice yelling inside my head, "I knew this wasn't a good idea...Oh my god, I'M FUCKING GOING DOWN ON TV!"

I have no idea what I'm saying anymore. I'm simply babbling in a kind of castrated Morse Code, "No, Ma'am, sorry, Ma'am, no..." Finally, I blurt out over the Judge's gusher of damnation, "Ma'am, I don't understand, but I am extremely sorry and I apologize!"

The Judge suddenly stops screaming. She sits back, keeping her fierce look of loathing fixed on me. I think I'm about to cry. The Judge shifts her glance away from me for one darting second, over at Toomey. I glance over too, and see Toomey grinning like a demonic cat. The Judge announces to both of us, "I want to see everything! All police reports and court documents! Now!" Judge J- looks surprised at the amount of paper handed up to her, which she derisively refers to as "voluminous".

We wait while the Judge reads. We stand there for a good fifteen minutes, as Toomey gloats and I try not to wet my pants. The Judge reviews everything, quickly and thoroughly. I don't know what to make of this because Judge J- is the only court-related person, in all these months, to have any interest in reading the police reports. But still, her only reaction while reading the reports is to periodically look up, lift a disgusted eyebrow, and scowl at me with more burning hatred.

I'm starting to sweat. Finally, the Judge gives a sickened moan and shoves the stack of paper aside. She takes a deep breath and frowns at me like I'm scum, "Mr. Bevilacqua, why don't you tell me what happened that day..."

"Um..." I stammer, angry with myself as I hear my voice cracking. The Judge roars, "WELL?! WHAT HAPPENED?!" Quivering, I start talking fast, "It was Sunday, and I was crossing the street near my apartment..." The heinous tale pours from my mouth, through the car sideswiping me, Toomey giving me the finger then taking off, but I'm terrified that the volcano of judicial spite is going to erupt again. Remembering the advice of Roz, I try not to talk too much, but every time I pause, the Judge yells "THEN WHAT?!" Each time, I jump, quickly gasp, and continue the story.

As I approach the part of the tale where Tam is introduced, I suspect that Judge J- will want to hear from her. I gesture towards Tam and say, "And that's when my girlfriend Tamara walked out of the store." The Judge thunders from above, "THEN WHAT HAPPENED?!" So I keep talking, for what seems like years, until my mouth is so dry that I reach for the water that is on the table before me. The Judge groans impatiently as I take a quick gulp, then I continue my story under her neutering stare.

"Are you done?!" the enraged Judge yells and I nod, trembling. "Good!" she yells, "Because I have some questions for you!" The Judge asks me if I was angry after the car hit me. Too afraid to answer, I simply nod again. She explodes, "ARE YOU GETTING SMART WITH ME?!"

"No, Ma'am."

The Judge shouts, "YOU THINK YOU'RE SMART?!" My rambling apologies start again and, with a dismissive wave of her hand, the Judge yells, "Alright, shut up!" She asks me why I didn't take Lauren Toomey's license plate number and immediately call the police, instead of speaking to her directly. In my head, I'm thinking it's because I wasn't hurt and simply wanted an apology. So I respond, "Yes Ma'am, I regret that now. May I explain?"

The Judge puffs up, clearly going for a big one, then bellows with enough force to take the varnish off the bench, "NO! YOU MAY NOT EXPLAIN!" And this is it, my watershed moment. I realize that it's over. She hates me, I'm going down. This was the dumbest idea I've ever had in my entire stupid fucking life, and I'm just going to stand here until it's over, then go home and drown myself in the Santa Monica Bay like Frederic March in *A STAR IS BORN*, only without the swelling violins because I don't deserve them. I regret every decision I've ever made that led me to this place. I regret my whole wasted life and its path of useless efforts and pointless endeavors. I regret it all.

It's over, and I find myself leaving my body for the second time today. I'm floating over the courtroom set, past the camera crane that takes us in and out of commercials. The Judge is still yelling at me but I'm no longer listening. I'm drifting over the lighting grid, watching the proceedings from above.

Now Judge J- asks Toomey to explain what really happened, only the Judge refers to her as "Ms. Bennett". Toomey begins her strange tale of how she was driving between eight and ten miles an hour when I assailed her car, shouting and flashing my middle finger at her. Toomey describes how I followed her home and then viciously attacked her. The Judge seems sympathetic, nodding as she listens. Toomey continues with an account of how, injured and unspeakably terrified, she bravely followed me through the streets to apologize.

The sound of my pounding heartbeat floods my eardrums as, down below, the Judge smiles kindly on Lauren Toomey. "Ms. Bennett, it says in the report that you were on your way home from taking your medical board exams. So you're a doctor?" Judge J- asks, impressed.

"Yes, Ma'am, that is correct. I am a doctor," Toomey smugly replies.

"And your exams were so demanding that you hadn't had time to sleep for days. Then at the airport, they lost your luggage. So the day in question was stressful for you?" the Judge asks, oozing compassion.

"Yes, your Honor, it was extremely stressful. So I was even more vulnerable to this man's violent attack," Toomey says.

"I see..." the Judge nods, "So that's when you hit him with your car."

Toomey's eyes glaze over, "No, I didn't hit him. He ran at my car, attacking me."

Judge J-'s sympathetic smile suddenly turns sinister. "Oh, I don't believe that," the Judge growls, "I don't believe that for one second."

Floating above the studio, I feel a tug on my shoulder. The other sinister Steve from the mirror appears, "Hey dickhead, better get down there. This just got interesting." With a shove, my second-self forces me back down to the floor, as Judge J- starts screaming again. Only this time, she's not screaming at me.

"I think you did hit him!" the Judge shrieks, "And you heard him yell?"

"Oh yes," Toomey dramatically responds.

"And you didn't stop?" the Judge pointedly asks.

"No!" Toomey declares with a theatrical gesture, "I was far too afraid. He was irate."

"I would be too if you hit me with your car and then flipped me off! It says right here, in your statement to the police, that you flashed your middle finger at him. Not him, you! You hit this man with your car, Doctor Bennett!" Judge J- yells, with an ironic inflection on the word 'doctor'. Am I hallucinating this?

Toomey's eyes flash with lunatic fire. "He attacked me!" she screams, pointing a wicked finger at my head, "He ran to my car, swinging his fists. He scratched my face and smashed my sunglasses!"

Judge J- looks at me, furious, "Did you?!"

"Uh, no," I stammer, "Those sunglasses were-"

"Alright, SHUT UP!" the Judge blasts at me. Judge J- looks back at Toomey, pounding her finger on the police report, "Where in this report does it say that you had injuries?!"

Toomey replies, "It says the police took photographs of the injuries inflicted by this man when he assaulted me."

"Where?!" the Judge demands to know. Judge J- angrily scans the report. Chuck the Bailiff gives me a snide look, which according to Roz means certain doom, and he steps forward to help Judge J- search. Chuck points to a section of the report. "It's right here, your Honor," he says, overstepping his duties if you ask me.

The Judge irritably scrutinizes the report, "It says they took photographs, it doesn't describe any injuries."

"I had injuries! Injuries from this man's violent attack!" Toomey shrieks, "And I can prove it!"

"How?" Judge J- asks.

"Because I have the photographs of my injuries right here!"

My heart stops. Breaking Roz's rules of Judge J- engagement, I look over at Toomey, as she pulls out the same brown envelope that boob Ned Price had back in court. That's the property of the Santa Monica Court. How many Jack 'n Cokes did Toomey have to buy Noreen McDonough to get her hands on that?

"Bring me the photographs!" the Judge commands. I'm cringing in anticipation as Judge J- flips through Toomey's photos. The Judge looks shocked. "Injuries?!" the Judge roars, "I don't see any injuries! I see pimples! I see bad skin! But I don't see one scratch!"

Toomey announces like a martyr, "I just thank god that my injuries weren't more serious!"

The Judge pauses, suddenly unnerved. She glances over at me, wondering. I think the depths of Toomey's lunacy just started to sink in. Undaunted, the Judge looks back at Toomey. "There are no injuries in these photographs! None!" she screams, "Only an idiot would believe this man assaulted you on the basis of these photographs!" Chalk up another one for the Santa Monica City Attorney's Office.

"He did assault me!" Toomey shrieks.

"That's a lie!" the Judge explodes, "I don't believe this man attacked you! I don't believe he ever laid his hands on you!" My jaw drops open. Can this be? Is someone actually having an appropriate reaction to this bullshit since it first spewed from Toomey's foul mouth? Judge J- takes a breath and asks Toomey, "What did you do after the encounter at the car?"

Toomey braces herself, preparing to recount more of her traumatic ordeal. "Well, I was so terrified-"

"That you followed him?!" the Judge interrupts, "That's ridiculous! How terrified could you have been? Following him through the streets, screaming threats at him?!"

"I was upset!" she cries.

"Why were you upset?!" shouts the Judge, "He's the one who got hit by a car! And now he's being stalked through the streets by a lunatic!" The court set starts to spin in a dizzying swirl, as Judge J- grows into a tornado of fury. "YOU WERE ACTING LIKE A NUT!" she howls at Toomey.

"I was not!" Toomey protests.

The Judge thrusts her damning finger at Toomey, roaring, "NUT! NUT! NUT! What kind of a doctor are you?! Then you call the police and report a felony strongarm robbery! THAT WAS A LIE!"

"He did rob me!" Toomey shrieks, "He took a piece of paper from my hands!"

"That's not a robbery! It's a lie! You!" The Judge points at me, "You took the paper?!"

"Yes," I squeak, afraid to move.

"And what did you do with it?!" the Judge yells as her frenzy of carnage builds.

"Uh, I ripped it up and threw it in the trash," I timidly admit, "But I dug it out of the trash and gave it to the police. And I only took it because-"

"SHUT UP!" the Judge booms, "I know why you took it!"

Toomey chimes in, "See?! He even admits it!"

"He took that piece of paper because you were making threats against..." the Judge now points her ferocious finger at Tam, "YOU! Get up here!"

With an intro like that, I expected Tam to turn into a pillar of salt before our eyes. But no! Tam totally rises to the occasion. Without hesitation, she glides to the table with a graceful, "Yes, your Honor?"

Judge J-'s eyes seethe with rage as she looks at Toomey, "He took that piece of paper because you were threatening her. I wouldn't want a nut like you to know where my girlfriend lives either!" Toomey continues arguing but it fades into white noise as I stare spellbound at Judge J-. Who is this amazing woman? This modern-day Solomon! In a few minutes, this Judge has untangled months of lies and subterfuge created by Toomey and perpetuated by the self-serving circus clowns of the Santa Monica Court. This TV 'court' is smarter and more effective than any genuine court I've experienced. Is syndicated television the last refuge of true justice in America?

Judge J-'s cannonade continues, "I can't believe your stupid lies forced this man to spend over twelve thousand dollars in legal fees. Only a moron would believe your story. This man's not a nut! He's not a hothead! He may not be the smartest guy on the block, but I don't think he acted inappropriately at all!" I have a feeling that the Judge proclaiming that I'm "not a nut" and didn't act "inappropriately" are about the highest compliments you can get on this show. I am now totally enamored of this brilliant, marvelous, wise woman.

Judge J- keeps screaming at Toomey in a vain attempt to break through the madness. "You should have apologized immediately for hitting him with your car!" Toomey's eyes are frosted with a psychotic sheen as she yells, "No, I shouldn't have!"

The Judge stops, at a loss. Like all who come into contact with her, Judge J- keeps underestimating the tower of pissy insanity that is Lauren Toomey. The entire audience sits frozen and silent, transfixed by Toomey's psychosis. With a sigh, the Judge valiantly proceeds, "Not only did you lie to the police about this man assaulting you, you also made false accusations about her."

Toomey gets indignant, "I did not! I said nothing about her!" The Judge holds up the police report, amazed that she needs to remind Toomey of the fifteen-page account detailing how Tamara drove the getaway vehicle in a felony strongarm robbery. "Oh, you said plenty about her."

"I didn't accuse her of anything!" Toomey defiantly yells.

"YES, YOU DID!" the Judge roars.

Her head held high, Toomey declares, "I said nothing about her. It must have been the police who put that in." The Judge gags in frustration, "That's absurd! Of course it was you! This event and this whole police report of lies were entirely propelled by you!"

"No!" Toomey insists, maintaining a hateful scowl under the crazy wig. And I suddenly wonder, why the hell would Toomey go to all that trouble to disguise herself with the makeup, wig, and bizarre tent-dress, if she's just going to whip out a bunch of photos of what she really looks like?

Exasperated, Judge J- throws up her hands, "And you have the nerve to bring a lawsuit against this man?! Emotional distress?! He's the one who should have emotional distress, dealing with a wacko like you! I'm dismissing your counterclaim outright, because it's preposterous."

Toomey protests, "You're-"

"QUIET!" bellows the Judge, "I find that you are entirely responsible for his legal costs! You were the precipitating factor in this horrible incident; your road rage, your foul temper and your absurd lies that no police officer or prosecutor should have ever believed for one second!" From the side, a camera rushes toward my head, as Judge J-angrily looks my way. "However, the most I can give you is five thousand dollars."

I am mesmerized by this Goddess of Justice. My mouth hangs open as I gaze upon her. "WELL?!" the Judge yells, "Do you understand?!"

"What? Oh, yes, Ma'am! Thank you." I bow slightly without meaning to, and then grimace with embarrassment for having just bowed.

"Sit down!" the Judge yells with disgust. As I slink back to the bench, the Judge points at Tam, "Now you! Tell me what the police did after this nut accused you of being involved in the 'strongarm robbery'."

"I didn't-" Toomey starts to yell but the Judge cuts her off with an inarguable "SILENCE!"

The audience gasps with shock as Tam describes how the police stormed the apartment and handcuffed her while they brought Toomey around to identify the car. Judge J- growls, "You mean, the red, four-door car?" Damn, she caught everything in those reports.

Toomey pipes up, "I was tired from-"

"I said SILENCE!" The Judge's face grows lava-red again, then she pauses to rub her temples. Growing tired of this whole mess, she asks Tam, "Then it was over, right?"

"Well, not exactly," Tam explains, "Because for the months that he was in court, the City Attorney kept suggesting that they might bring charges against me as well."

Judge J- glares at Toomey, "I wonder why that was?!" The Judge likes Tam, I can tell. And why not? Tam's well spoken and she's not wearing a silly disguise, thus providing an excellent counterpoint to Toomey's bone-chilling dementia and my maybe-he-did-and-maybe-he-didn't dumb guy demeanor. The Judge sighs, "You're asking for five thousand dollars as well."

"Yes," Tam replies.

The Judge sighs wearily, "I'll give you half."

"Fair enough, thank you," Tam smiles. The Judge smiles a little, but that smile sinks when her eyes find me, "You, get back here!"

I jump to my feet with a "Yes, Ma'am" when what I really want to say is "God bless you, you heroic voice of reason! You represent all that is good."

The Judge makes some concluding comments, but I'm not sure what she's saying. I'm thunderstruck at how this fake TV court proved to be light years better than our country's existing justice system. The Judge dismisses us and, despite myself, I again do a little half bow, regretting it as it's happening, and say "Thank you" one last time. Then we turn and hurry through the gate. People in the audience smile at us and some even applaud. As we reach the back of the aisle, Cassandra appears in our path. "You have to come here now!" she urgently orders us.

Because the fun isn't over yet...

justice starts after the young and the restless...

"What is gayer than believing in a household god?" – Kafka

Here's the deal...After Judge J- announces her verdict, you're led to a different part of the stage and placed in front of prop "courtroom doors" in some imagined corridor outside the renowned hall of justice. The producers ask one litigant about the outcome of the case, while the others stand in the background, then they reverse the players and do it again.

Tamara and I wait at the prop courtroom doors while the announcer interviews Lauren Toomey, who's in a major huff, spouting some incomprehensible bile about how the judge's verdict is a case of criminal harassment. Suddenly, the prop doors behind us fly open, and a man pounces on me, grabbing my neck and shouting that he's going to kill me. Three hulking security guards leap forward and stomp the madman to the floor. Scared shitless, I duck behind a plastic potted plant and yell, "Who the hell is that?!"

"Oh my god, could that be the 'husband'?" Tam wonders aloud. My attacker is not the ponytailed freak who was making faces at me inside. Oddly, Lauren Toomey doesn't acknowledge this man at all. Restrained by the guards, my mystery attacker keeps ranting violent threats, so one guard puts his hand over the man's mouth. Cassandra cuts short Toomey's interview, then moves me and Tam before the camera, a few feet from where the crazed man fights to carry out his mission.

The announcer, who has the deep resonant voice of a seasoned broadcast veteran but looks like a young surfer dude, asks me how I feel. I start to answer when the madman shakes the guard's hand off his mouth and resumes yelling that I need to die. The guards gag the man again, and the announcer assures me that I needn't worry about the screaming violent psycho four feet away. I try to comment on the case, but my fearful eyes are locked on the maniac who wants to kill me.

Cassandra marches forward, flanked by more security guards, and announces that we're done. She grabs my shoulder, yelling, "This way! Hurry!" The guards form a human barrier around Tam and me, as Cassandra guides us to another tiny holding pen made of black cloth. Cassandra tells us to wait there, and two guards block the entrance. We can hear violent shouts and scuffling outside the cloth walls. I hear Lauren Toomey scream that she's going to sue the show, and then, amazingly enough, I hear Toomey shrieking that she's going to call the police and tell them that she was just assaulted, followed by Cassandra yelling emphatically, "No, you're not!" I can't believe Toomey would revisit her favorite threat after everything that just went down, but I guess the thing about Lauren Toomey is, she never gets any less fucking crazy.

The sweet old sound man comes to retrieve our microphones, "How you folks doing?" Tensely listening to the brutal noises behind the cloth, I say nothing. The old man pats my shoulder, "You did good out there."

"You think?" I ask, as a loud crash outside makes me jump.

The man nods, "I told you, you had nothing to worry about."

"Yeah. How'd you know?" I ask him.

"You folks seem nice enough," he replies, "But that wig lady, she's batshit." Cassandra bursts in with more guards and shouts, "Okay, now!"

"Thanks, Cassandra, for everything," I say as we emerge from the holding pen. On edge like a ninja, Cassandra's eyes dart around, "Glad it worked out for you, Steve. Let's move!"

Cassandra leads the way through the dark stage. From behind a closed door, I hear Toomey's murderous screaming and what sounds like a chair hitting a wall. I stare at the door, worried, as Cassandra pulls me forward, "You have to get out of here!"

"Who's that guy who threatened-"

Cassandra cuts me off, "We don't have time! We're holding them here for thirty minutes. After that, you're on your own!"

"How afraid should I be?" I ask Cassandra.

Cassandra gives me a grave look, "Learn from the past, Steve. If anything happens outside this stage, call the police immediately!"

People suddenly emerge out of the darkness. There are a lot of them, it must be the entire staff of the show. They join hands, making two human chains to create a corridor through the cluttered stage. I hesitate, confused by the blur of activity but Cassandra shoves me. "Go!" she commands.

Tamara yanks my arm, "We're getting the fuck out of here!"

Tam and I run through the human gauntlet as it twists through the dark stage. The staffers' linked arms guide us like a weird mime version of a birth canal, until we slam through a door and are reborn into the hot Hollywood sun. We stop in our tracks, blinded, and with absolutely no idea where we just came out.

Disoriented and struggling to regain my sight, it hits me. I yell, "It's over, and WE WON!" I pick Tam up and spin her around, shouting "We won! We won!" I give Tam a huge kiss, but she yanks free and announces, "We have to get away from here, now! Where the hell are we?"

I look around, "I don't know..." Tam looks afraid, of both Toomey and this bold new loon who just surfaced. We walk quickly, trying to get our bearings. Soon we find the car and flee. Once on the freeway, Tam screams with glee, "That was amazing!"

"Judge J- is the greatest!" I exclaim, "I don't even care that she yelled at me so much. Then again, why did she yell at me so much?"

"I know!" Tam announces, suddenly an expert, "Obviously, she wanted to see how belligerent you get when you're attacked. The only believable thing about Toomey's bullshit story was that, after she hit you with her car, you were so pissed off that you clobbered her."

"You think?" I ask.

"Either that," Tam says, "Or she was just doing it for the show."

"I don't care," I laugh, "I think Judge J- is tremendous."

When the show finally airs a few months later, they end up cutting out most of the beginning when the Judge screams at me relentlessly. Which means that the episode starts right after that, when I'm standing there with my mouth hanging open like a big dummy. I look like a moron, completely shellshocked and for no apparent reason. I'm watching the show alone in our apartment on the afternoon that it's broadcast. Irresistibly compelled to watch, within seconds I'm curled up fetal-style on the floor, squirming and moaning. My mouth hangs open as I watch myself on the screen with my mouth hanging open, until finally I shout at myself on the TV, "For the love of god, would you close your goddamned mouth?!"

Ignoring the phone that's ringing off the hook, I keep watching the televised screaming match in the 'court'. They periodically flash captions under my clueless face. Caption-wise, I start out as "ACCUSED OF ASSAULT" but evolve to "HIT BY DEFENDANT'S CAR" and finally become "VICTIM OF FALSE CHARGES". Ah, vindication via afternoon TV!

The episode also cuts out a lot of the Judge yelling at Toomey, but they needed to. That verbal bloodbath lasted for over an hour, more than twice the length of the show, with most of that time spent while Judge J- ripped Toomey's dumb lying head off.

Rosalyn B- goes absolutely bonkers on the air date, calling over thirty times, shrieking with delirious joy. Roz canceled all of her patients for that day, and then decided to have a party and invite all of her patients who'd had their appointments canceled. Roz's boyfriend, who works at a large Wall Street brokerage house, requested that one of their TV monitors be switched from their usual business channel to the Judge J- Show. When he explained why, the whole firm got hopped up about it. So for a half hour that afternoon, one Wall Street brokerage house had all of their TV monitors tuned to Judge J- and everybody cheered as the guy who got nailed by a car finally found justice.

I continue to ignore the ringing phone as the show continues. I hear Tam's boss through the answering machine, saying that they're watching at the office, and Tam's gone catatonic. She's not responding, and he's a little worried. When the episode finally ends, I hear Dave the Actor and Amy Nextdoor yelling for me from outside, and I step out to a standing ovation from my neighbors, each standing in front of their door.

But one voice yelling through the answering machine makes me stop. "Who the hell is Anne Bennett?!" It's Phil! I dive for the phone.

"Hey!" I say, "So you watched it, huh?"

"Of course I watched it!" Phil screams, "That was the coolest thing ever!"

"I looked like an idiot with my mouth hanging open!" I laugh into the phone.

"Who cares?! The truth finally came out and Toomey got hers! I love Judge J-! I wish all judges were that smart."

"I, too, am loving Judge J-," I proclaim.

"But what the hell's up with Anne Bennett?!" Phil giggles, "That's not her name!"

"It was the only way she'd go on the show, if they let her use the phony name. I didn't even notice she was using a fake first name until you pointed it out just now. Does it matter?"

"Nothing matters now, bud. You won. And I'm proud of you."

"Thanks! It is amazing. When the real-life courts fail you, you can still go on afternoon TV to find salvation. I love America!"

Phil laughs, "You really aren't like my other clients."

"Why? Lots of your clients are on TV, all the famous ones."

"One, they're on plain old regular TV, not on Judge J-. Two, the famous people are always guilty. Three, and this is the big one, you're the only client I've ever had who took the complaining witness and completely disgraced her on national television. I love that!"

Phil's dying to hear every detail about the show, so I tell him more about it, including the part by the courtroom doors when the strange unidentified man threatened to kill me. Phil reminds me of my promise to him on the day we first met, that if anything ever happens in the future, that I will "reserve my right to remain silent" until I speak to him.

"Phil, I promise. Swear to god, trust me on that."

But now we're back on the afternoon of the taping, at the Rose Café where Liz is jumping out of her skin, hanging on every gory detail. Liz's eyes bug out with twisted glee as I tell her about Toomey showing up in her weird disguise. Now Liz is all worked up about the mysterious stranger who crashed through the prop doors and lunged at me.

"I think it's the husband," I tell her.

"Steve, you're so stupid. There is no husband."

"Then who the hell was it?"

Liz doesn't respond. She simply grins, the devious gears in her head grinding away. I decide to leave her to this. "Alright, I'm heading out..."

"Home?" she asks.

"No, I need to think about this. It hasn't really sunk in yet that I have my life back, for what that's worth."

I leave the Rose and head for the beach, trying to comprehend that this nightmare is truly over. I am finally emancipated from Lauren Toomey, Noreen McDonough, and all the soul-sucking monsters who spent the past year trying to destroy my life.

The setting sun has sunk to that excruciating angle where it slices straight through the optic nerve into the brain. While it will soon be a lovely sunset, right now it's a painful blinding red spot in everyone's face. I'm standing at the corner of Rose and Pacific, waiting for the light to turn green. When it does, I step off the curb and start crossing the street when, astoundingly enough, I hear the screech of brakes and a beige Cadillac swerves around the corner and fucking hits me.

The Caddy sideswipes my thigh and knocks me back, just like before. But this time, I don't make a sound. My heart turns to stone and my knees get weak. I am terrified, not of being killed by the speeding car, but of whatever's about to happen next and how long it will ravage my life. The Cadillac skids to a halt. The door opens and a well-dressed woman, probably in her early sixties, gets out of the car and yells. I'm afraid to listen.

However, upset as she is, this woman yells, "Oh my god! The sun was in my eyes, and I didn't see you! Are you hurt?!" The poor woman is shaking. I hold up my hand, just in case she decides to take a swing at me. "I'm okay," I tell her, "You just brushed me. I'm not hurt."

The woman covers her mouth, "I'm so sorry."

"I'm alright. Really," I assure her, still standing back.

"Can I give you a ride somewhere? Take you home? Are you sure you're not hurt?" Her Cadillac is blocking a lane of Pacific Avenue, and by now the delightful assholes of L.A. are honking, yelling obscenities, and flashing their meaningless fingers at this woman. She ignores all of it, keeping her distraught eyes on me. I smile, "Ma'am, I'm fine."

"Isn't there anything I can do?" she asks.

"No, it's alright," I tell her, "You better go, you're blocking the street here."

"Well, okay..." she says uncertainly.

"But...thank you," I sigh, relieved.

And there you go, she hits me with her car and I thank her. And I'm happy to, because I now know how this situation could have gone. I give the woman a friendly wave as she drives off, while thanking god that she has no connection to the Medical Board of California. Then I go down to the beach.

I walk along the water's edge, watching the sun set and trying to process the last year of my life. Today is June 20th, so it's actually been 13 months and 13 days since Toomey's car sideswiped me. That brief, horrible moment conquered my life for over a year and now, just as suddenly, it's over. Things will go back to their former strange state before they were brutally interrupted by something far stranger. As the concept sinks into my skull, I'm so overcome with joy that I'm almost skipping.

At the edge of the vast ocean, I think I've finally reached the end of the seemingly infinite spite of Lauren Toomey. I never thought I'd be so excited for my life to return to the complete mess it was last May. But now I have a chance to finally tackle that and turn it around.

With the money from Judge J-, I pay back the generous souls who contributed to my legal defense fund. Almost all of it, anyway. There are still a few outstanding balances that I'm working on.

The movie is eventually finished and we take it on the festival circuit, where it does well enough. The world of film festivals is one seriously twisted racket, but that's a whole other story. At home, things with Tam return to normal. She seems recovered from the many traumas thrust upon her over the course of this ordeal, although I still call her "Wheels" from time to time.

As for all the lovely folks involved with this thing, it remains open how much of what happened was due to malice, how much due to incompetence, and how much simply due to dumb luck and bad timing. I think more was due to malice than they'd ever admit, but maybe that's just me.

And Santa Monica still lies just a few hundred feet away, thriving in its sunny scorn. William Faulkner once said, "The fundamental virtue of humanity is its capacity to endure." While conjuring up centuries of profound perseverance in the Deep South, I wonder if the old boy actually had this insight during his time in Santa Monica. You see the condemning legions walking around Santa Monica every day. They'd be attractive except for that distinctive pinched look they all wear. It's a beautiful day but they don't seem to notice, because they're obsessively solving some problem that only exists in theory, yet still requires their complete, ardent devotion.

The place is named after Saint Monica, who was Saint Augustine's mother, which I find ironic. According to her son, Saint Monica's deepest virtues were her steadfast ability to see the best in people, and her unshakable belief that the world is good. Santa Monica, with its unfathomable labyrinth of regulations, always assumes the worst about people. Here in Venice, people are more free to make their own decisions, for better or worse. Maybe some wrong things will occur, but life in general is easier because it doesn't require perpetual research into arbitrary guidelines. Saint Monica held out for decades, hoping that her son would give up his life of depraved debauchery. And he did. He even became Saint Augustine, a pillar of the early Church. The point is, Saint Monica did not form a committee to enact a litany of nitpicking regulations in an attempt to whittle down Augustine's party-boy lifestyle. She had faith in the whole.

I walk along the shoreline, wondering. Maybe God does love an optimist, even though it doesn't seem like it most of the time. Sure, it's courting a lifelong waltz with disappointment, but I now realize, deeper than ever, that as bad as things seem, they can always get worse. You're not a chump for appreciating what little is right at any given moment. So if I believe it's a good thing that my taillight got cracked in a parking lot because that's how I discovered the other one was already broken, then so be it, despite the chronic aggravation it causes for my girlfriend. Maybe it makes me an idiot...and then again, maybe not.

I feel a heady whoosh of ecstasy as I step into the water. Behind me, on the sand, I see the gigantic shoes of the towering sickly writer. I see Detective Bender dancing with the ghost pirates. Scabby goblins form a kickline around Phil Damascus, while Officer Hink leads a conga line of mangled samurai. Cackling witches, crazed dictators, laughing rabbits, Lauren Toomey...all at the cosmic beach party, hosted by Blodg, who's flirting with Noreen McDonough, who's too drunk to notice. I see it all.

The Judge on High swoops down, more imperious than the crimson sky, her long robes billowing behind her. Like a furious dive-bomber, she commands the grotesque creatures to stop their pointless nonsense.

I am soaring toward the sun...spinning into the clouds...swimming with the dolphins...crashing with the waves.

I am free.

Made in the USA
Lexington, KY
05 October 2014